WORLD WAR II

PEOPLE, POLITICS, AND POWER

AMERICA AT WAR

WORLD WAR II

PEOPLE, POLITICS, AND POWER

EDITED BY WILLIAM L. HOSCH, ASSOCIATE EDITOR, SCIENCE AND TECHNOLOGY

Britannica®
Educational Publishing

IN ASSOCIATION WITH

ROSEN
EDUCATIONAL SERVICES

LONGWOOD PUBLIC LIBRARY

Published in 2010 by Britannica Educational Publishing
(a trademark of Encyclopædia Britannica, Inc.)
in association with Rosen Educational Services, LLC
29 East 21st Street, New York, NY 10010.

Distributed exclusively by Rosen Educational Services.
For a listing of additional Britannica Educational Publishing titles, call toll free (800) 237-9932.

First Edition

Britannica Educational Publishing
Michael I. Levy: Executive Editor
Marilyn L. Barton: Senior Coordinator, Production Control
Steven Bosco: Director, Editorial Technologies
Lisa S. Braucher: Senior Producer and Data Editor
Yvette Charboneau: Senior Copy Editor
Kathy Nakamura: Manager, Media Acquisition
William L. Hosch: Associate Editor, Science and Technology

Rosen Educational Services
Hope Lourie Killcoyne: Senior Editor and Project Manager
Joanne Randolph: Editor
Nelson Sá: Art Director
Matthew Cauli: Designer
Introduction by Therese Shea

Library of Congress Cataloging-in-Publication Data

World War II: people, politics, and power / edited by William L Hosch.
    p. cm.—(America at war)
"In association with Britannica Educational Publishing, Rosen Educational Services."
Includes index.
ISBN 978-1-61530-008-2 (library binding)
1. World War, 1939–1945—Juvenile literature. I. Hosch, William L. II. Title: World War Two.
D743.7.W678 2010
940.53—dc22

2009033541

Manufactured in the United States of America

On the cover: American troops roll past the Arc de Triomphe after the liberation of Paris,
August 1944. *National Archives and Records Administration*

Evening Standard

La Coquille

No. 35,000 — LONDON, FRIDAY, SEPTEMBER 1, 1939 — ONE PENNY

GERMANS INVADE AND BOMB POLAND BRITAIN MOBILISES

Warsaw, Cracow, Nine Other Towns Bombed: Danzig is "Annexed"

FRANCE DECLARES "STATE OF SIEGE"

GERMANY INVADED POLAND TO-DAY. COMPLETE MOBILISATION HAS BEEN ORDERED IN BRITAIN.

Orders in Council for the complete mobilisation of the Navy, Army and Air Force, were signed by the King at a Privy Council to-day. The King also approved other Orders in Council dealing with the emergency.

Warsaw has been bombed. Other German aircraft raided Korsk, Gdenia, Thorn, Bialystock, Grodno, Dilkko and Bydgoszcz. A few hours later, Cracow, Katowice and Czestowice were bombed.

THE EVENING STANDARD LEARNS THAT THE POLISH AMBASSADOR SAW LORD HALIFAX TO-DAY. HE INFORMED THE FOREIGN SECRETARY OF THE GERMAN ATTACK UPON POLAND, WHICH HE SAID CONSTITUTED A CASE OF DIRECT AGGRESSION, AND HE INVOKED THE ANGLO-POLISH TREATY.

French aid has also been invoked.

The French Cabinet met for an hour and 35 minutes. They decided to call Parliament immediately, to order general mobilisation of Army, Navy and Air Force beginning to-morrow, and to proclaim a "state of siege."

The Germans attacked without having delivered any ultimatum.

Attack On Both Sides

They are striking at the "Corridor" both from the East and the West—from the East at the town of Dzialdowo, on the East Prussian frontier, and from the West at Chojnice, about 60 miles from Danzig.

Dzialdowo is about 80 miles north-west of Warsaw.

(Continued on PAGE FOUR)

Air Raid Warning System In Force

L.C.C. authorities have been instructing all over the area, and Sunday evening they held exercises.

Every hint on the mounting of barrage stoops and balloons is prescribed, except for putting all real experience.

"BRITAIN WILL FULFIL HER OBLIGATIONS"

Parliament Meeting To-night

THE BRITISH CABINET MET TO-DAY. THEY BROKE UP AFTER ONE HOUR AND FIFTY MINUTES.

BOTH HOUSES OF PARLIAMENT ARE MEETING AT SIX O'CLOCK TO-NIGHT. THE PRIME MINISTER IS MAKING A FULL STATEMENT IN THE COMMONS, AND AFTERWARDS THE HOUSE IS BEING ASKED TO PASS EMERGENCY LEGISLATION AT ONCE, AND SO THE LORD CHANCELLOR WILL REGISTER IN MAKING A STATEMENT IN THE LORDS.

MEMBERS OF PARLIAMENT WILL BE IN POSSESSION OF THE CORRESPONDENCE BETWEEN GREAT BRITAIN AND GERMANY WHICH BILL OF PUBLISHED AS A WHITE PAPER.

It was pointed out to official circles in London to-day that if the proclamation by the German people by Herr Hitler proved untrue, as it would seem to mean, that Germany has declared war on Poland, it can be stated on the highest authority that Great Britain and France are definitely determined to fulfil to the utmost

(Continued on PAGE FOUR)

227

238

241

CONTENTS

23

38

125

155

166

191

World War II—fought between 1939 and 1945—was the most widespread and deadly war in recorded history. Beginning just 20 years after World War I, three countries in particular aggressively sought power: Germany, Italy, and Japan. However, by the war's end, most of the world's nations had fought with or against this "Axis" coalition. Within these pages, readers will gain insight to a war that shifted world power in unexpected ways, tested the mettle of soldier and civilian alike, and cost the lives of millions upon millions of people.

In 1919, the Treaty of Versailles stripped much from the defeated nations of World War I. Germany lost territory, military strength, and great wealth. Adolf Hitler rode the rising tide of the German public's postwar discontent, becoming the leader of the Nationalist Socialist—or Nazi—Party. In 1934, Hitler became the German dictator—the Führer. Fascism tightened its grip on Germany as its leaders wielded propaganda as both a powerful weapon and a lure. In March 1935, Germany began rebuilding its military overtly, the next year sending troops into the Rhineland, a demilitarized area along France's border. These actions made France, along with many other European countries, anxiously speculate the extent of Hitler's ambition.

Unlike Germany, Italy fought on the victor's side of World War I. However, Italians were disappointed that their nation did not benefit from postwar reparations as others had. In the subsequent years, Benito Mussolini constructed a Fascist government, first becoming prime minister in 1922. Eventually, he became a dictator known as Il Duce, or "The Leader." Italy's imperialist objectives were made known in October 1935 with the invasion of Ethiopia. The following year Mussolini and Hitler forged an alliance, later called the "Axis." They battle-tested strategies and weapons during the Spanish Civil War of the mid-1930s.

Meanwhile, Japan's growing population desired more natural resources and additional territory. In 1931, Japan seized Manchuria in northeast China; an all-out war began several years later. In 1937, Japan signed the Anti-Comintern Pact, essentially uniting with Germany and Italy against Communist Soviet Union, the nearest powerful nation capable of halting Japanese imperialism.

In March 1938, Germany annexed Austria and appeared poised to occupy Czechoslovakia. Hoping to avoid war, Great Britain, France, Italy, and Germany entered into the Munich Pact, giving western Czechoslovakia to Germany in exchange for peace. On August 23, 1939, Hitler and Soviet leader Joseph Stalin signed a surprising treaty of nonaggression; an invasion of Poland seemed likely.

London's Evening Standard *announces Germany's invasion of Poland, September 1, 1939.* Hulton Archive/Getty Images

Great Britain and France, uniting as the core "Allied" powers, promised retribution.

On September 1, 1939, German forces stormed into Poland, revealing the power of blitzkrieg, or "lightning war." Air strikes of low-flying dive bombers destroyed communication and transportation centres, while tanks and troops pushed deep into enemy territory at great speed. After the slow-moving trench warfare of World War I, blitzkrieg was unprecedented. Germany's aggression surprised few, but its tactics and technology were unanticipated. Consider that Great Britain did not have a single armoured division, while Germany commanded 2,400 tanks in 1939. Hitler had been preparing for war while the Allies had been avoiding it. On September 17, the Soviet Union invaded eastern Poland, revealing that the Soviets and Germans had agreed to partition the country in their pact.

In the spring of 1940, the German Wehrmacht ("armed forces") exploded into action. After an invasion of Norway and Denmark, they ploughed through the Netherlands and Belgium. On May 10, a German offensive force attacked France through the forests of the Ardennes, a maneuvre previously not thought possible by Allied strategists. More than 300,000 British, French, and Belgian soldiers were evacuated from the port of Dunkirk. Shortly after, Mussolini—eager to show support for Germany—declared war against the Allies and sent troops to France. The Axis took Paris on June 14.

Shortly before the collapse of France, Winston Churchill became the prime minister of Great Britain. From July to September 1940, the Battle of Britain raged in the skies. German General Hermann Göring sought to cripple the nation first with air raids, followed by an invasion. The Royal Air Force used radar to detect attacks, thereby enabling British fighters to shoot down Luftwaffe bombers faster than they could be replaced.

Meanwhile, Hungary, Romania, and Slovakia became part of the Axis, joining Germany, Italy, and Japan. Greece and Yugoslavia fell by spring of 1941. On the battlefront in North Africa, Italian and British forces battled in present-day Libya and Egypt. When Nazi General Erwin Rommel and the Afrika Korps joined the Italian forces in 1941, all British gains were lost. However, the Allies held territory in East Africa and the Middle East, ensuring the security of the Suez Canal.

In June 1941, about three million German soldiers invaded the Soviet Union in the largest military campaign in history. Had the Wehrmacht triumphed, the Third Reich would have been the largest empire in the world. The Axis captured Kiev—killing, wounding, and capturing more than one million Soviets. Though the Germans nearly reached Moscow by November, miscalculations and a Soviet counterattack drove them back, and they were never able to regain as much ground or strength.

In the Pacific theatre of war, Japan used Germany's success in Europe as an opportunity to attack European colonies in

After capturing the Philippines in the spring of 1942, the Japanese force-marched American and Filipino prisoners of war in what became known as the Bataan Death March. MPI/ Hulton Archive/Getty Images

Asia, starting with southern Indochina in July 1941. Recognizing the United States as a major obstacle, Admiral Yamamoto Isoroku planned a surprise assault. On December 7, 1941, dive-bombers attacked Pearl Harbor naval station in Hawaii as well as the Philippines, for a time crippling the U.S. Pacific naval and air forces.

Though the United States declared war the day after the Pearl Harbor offensive, the first half of 1942 was a time of one Axis victory after another. The Japanese outmanned Allied forces in Asia as the Allied powers concentrated on Europe. By summer, Japan held the Philippines and several Allied Pacific strongholds. Mainland China remained in peril. Chiang Kai-shek's Chinese army, under American command, lost Burma by the end of the year.

However, in June 1942, U.S. intelligence learned of the intention of Japanese forces to conquer Midway Island and demolish the American fleet. U.S. forces mounted their own surprise strike, destroying Japan's first line of aircraft carriers. Beginning with Guadalcanal in August 1942, Allied forces advanced on Japanese holds, one island at a time. Japan abandoned Guadalcanal by February.

After a harsh winter on the Eastern Front, a renewed offensive for the city of Stalingrad was a seminal point for the German forces. In late August 1942, one of the deadliest battles commenced, forcing a massive German retreat and the relinquishing of territory won that summer.

In October 1942, British General Bernard Montgomery's Eighth Army attacked Rommel's Afrika Korps near el-Alamein, eventually pushing Axis forces out of Egypt into Tunisia. Major General Dwight Eisenhower coordinated the overtaking of northwest Africa in late 1942. Victories in Morocco and Algeria placed the Axis in the middle of two major Allied forces. By mid-1943, all of North Africa was in Allied hands. Churchill and Roosevelt met in Casablanca to discuss further offensive action in Sicily and Asia.

In July 1943, Hitler's Wehrmacht executed one more assault against the Soviets. The Battle of Kursk, the largest tank battle in history, resulted in a decisive German loss. Also in July, on the Western Front, Sicily fell to the Allied forces of Montgomery and American General George Patton. By early September 1943,

Mussolini had fallen from power. Though Italy formally surrendered, Germans continued fighting within its borders.

Beginning in late 1943, Hitler's strategy was to fortify German forces in western Europe at the expense of the Eastern Front. In December, Russia began a winter offensive, pushing the Germans out of their country. One advantage of Germany waging war against the Soviet Union had been a new cooperation between Allied and Soviet forces. However, the relationship became strained. Stalin intended to keep control of Soviet-occupied Poland and was interested in other German-held territories as well. The Allies wished to stop the spread of Communism, yet needed the strength of the Soviet Red Army. On November 1943, Churchill, Roosevelt, and Stalin met in Cairo, Egypt. It was decided that Eisenhower would take Allied forces into France while the Soviet Red Army would simultaneously attack the German Eastern Front.

In the first half of 1944, the Allies in the Pacific gained western New Guinea. In June, the Battle of the Philippine Sea was decidedly disastrous for the Japanese fleet, and the Imperial navy retreated northward toward Okinawa. In July, the loss of Saipan in the Marianas was such a blow that Japanese Prime Minister Tōjō Hideki and his entire cabinet resigned.

Bombed by the Japanese on December 7, 1941, the USS Shaw, *dry docked in the Pearl Harbor Naval Yard, was quickly engulfed in flames.* Lawrence Thornton/Hulton Archive/Getty Images

American forces continued to advance in the Philippines despite kamikaze fighters, winning the Battle of Leyte Gulf by the end of 1944. Meanwhile, the Allies made headway in Burma and China.

"Operation Overlord"—the Allied invasion of northern France—took place on June 6, 1944. Though fully expected by the Wehrmacht, the Germans didn't know just where or when it would be, and they were ultimately overwhelmed as the largest armada ever assembled delivered more than 150,000 soldiers to the beaches of Normandy. Allied land forces moved south, aided by air support. With additional American and French troops, the Allies had northern France in two months. On August 25, Paris was liberated. Hitler refused to withdraw from France, resulting in hundreds of thousands of German soldiers becoming Allied prisoners.

The progress of the Soviet armies on the Eastern Front made it imperative for the Allies to come to terms with Stalin about the fate of eastern Europe. Churchill and Roosevelt met for their second Quebec Conference, code-named "Octagon," on September 11, 1944. A plan was formed to divide Germany into Allied zones of occupation.

On December 24, 1944, Hitler organized his last major attack, using all soldiers and weapons available on the Western Front. This last offensive through the Ardennes became known as the Battle of the Bulge. It was meant to divide the Allied forces; however, by January, high casualties forced the Germans back into their own territory. In addition, the Allied

air offensive under U.S. General Carl Spaatz had major success, destroying Germany's production of synthetic oil for its war machine.

By early 1945, Allied bombings and raids had paralyzed German transportation. The Red Army under Georgy Zhukov had little trouble piercing the Eastern Front and capturing Warsaw in January 1945 and Berlin by late April. By then, Allied units had crossed the Rhine into Germany. Hitler encouraged suicide attacks and the destruction of German resources so that the Allies would have nothing to gain; many now turned against their Führer.

Several fateful changes in leadership rapidly occurred. On April 12, 1945, U.S. President Franklin Roosevelt died, succeeded by Harry Truman. Then, Benito Mussolini was executed on April 28. Two days later Hitler committed suicide, replaced by Karl Dönitz. His successor did everything in his power to surrender the 1.8 million German troops to Allies, fearing Soviet retribution. At midnight on May 8, 1945, the war in Europe was officially over.

From July to August 1945, the Allied leaders—Stalin, Truman, and Churchill (later replaced by Clement Attlee)—met at Potsdam, occupied Germany. Operations against Japan were discussed, and a declaration called on that nation to surrender. Stalin also persuaded Truman and Attlee to consent to Soviet reparation demands.

Back in the Pacific theatre, Allied forces had defeated the Japanese in Burma by May 1945, but war raged on. Despite a heavy bombing campaign, American forces were compelled to land on the tiny island of Iwo Jima, resulting in a significant loss of lives. The next invasion—the target Okinawa—was the largest amphibious operation of the Pacific War. Okinawa was in Allied hands by July. Douglas MacArthur, now in command of all Pacific army units, prepared for a Japanese invasion.

With so many soldiers and civilians already killed, President Harry Truman made the controversial decision to "shorten the agony of battle." On August 6, 1945, the most destructive weapon ever released by man—an atomic bomb—was dropped on Hiroshima. Another bomb followed on August 9, 1945, falling this time on Nagasaki. With close to 120,000 people killed in two days, Japan surrendered on August 15.

The aftermath of World War II was overwhelming. The total number of dead varies anywhere from 35 million to 60 million; maybe as many as 30 million civilians across 61 nations died. Few have ventured to calculate the total number of wounded or disabled.

The most horrifying events of World War II are known by a single word—Holocaust. Since Hitler's rise, he fomented Jewish persecution. Nazi task forces were created to wipe out the Jews—whom the Nazis depicted in racial terms—this, though Judaism is a religion. Many Jews were forced into concentration camps, such as the notorious Auschwitz. When the prisoners became too weak to work, they were sent to the gas chambers. Some six million Jews were murdered by 1945. For these crimes, as well as atrocities such as the Bataan Death March, German and Japanese war criminals stood trial.

To tackle the reconstruction of Europe and Japan, the Marshall Plan of 1947 provided money for non-Soviet territories. In an effort to keep more nations from falling under Soviet control, the North Atlantic Treaty Organization (NATO) was created in 1947. As Winston Churchill described it, an "Iron Curtain" had fallen between the United States and the Soviet Union. The "Cold War" was hostile, but with few major conflicts. Eventually, the Soviet Union would disband.

World War II cannot be designated as the "war to end all wars," just as the World War I had not been. Wars continue to be fought for causes both honourable and corrupt. Yet as this book shows, haunting images of World War II remain —from crumbling buildings to emaciated bodies—to remind and caution us to weigh the consequences of human conflict.

CHAPTER 1

THE ORIGINS OF WORLD WAR II, 1929–39

The 1930s were a decade of unmitigated crisis culminating in the outbreak of a second total war. The treaties and settlements of the first postwar era collapsed with shocking suddenness under the impact of the Great Depression and the aggressive revisionism of Japan, Italy, and Germany. By 1933 hardly one of the economic structures raised in the 1920s still stood. By 1935 Adolf Hitler's Nazi regime had torn up the Treaty of Versailles and by 1936, the Locarno treaties as well. Armed conflict began in Manchuria in 1931 and spread to Abyssinia in 1935, Spain in 1936, China in 1937, Europe in 1939, and the United States and U.S.S.R. in 1941.

The context in which this collapse occurred was an "economic blizzard" that enervated the democracies and energized the dictatorial regimes. Western intellectuals and many common citizens lost faith in democracy and free-market economics, while widespread pacifism, isolationism, and the earnest desire to avoid the mistakes of 1914 left Western leaders without the will or the means to defend the order established in 1919.

The militant authoritarian states on the other hand—Italy, Japan, and (after 1933) Germany—seemed only to wax stronger and more dynamic. The Depression did not cause the rise of the Third Reich or the bellicose ideologies of the German, Italian, and Japanese governments (all of which pre-dated the 1930s), but it did create the conditions for the

Nazi seizure of power and provide the opportunity and excuse for Fascist empire-building. Hitler and Benito Mussolini aspired to total control of their domestic societies, in part for the purpose of girding their nations for wars of conquest, which they saw, in turn, as necessary for revolutionary transformation at home. This ideological meshing of foreign and domestic policy rendered the Fascist leaders wholly enigmatic to the democratic statesmen of Britain and France, whose attempts to accommodate rather than resist the Fascist states only made inevitable the war they longed to avoid.

THE ECONOMIC BLIZZARD

The Smoot–Hawley Tariff, the highest in U.S. history, became law on June 17, 1930. Conceived and passed by the House of Representatives in 1929, it may well have contributed to the loss of confidence on Wall Street and signaled American unwillingness to play the role of leader in the world economy. Other countries retaliated with similarly protective tariffs, with the result that the total volume of world trade spiraled downward from a monthly average of $2,900,000,000 in 1929 to less than $1,000,000,000 by 1933. The credit squeeze, bank failures, deflation, and loss of exports forced production down and unemployment up in all industrial nations. In January 1930 the United States had 3,000,000 idle workers, and by 1932 there were more than 13,000,000. In Britain 22 percent of

the adult male work force lacked jobs, while in Germany unemployment peaked in 1932 at 6,000,000. All told, some 30,000,000 people were out of work in the industrial countries in 1932.

Panicky retrenchment and disunity also rendered the Western powers incapable of responding to the first violation of the post–World War I territorial settlements. On Sept. 10, 1931, Viscount Cecil assured the League of Nations that "there has scarcely ever been a period in the world's history when war seemed less likely than it does at the present." Just eight days later officers of Japan's Kwantung Army staged an explosion on the South Manchurian Railway to serve as pretext for military action. Since 1928, China had seemed to be achieving an elusive unity under Chiang Kai-shek's Nationalists (KMT), now based in Nanjing. While the KMT's consolidation of power seemed likely to keep Soviet and Japanese ambitions in check, resurgent Chinese nationalism also posed a threat to British and other foreign interests on the mainland. By the end of 1928, Chiang was demanding the return of leased territories and an end to extraterritoriality in the foreign concessions. On the other hand, the KMT was still split by factions, banditry continued widespread, the Communists were increasingly well-organized in remote Jiangxi, and in the spring of 1931 a rival government sprang up in Canton. To these problems were added economic depression and disastrous floods that took hundreds of thousands of lives.

Japan, meanwhile, suffered from the Depression because of its dependence on trade, its ill-timed return to the gold standard in 1930, and a Chinese boycott of Japanese goods. But social turmoil only increased the appeal of those who saw in foreign expansion a solution to Japan's economic problems. This inter-weaving of foreign and domestic policy, propelled by a rabid nationalism, a power-ful military-industrial complex, hatred of the prevailing distribution of world power, and the raising of a racist banner (in this case, antiwhite) to justify expansion, all bear comparison to European Fascism. It was when the parliamentary government in Tokyo divided as to how to confront this complex of crises that the Kwantung Army acted on its own, invading Man-churia. Manchuria, rich in raw materials, was a prospective sponge for Japanese emigration (250,000 Japanese already resided there) and the gateway to China proper. The Japanese public greeted the conquest with wild enthusiasm.

China appealed at once to the League of Nations, which called for Japanese withdrawal in a resolution of October 24. But neither the British nor U.S. Asiatic fleets (the latter comprising no battleships and just one cruiser) afforded their gov-ernments (obsessed in any case with domestic economic problems) the option of intervention. The tide of Japanese nationalism would have prevented Tokyo from bowing to Western pressure in any case. In December the League Council appointed an investigatory commission under Lord Lytton, while the United States contented itself with propounding the Stimson Doctrine, by which Washington merely refused to recognize changes born of aggression. Unperturbed, the Japanese prompted local collaborators to proclaim, on Feb. 18, 1932, an indepen-dent state of Manchukuo, in effect a Japanese protectorate. In March 1933, Japan announced its withdrawal from the League of Nations, which had been tested and found impotent, at least in East Asia.

The League also failed to advance the cause of disarmament in the first years of the Depression. The London Naval Conference of 1930 proposed an extension of the 1922 Washington ratios for naval tonnage, but this time France and Italy refused to accept the inferior status assigned to them. In land arma-ments, the policies of the powers were by now fixed and predictable. Fascist Italy, despite its financial distress, was unlikely to take disarmament seriously, while Germany, looking for foreign-policy triumphs to bolster the struggling Republic, demanded equal treatment. Either France must disarm, they said, or Germany must be allowed to expand its army. The League Council nonetheless summoned delegates from 60 nations to a grand Disarmament Conference at Geneva beginning in February 1932. When Germany failed to achieve satis-faction by the July adjournment it withdrew from the negotiations.

Negotiations were delayed by a sudden initiative from Mussolini in March. He called for a pact among Germany, Italy, France, and Britain to grant Germany equality, revise the peace treaties, and establish a four-power directorate to resolve international disputes. Mussolini appears to have wanted to downgrade the League in favour of a Concert of Europe, enhancing Italian prestige and perhaps gaining colonial concessions in return for reassuring the Western powers. The French watered down the plan until the Four-Power Pact signed in Rome on June 7 was a mass of anodyne generalities. Any prospect that the new Nazi regime might become part of collective security agreements disappeared on Oct. 14, 1933, when Hitler denounced the unfair treatment accorded Germany at Geneva and announced its withdrawal from the League of Nations.

THE TREATY OF VERSAILLES IS SHREDDED

THE RISE OF HITLER

The National Socialist German Workers' Party (Nazis) exploited the resentment and fear stemming from Versailles and the Depression. Its platform was a clever, if contradictory, mixture of socialism, corporatism, and virulent assertion in foreign policy. The Nazis outdid the Communists in forming paramilitary street gangs to intimidate opponents and create an image of irresistible strength, but unlike the Communists, who implied that war veterans had been dupes of capitalist imperialism, the Nazis honoured

the Great War as a time when the German *Volk* had been united as never before. The army had been "stabbed in the back" by defeatists, they claimed, and those who signed the Armistice and Versailles agreements had been criminals. What was worse, they claimed, was the continued conspiracy against the German people by international capitalists, Socialists, and Jews. Under Nazism alone, they insisted, could Germans again unify under "ein Reich, ein Volk, ein Führer" and get on with the task of combating Germany's real enemies. This amalgam of fervent nationalism and rhetorical socialism, not to mention the charismatic spell of Hitler's oratory and the hypnotic pomp of Nazi rallies, was psychologically more appealing than flaccid liberalism or divisive class struggle. In any case, the Communists (on orders from Moscow) turned to help the Nazis paralyze democratic procedure in Germany in the expectation of seizing power themselves.

Heinrich Brüning resigned as chancellor in May 1932, and the July elections returned 230 Nazi delegates. After two short-lived rightist cabinets foundered, German President Paul von Hindenburg appointed Hitler chancellor on Jan. 30, 1933. The president, parliamentary conservatives, and the army all apparently expected that the inexperienced, lower-class demagogue would submit to their guidance. Instead, Hitler secured dictatorial powers from the Reichstag and proceeded to establish, by marginally legal means, a totalitarian state. Within two years the regime had outlawed all

Adolf Hitler, leader of the Nazi Party, arrives at a rally in Nürnberg in September of 1933. Officers, including Rudolf Hess, follow closely behind. Keystone/Hulton Archive/Getty Images

other political parties and coopted or intimidated all institutions that competed with it for popular loyalty, including the German states, labour unions, press and radio, universities, bureaucracies, courts, and churches. Only the army and foreign office remained in the hands of traditional elites. But this fact, and Hitler's own caution at the start, allowed Western observers fatally to misperceive Nazi foreign policy as simply a continuation of Weimar revisionism.

Hitler's worldview dictated a unity of foreign and domestic policies based on total control and militarization at home and war and conquest abroad. In *Mein Kampf* he ridiculed the Weimar politicians and their "bourgeois" dreams of restoring the Germany of 1914. Rather, the German Volk could never achieve their destiny without Lebensraum ("living space") to support a vastly increased German population and form the basis for world power. Lebensraum, wrote Hitler in *Mein Kampf*, was to be found in the Ukraine and intermediate lands of eastern Europe. This "heartland" of the Eurasian continent (so named by the geopoliticians Sir Halford Mackinder and Karl Haushofer) was especially suited for conquest since it was occupied, in Hitler's mind, by Slavic *Untermenschen* (subhumans) and ruled from the centre of the Jewish-Bolshevik conspiracy in Moscow. By 1933 Hitler had apparently imagined a step-by-step plan for the realization of his goals. The first step was to rearm, thereby restoring complete freedom of maneuver to Germany. The next step was to achieve Lebensraum in alliance with Italy and with the sufferance of Britain. This greater Reich could then serve, in the distant third step, as a base for world dominion and the purification of a "master race." In practice, Hitler proved willing to adapt to circumstances, seize opportunities, or follow the wanderings of intuition. Sooner or later politics must give way to war, but because Hitler did not articulate his ultimate fantasies to the German voters or establishment, his actions and rhetoric seemed to imply only restoration, if not of the Germany of 1914, then the Germany of 1918, after Brest-Litovsk. In fact, his program was potentially without limits.

To be sure, Mussolini was gratified by the triumph of the man he liked to consider his younger protégé, Hitler, but he also understood that Italy fared best while playing France and Germany against each other, and he feared German expansion into the Danubian basin. In September 1933 he made Italian support for Austrian Chancellor Engelbert Dollfuss conditional on the latter's establishment of an Italian-style Fascist regime. In June 1934 Mussolini and Hitler met for the first time, and in their confused conversation (there was no interpreter present) Mussolini understood the Führer to say that he had no desire for *Anschluss*. Yet, a month later, Austrian Nazis arranged a putsch in which Dollfuss was murdered. Mussolini responded with a threat of force (quite likely a bluff) on the Brenner Pass and thereby saved Austrian independence. Kurt von Schuschnigg, a pro-Italian Fascist, took over in Vienna. In Paris and London it seemed that Mussolini was one leader with the will and might to stand up to Hitler.

Joseph Stalin, meanwhile, had repented of the equanimity with which he had witnessed the Nazi seizure of power. Before 1933, Germany and the U.S.S.R. had collaborated, and Soviet trade had been a rare boon to the German economy in the last years of the Weimar Republic. Still, the behaviour of German Communists contributed to the collapse of parliamentarism, and now Hitler had shown that he, too, knew how to crush dissent and master a nation. The Communist line shifted in 1934–35 from condemnation of social democracy, collective security, and Western militarism to collaboration with other anti-Fascist forces in "Popular Fronts," alliance systems, and rearmament. The United States and the U.S.S.R. established diplomatic relations for the first time in November 1933, and in September 1934 the Soviets joined the League of Nations, where Maksim Litvinov became a loud proponent of collective security against Fascist revisionism.

Thus, French foreign minister Louis Barthou's plan for reviving the wartime alliance from World War I and arranging an "Eastern Locarno" began to seem plausible—even after Oct. 9, 1934, when Barthou and King Alexander of Yugoslavia were shot dead in Marseille by an agent of Croatian terrorists. The new French foreign minister, the rightist Pierre Laval, was especially friendly to

Soviet leader Joseph Stalin at work in his office. A portrait of German philosopher Karl Marx, whose theories are credited as the foundation for communism, hangs on the wall over Stalin's head. James Abbe/Hulton Archive/Getty Images

Rome. The Laval–Mussolini agreements of Jan. 7, 1935, declared France's disinterest in the fate of Abyssinia in implicit exchange for Italian support of Austria. Mussolini took this to mean that he had French support for his plan to conquer that independent African country. Just six days later the strength of German nationalism was resoundingly displayed in the Saar plebiscite. The small, coal-rich Saarland, detached from Germany for 15 years under the Treaty of Versailles, was populated by miners of Catholic or social democratic loyalty. They knew what fate awaited their churches and labour unions in the Third Reich, and yet 90 percent voted for union with Germany. Then, on March 16, Hitler used the extension of French military service to two years and the Franco-Soviet negotiations as pretexts for tearing up the disarmament clauses of Versailles, restoring the military draft, and beginning an open buildup of Germany's land, air, and sea forces.

In the wake of this series of shocks Britain, France, and Italy joined on April 11, 1935, at a conference at Stresa to reaffirm their opposition to German expansion. Laval and Litvinov also initialed a five-year Franco-Soviet alliance on May 2, each pledging assistance in case of unprovoked aggression. Two weeks later a Czech-Soviet pact complemented it. Laval's system, however, was flawed; mutual suspicion between Paris and Moscow, the failure to add a military convention, and the lack of Polish adherence meant that genuine Franco-Soviet

military action was unlikely. The U.S.S.R. was in a state of trauma brought on by the Five-Year Plans; the slaughter and starvation of millions of farmers, especially in the Ukraine, in the name of collectivization; and the beginnings of Stalin's mass purges of the government, army, and Communist Party. It was clear that Russian industrialization was bound to overthrow the balance of power in Eurasia, hence Stalin was fearful of the possibility of a preemptive attack before his own militarization was complete. But he was even more obsessed with the prospect of wholesale rebellion against his regime in case of invasion. Stalin's primary goal, therefore, was to keep the capitalist powers divided and the U.S.S.R. at peace. Urging the liberal Western states to combine against the Fascists was one method. Exploring bilateral relations with Germany, as in the 1936 conversations between Hjalmar Schacht and Soviet trade representative David Kandelaki, was another.

Italy and Britain looked askance at the Franco-Soviet combination, while Hitler in any case sugar-coated the pill of German rearmament by making a pacific speech on May 21, 1935, in which he offered bilateral pacts to all Germany's neighbours (except Lithuania) and assured the British that he, unlike the Kaiser, did not intend to challenge them on the seas. The Anglo-German Naval Agreement of June 18, which countenanced a new German navy though limiting it to not larger than 35 percent the size of the

British, angered the French and drove a wedge between them and the British.

ITALIAN AGGRESSION

The Stresa Front collapsed as soon as Paris and London learned the price Mussolini meant to exact for it. By 1935 Mussolini had ruled for 13 years but had made little progress toward his "new Roman Empire" that was to free Italy from the "prison of the Mediterranean." What was more, Il Duce concluded that only the crucible of war could fully undermine the monarchy and the church and consummate the Fascist revolution at home. Having failed to pry the French out of their North African possessions, Mussolini fixed on the independent African empire of Abyssinia (Ethiopia). Italy had failed in 1896 to conquer Abyssinia, thus to do so now would erase a national humiliation. This spacious land astride Italy's existing coastal colonies on the Horn of Africa boasted fertile uplands suitable for Italy's excess rural population, and Mussolini promised abundant raw materials as well. The conquest of Abyssinia would also appear to open the path to the Sudan and Suez.

An Abyssinian soldier has his head bandaged by native members of the British Red Cross. The ill-equipped Abyssinian army was no match for the Italian forces when Mussolini invaded in October 1935. Popperfoto/Getty Images

Finally, this landlocked, semifeudal kingdom seemed an easy target. In fact, Emperor Haile Selassie had begun a modernization program of sorts, but this only suggested that the sooner Italy struck, the better.

The Italian army was scarcely prepared for such an undertaking, and Mussolini made matters worse by ordering ill-trained blackshirt brigades to Africa and entrusting the campaign to a Fascist loyalist, Emilio De Bono, rather than to a senior army officer. The military buildup at Mitsiwa left little doubt as to Italian intentions, and Britain tried in June to forestall the invasion by arranging the cession of some Abyssinian territories. But Mussolini knew that the British Mediterranean fleet was as unready as his own and expected no interference.

De Bono's absurdly large army invaded Ethiopia from Eritrea on Oct. 3, 1935. Adwa, the site of the 1896 debacle, fell in three days, after which the advance bogged down and Mussolini replaced De Bono with Marshal Pietro Badoglio. The League Council promptly declared Italy the aggressor (October 7), whereupon France and Britain were caught on the horns of a dilemma. To wink at Italy's conquest would be to condone aggression and admit the bankruptcy of the League. On the other hand, to resist would be to smash the Stresa Front and lose Italian help against the greater threat, Germany. The League finally settled on economic sanctions but shied away from an embargo on oil, which would have grounded the Italian army and air force, or closure of the Suez Canal, which would have cut the Italian supply line. The remaining sanctions only vexed Italy without helping Abyssinia. Germany, no longer a League member, ignored the sanctions and so healed its rift with Rome.

In December, Laval and Sir Samuel Hoare, the British foreign secretary, contrived a secret plan to offer Mussolini most of Abyssinia in return for a truce. This Hoare–Laval Plan was a realistic effort to end the crisis and repair the Stresa Front, but it also made a mockery of the League. When it was leaked to the press, public indignation forced Hoare's resignation. The Italians finally took the fortress of Mekele on November 8, but their slow advance led Mussolini to order a major offensive in December. He instructed Badoglio to use whatever means necessary, including terror bombing and poison gas, to end the war.

THE FIRST GERMAN MOVE

Hitler observed the Abyssinian war with controlled glee, for dissolution of the Stresa Front—composed of the guarantors of Locarno—gave him the chance to reoccupy the Rhineland with minimal risk. A caretaker government under Albert Sarraut was in charge of France during a divisive electoral campaign dominated by the leftist Popular Front, and Britain was convulsed by a constitutional crisis stemming from King Edward VIII's insistence on marrying an American divorcée. On March 7, 1936, Hitler ordered a token force of 22,000 German soldiers across the bridges of the Rhine. Characteristically, he chose a weekend for his sudden move and then softened the blow with offers of nonaggression pacts and a new demilitarized zone on both sides of the frontier. Even so, Hitler assured his generals that he would retreat if the French intervened.

German reoccupation and fortification of the Rhineland was the most significant turning point of the interwar years. After March 1936 the British and French could no longer take forceful action against Hitler except by provoking the total war they feared. The French Cabinet also concluded that it should do nothing without the full agreement of the British. But London was not the place to look for backbone. Prime Minister Stanley Baldwin shrugged, "They might succeed in smashing Germany with the aid of Russia, but it would probably only result in Germany going Bolshevik," while the editor of *The Times* asked, "It's none of our business, is it? It's their own back-garden they're walking into." By failing to respond to the violation, however, Britain, France, and Italy had broken the Locarno treaties just as gravely as had Germany.

The strategic situation in Europe now shifted in favour of the Fascist powers. In June, Mussolini appointed as foreign minister his son-in-law Galeazzo Ciano, who concluded an agreement with Germany on July 11 in which Italy acquiesced in Austria's behaving hence-forth as "a German state." The Rome–Berlin Axis followed on November 1, and the German–Japanese Anti-Comintern Pact, another vague agreement ostensibly directed at Moscow, on November 25. Finally, Belgium unilaterally renounced its alliance with France on October 14 and returned to its traditional neutrality in hopes of escaping the coming storm. As a direct result of the Abyssinian imbroglio, the militant revisionists had come together and the status quo powers had splintered.

Meanwhile, on May 5, 1936, Italian troops had entered Addis Ababa and completed the conquest of Abyssinia, although the country was never entirely pacified, despite costly and brutal repression. The Abyssinian war had been a disaster for the democracies, smashing both the Stresa Front and the credibility of the League. As the historian A.J.P. Taylor wrote, "One day [the League] was a powerful body imposing sanctions, seemingly more effective than ever before; the next day it was an empty sham, everyone scuttling from it as quickly as possible." In December 1937, Italy, too, quit the League of Nations.

BRITISH APPEASEMENT AND AMERICAN ISOLATIONISM

THE CIVIL WAR IN SPAIN

The Spanish Civil War highlighted the contrast between democratic bankruptcy and totalitarian dynamism. In 1931 the Spanish monarchy gave way to a republic whose unstable government moved steadily to the left, outraging the army and church. After repeated provocations on both sides, army and air force officers proclaimed a Nationalist revolt on July 17, 1936, that survived its critical early weeks with logistical help from Portugal's arch-conservative premier, António Salazar. The Nationalists, rallying behind General Francisco Franco, quickly seized most of Old Castile in the north and a beachhead in the south extending from Córdoba to Cádiz opposite Spanish Morocco, where the insurrection had begun. But the Republicans, or loyalists (a Popular Front composed of liberals, Socialists, Trotskyites, Stalinists, and anarchists), took up arms to defend the Republic elsewhere and sought outside aid against what they styled as the latest Fascist threat. Spain became a battleground for the ideologies that were wrestling for mastery of Europe.

The civil war posed a dilemma for France and Britain, pitting the principle of defending democracy against the principle of noninterference in the domestic affairs of other states. The ineffectual Blum at first fraternally promised aid to the Popular Front in Madrid, but he reneged within a month for fear that such involvement might provoke a European war or a civil war in France. The British government counseled nonintervention and seemingly won Germany and Italy to that position, but Hitler, on well-rehearsed anti-Bolshevik grounds,

hurriedly dispatched 20 transport planes that allowed Franco to move reinforcements from Morocco. Not to be outdone, Mussolini sent matériel, Fascist "volunteers," and, ultimately, regular army formations. The Italians performed miserably (especially at Guadalajara in March 1937), but German aid, including the feared Condor Legion, was effective. Hitler expected to be paid for his support, however, with economic concessions, and he also saw Spain as a testing-ground for Germany's newest weapons and tactics. These included terror bombing such as that over Guernica in April 1937, which caused far fewer deaths than legend has it but which became an icon of anti-Fascism through the painting of Pablo Picasso. International aid to the Republicans ran from the heroic to the sinister. Thousands of leftists and idealistic volunteers from throughout Europe and America flocked to International Brigades to defend the Republic. Material support, however, came only from Stalin, who demanded gold payment in return and ordered Comintern agents and commissars to accompany the Soviet supplies. These Stalinists systematically murdered Trotskyites and other "enemies on the left," undermined the radical government of Barcelona, and exacerbated the intramural confusion in Republican ranks. The upshot of Soviet intervention was to discredit the Republic and thereby strengthen Western resolve to stay out.

The war dragged on through 1937 and 1938 and claimed some 500,000 lives before the Nationalists finally captured

Barcelona in January 1939 and Madrid in March. During the final push to victory, France and Britain recognized Franco's government. By then, however, the fulcrum of diplomacy had long since shifted to central Europe. The Nationalist victory did not, in the end, redound to the detriment of France, for Franco politely sent the Germans and Italians home and observed neutrality in the coming war, whereas a pro-Communist Spain might have posed a genuine threat to France during the era of the Nazi–Soviet pact.

JAPAN'S AGGRESSION IN CHINA

The first major challenge to American isolationism, however, occurred in Asia. After pacifying Manchukuo, the Japanese turned their sights toward North China and Inner Mongolia. Over the intervening years, however, the KMT had made progress in unifying China. The Communists were still in the field, having survived their Long March (1934–35) to Yan'an in the north, but Chiang's government, with German and American help, had introduced modern roads and communications, stable paper currency, banking, and educational systems. How might Tokyo best round out its continental interests: by preemptive war or by cooperating with this resurgent China to expel Western influence from East Asia? The chief of the operations section of the Japanese general staff favoured collaboration and feared that an invasion of China proper would bring war with the Soviets or the Americans, whose

economic potential he understood. Supreme headquarters, however, preferred to take military advantage of apparent friction between Chiang and a North China warlord. In September 1936, when Japan issued seven secret demands that would have made North China a virtual Japanese protectorate, Chiang rejected them. In December Chiang was kidnapped by the commander of Nationalist forces from Manchuria, who tried to force him to suspend fighting the Communists and to declare war on Japan. Called the Xi'an Incident, this kidnapping demonstrated the unlikelihood of Chinese collaboration with the Japanese program and strengthened the war party in Tokyo. As in 1931, hostilities began almost spontaneously and soon took on a life of their own.

An incident at the Marco Polo Bridge near Beijing (then known as Beiping) on July 7, 1937, escalated into an undeclared Sino-Japanese war. Contrary to the Japanese analysis, both Chiang and Mao Zedong vowed to come to the aid of North China, while Japanese moderates failed to negotiate a truce or localize the conflict and lost all influence. By the end of July the Japanese had occupied Beijing and Tianjin. The following month they blockaded the South China coast and captured Shanghai after brutal fighting and the slaughter of countless civilians. Similar atrocities accompanied the fall of Nanjing on December 13. The Japanese expected the Chinese to sue for peace, but Chiang moved his government to Hankou and continued to resist the "dwarf bandits" with hit-and-run tactics that sucked the invaders in more deeply. The Japanese could occupy cities and fan out along roads and rails almost at will, but the countryside remained hostile.

World opinion condemned Japan in the harshest terms. The U.S.S.R. concluded a nonaggression pact with China (Aug. 21, 1937), and Soviet-Mongolian forces skirmished with Japanese on the border. Britain vilified Japan in the League, while Roosevelt invoked the Stimson Doctrine in his "quarantine speech" of October 5. But Roosevelt was prevented by the Neutrality acts from aiding China even after the sinking of U.S. and British gunboats on the Yangtze.

On March 28, 1938, the Japanese established a Manchukuo-type puppet regime at Nanjing, and spring and summer offensives brought them to the Wuhan cities (chiefly Hankou) on the Yangtze. Chiang stubbornly moved his government again, this time to Chongqing, which the Japanese bombed mercilessly in May 1939, as they did Guangzhou (Canton) for weeks before its occupation in October. Such incidents, combined with the Nazi and Fascist air attacks in Spain and Abyssinia, were omens of the total war to come. The United States finally took a first step in opposition to Japanese aggression on July 29, 1939, announcing that it would terminate its 1911 commercial treaty with Japan in six months and thereby cut off vital raw materials to the Japanese war machine. It was all Roosevelt could do under existing law, but it set in motion the events that would lead to Pearl Harbor.

Anschluss and the Munich Pact

The German-Austrian Union

Heightened assertiveness also characterized foreign policies in Europe in 1937. But while Hitler's policies involved explicit preparations for war, Britain's consisted of explicit attempts to satisfy him with concessions. The conjuncture of these policies doomed the independence of Austria, Czechoslovakia, and Poland, and set Europe on a slippery slope to war.

By the end of 1936, Hitler and the Nazis were total masters of Germany with the exceptions of the army and the foreign office, and even the latter had to tolerate the activities of a special party apparatus under the Nazi "expert" on foreign policy, Joachim von Ribbentrop. Nazi prestige, bolstered by such theatrics as the Berlin Olympics, the German pavilion at the Paris Exhibition, and the enormous Nürnberg (Nuremberg) party rallies, was reaching its zenith. In September 1936, Hitler imitated Stalin again in his proclamation of a Four-Year Plan to prepare the German economy for war under the leadership of Hermann Göring. With the Rhineland secured, Hitler grew anxious to begin his "drive to the east," if possible with British acquiescence. To this end he appointed Ribbentrop ambassador to London in October 1936 with the plea, "Bring me back the British alliance." Intermittent talks lasted a year, their main topic being the return of the German colonies lost at Versailles. But agreement was impossible, since Hitler's real goal was a free hand on the Continent, while the British hoped, in return for specific concessions, to secure arms control and respect for the status quo.

Meanwhile, Stanley Baldwin, having seen the abdication crisis through to a finish, retired in May 1937 in favour of Neville Chamberlain. The latter now had the chance to pursue what he termed "active appeasement": find out what Hitler really wants, give it to him, and thereby save the peace and husband British resources for defense of the empire against Italy and Japan. By the time of Lord Halifax's celebrated visit to Berchtesgaden in November 1937, Hitler had already lost interest in the talks and begun to prepare for the absorption (*Anschluss*) of Austria, a country in which, said Halifax, Britain took little interest.

On November 5, Hitler made a secret speech in the presence of the commanders of the three armed services, War Minister Werner von Blomberg, Foreign Minister Konstantin von Neurath, and Göring. The Führer made clear his

belief that Germany must begin to expand in the immediate future, with Austria and Czechoslovakia as the first targets, and that the German economy must be ready for full-scale war by 1943–45. Historians have debated whether the November 5

After its annexation in 1938, German soldiers—as well as the familiar flag of the Nazi Party—became a common sight in Austria. Hugo Jaeger/Time & Life Pictures/Getty Images

speech was a blueprint for aggression, a plea for continued rearmament, or preparation for the purges that followed. But there is no denying that the overheated Nazi economy had reached a critical turn with labour and resources fully employed and capital running short. Hitler would soon have to introduce austerity measures, slow down the arms program, or make good the shortages of labour and capital through plunder. Since these material needs pushed in the same direction as Hitler's dynamic quest for Lebensraum, 1937 merely marked the transition into concrete time-tables of what Hitler had always desired.

German intrigues in Austria had continued since 1936 through the agency of Arthur Seyss-Inquart's Nazi movement. When Papen, now ambassador to Vienna, reported on Feb. 5, 1938, that the Schuschnigg regime showed signs of weakness, Hitler invited the Austrian dictator to a meeting on the 12th. In the course of an intimidating tirade Hitler demanded that Nazis be included in the Vienna government. Schuschnigg, however, insisted that Austria remain "free and German, independent and social, Christian and united," and scheduled a plebiscite for March 13 through which Austrians might express their will. Hitler hurriedly issued directives to the military, and when Schuschnigg was induced to resign, Seyss-Inquart simply appointed himself chancellor and invited German troops to intervene. A last-minute Italian demarche inviting Britain to make colonial concessions in return for Italian support of Austria met only "indignant resignation" and Anthony Eden's irrelevant complaints about Italy's troops in Spain. A French plea for Italian firmness, in turn, provoked Ciano to ask: "Do they expect to rebuild Stresa in an hour with Hannibal at the gates?" Still, Hitler waited nervously on the evening of March 11 until he was informed that Mussolini would take no action in support of Austria. Hitler replied with effusive thanks and promises of eternal amity. In the nighttime invasion, 70 percent of the vehicles sent into Austria by the unprepared Wehrmacht broke down on the road to Vienna, but they met no resistance. Austrians cheered deliriously on the 13th, when Hitler declared Austria a province of the Reich.

The Taking of Czechoslovakia

The *Anschluss* outflanked the next state on Hitler's list, Czechoslovakia. Once again Hitler could make use of national self-determination to confuse the issue, as 3,500,000 German-speakers organized by another Nazi henchman, Konrad Henlein, inhabited the Czech borderlands in the Sudeten Mountains. Already on February 20, before the *Anschluss*, Hitler had denounced the Czechs for alleged persecution of this German minority, and on April 21 he ordered Keitel to prepare for the invasion of Czechoslovakia by October even if the French should intervene. Chamberlain was intent on appeasing Hitler, but this meant "educating" him to seek redress of grievances through

(From left to right) *Prime Ministers Lord Neville Chamberlain (U.K.), Édouard Daladier (France), German Chancellor Adolf Hitler, Benito Mussolini (Italy), and Italian Foreign Minister Count Ciano meet in Munich on September 30, 1938. At this meeting, a treaty was signed allowing Germany to annex Czechoslovakian territory called the Sudetenland.* AFP/ Getty Images

negotiation, not force. As the prospect of war increased, the British appeasers grew more frantic. Chamberlain then journeyed to Berchtesgaden and proposed to give the Germans all they demanded. Hitler, nonplussed, spoke of the cession of all Sudeten areas at least 80 percent German and agreed not to invade while Chamberlain won over Paris and Prague.

The French Cabinet of Édouard Daladier and Georges-Étienne Bonnet agreed, after the latter's frantic pleas to Roosevelt failed to shake American isolation. The Czechs, however, resisted handing over their border fortifications to Hitler until September 21, when the British and French made it clear that they would not fight for the Sudetenland. Chamberlain flew to Bad Godesberg the next day only to be met with a new demand that the entire Sudetenland be ceded to Germany within a week. The Czechs, fully mobilized as of the 23rd, refused, and Chamberlain returned home in a funk: "How horrible, fantastic, incredible it is that we should be digging trenches and trying on gas masks here because of a quarrel in a far-away country between people of whom we know nothing." But his sorrowful address to Parliament was interrupted by the news that Mussolini had proposed a conference to settle the crisis peacefully. Hitler agreed, having seen how little enthusiasm there was in Germany for war and on the advice of Göring, Joseph Goebbels, and the generals. Chamberlain and Daladier, elated, flew to Munich on September 29.

The awkward and pitiful Munich Conference ended on the 30th in a compromise prearranged between the two dictators. The Czechs were to evacuate all regions indicated by an international commission (subsequently dominated by the Germans) by October 10 and were given no recourse—the agreement was final. Poland took the opportunity to grab the Teschen district disputed since 1919. Czechoslovakia was no longer a viable state, and Beneš resigned the presidency in despair. In return, Hitler promised no more territorial demands in Europe and consultations with Britain in case of any future threat to peace. Chamberlain was ecstatic.

Hitler had no intention of honouring Munich, however. In October the Nazis encouraged the Slovak and Ruthene minorities in Czechoslovakia to set up autonomous governments and then in November awarded Hungary the 4,600 square miles (11,914 sq km) north of the Danube taken from it in 1919. On March 13, 1939, Gestapo officers carried the Slovak leader Monsignor Jozef Tiso off to Berlin and deposited him in the presence of the Führer, who demanded that the Slovaks declare their independence at once. Tiso returned to Bratislava to inform the Slovak Diet that the only alternative to becoming a Nazi protectorate was invasion. They complied. All that remained to the new president in Prague, Emil Hácha, was the core region of Bohemia and Moravia. It was time, said Hácha with heavy sarcasm, "to consult our friends in Germany." There Hitler subjected the elderly, broken-spirited man to a tirade that brought tears, a fainting spell, and finally a signature on a "request" that Bohemia and Moravia be incorporated into the Reich. The next day, March 16, German units occupied Prague, and Czechoslovakia ceased to exist.

CHAPTER 2

AXIS TRIUMPHANT, 1939–41

THE OUTBREAK OF WAR

By the early part of 1939 the German dictator Adolf Hitler had become determined to invade and occupy Poland. Poland, for its part, had guarantees of French and British military support should it be attacked by Germany. Hitler intended to invade Poland anyway, but first he had to neutralize the possibility that the Soviet Union would resist the invasion of its western neighbour. Secret negotiations led on August 23–24 to the signing of the German-Soviet Nonaggression Pact in Moscow. In a secret protocol of this pact, the Germans and the Soviets agreed that Poland should be divided between them, with the western third of the country going to Germany and the eastern two-thirds being taken over by the U.S.S.R.

Having achieved this cynical agreement, the other provisions of which stupefied Europe even without divulgence of the secret protocol, Hitler thought that Germany could attack Poland with no danger of Soviet or British intervention and gave orders for the invasion to start on August 26. News of the signing, on August 25, of a formal treaty of mutual assistance between Great Britain and Poland (to supersede a previous though temporary agreement) caused him to postpone the start of hostilities for a few days. He was still determined, however, to ignore the diplomatic efforts of the western powers to restrain him. Finally, at 12:40 PM on Aug. 31, 1939, Hitler ordered hostilities against Poland to start at 4:45 the next morning. The invasion began as ordered. In response, Great Britain and France declared war on Germany on September 3, at 11:00 AM and at 5:00 PM, respectively. World War II had begun.

INITIAL FORCES AND RESOURCES OF THE EUROPEAN COMBATANTS

In September 1939 the Allies, namely Great Britain, France, and Poland, were together superior in industrial resources, population, and military manpower. Yet the German Army, or Wehrmacht, because of its armament, training, doctrine, discipline, and fighting spirit, was the most efficient and effective fighting force for its size in the world. The index of military strength in September 1939 was the number of divisions that each nation could mobilize. Against Germany's 100 infantry divisions and six armoured divisions, France had 90 infantry divisions in metropolitan France, Great Britain had 10 infantry divisions, and Poland had 30 infantry divisions, 12 cavalry brigades, and one armoured brigade (Poland had also 30 reserve infantry divisions, but these could not be mobilized quickly). A division contained from 12,000 to 25,000 men.

Adolf Hitler reviewing troops on the Eastern Front, 1939. Heinrich Hoffmann, Munich

It was the qualitative superiority of the German infantry divisions and the number of their armoured divisions that made the difference in 1939. The firepower of a German infantry division far exceeded that of any French, British, or Polish division; the standard German division included 442 machine guns, 135 mortars, 72 antitank guns, and 24 howitzers. Allied divisions had a firepower only slightly greater than that of World War I.

Germany had six armoured divisions in September 1939. These armoured, or panzer, divisions comprised some 2,400 tanks. And though Germany would subsequently expand its tank forces during the first years of the war, it was not the number of tanks that Germany had, but the fact of their being organized into divisions and operated as such that was to prove decisive. While the allies had a large number of tanks (almost as many as Germany), they had no armoured divisions at that time. In accordance with the doctrines of General Heinz Guderian, the German tanks were used in massed formations in conjunction with motorized artillery to punch holes in the enemy line and to isolate segments of the enemy, which were then surrounded and captured by motorized German infantry divisions, while the tanks ranged forward to repeat the process: deep drives into enemy territory by panzer divisions were thus followed by mechanized infantry and foot soldiers. These tactics were supported by dive bombers that attacked and disrupted the enemy's supply and communications lines and spread panic and confusion in its rear, thus further paralyzing its defensive capabilities.

German Pz. IV (foreground) and Pz. III (background) tanks, 1942. U.S. Army photograph

German Junkers Ju 87 "Stuka" dive-bomber. UPI

Mechanization was the key to the German blitzkrieg, or "lightning war," so named because of the unprecedented speed and mobility that were its salient characteristics. Tested and well-trained in maneuvers, the German panzer divisions constituted a force with no equal in Europe.

The German Air Force, or Luftwaffe, was also the best force of its kind in 1939. It was a ground-cooperation force designed to support the Army, but its planes were superior to nearly all Allied types. In the rearmament period from 1935 to 1939 the production of German combat aircraft steadily mounted. The table on page 245 shows the production of German aircraft by year.

The standardization of engines and airframes gave the Luftwaffe an advantage over its opponents. Germany had an operational force of 1,000 fighters and 1,050 bombers in September 1939. The Allies actually had more planes in 1939 than Germany did, but their strength was made up of many different types, some of them obsolete. The table on page 245 shows the number of first-line military aircraft available to the Allies at the outbreak of war.

Great Britain, which was held back by delays in the rearmament program, was producing one modern fighter in 1939, the Hurricane. A higher-performance fighter, called the Spitfire, was just coming into production and did not enter the air war in numbers until 1940.

The value of the French Air Force in 1939 was reduced by the number of obsolete planes in its order of battle: 131 of the 634 fighters and nearly all of the 463 bombers. France was desperately trying to buy high-performance aircraft in the United States in 1939.

At sea the odds against Germany were much greater in September 1939 than in August 1914, since the Allies in 1939 had many more large surface warships than Germany had. At sea, however, there was to be no clash between the Allied and the German massed fleets but only the individual operation of German pocket battleships and commerce raiders.

ARMOURED DIVISIONS AND AIRPOWER

The experience of World War I seemed to vindicate the power of the defensive over the offensive. It was widely believed that a superiority in numbers of at least three to one was required for a successful offensive. Defensive concepts underlay the construction of the Maginot Line between France and Germany and of its lesser counterpart, the Siegfried Line, in the interwar years. Yet by 1918 both of the requirements for the supremacy of the offensive were at hand: tanks and planes. The battles of Cambrai (1917) and Amiens (1918) had proved that when tanks were used in masses, with surprise, and on firm and open terrain, it was possible to break through any trench system.

The Germans learned this crucial, though subtle, lesson from World War I. The Allies on the other hand felt that their victory confirmed their methods, weapons, and leadership, and in the interwar period the French and British armies were slow to introduce new weapons, methods, and doctrines. Consequently, in 1939 the British Army did not have a single armoured division, and the French tanks were distributed in small packets through- out the infantry divisions. The Germans, by contrast, began to develop large tank formations on an effective basis after their rearmament program began in 1935.

In the air the technology of war had also changed radically between 1918 and 1939. Military aircraft had increased in size, speed, and range, and for operations at sea, aircraft carriers were developed that were capable of accompanying the fastest surface ships. Among the new types of planes developed was the dive bomber, a plane designed for accurate low-altitude bombing of enemy strong points as part of the tank-plane-infantry combination. Fast low-wing monoplane fighters were developed in all countries; these aircraft were essentially flying platforms for eight to 12 machine guns installed in the wings. Light and medium bombers were also developed that could be used for the strategic bombardment of cities and military strongpoints. The threat of bomber attacks on both military and civilian targets led directly to the development of radar in England. Radar made it possible to determine the location, the distance, and the height and speed of a distant aircraft no matter what the weather was. By December 1938 there were five radar stations established on the coast of England, and 15 additional stations were begun. So, when war came in September 1939, Great Britain had a warning chain of radar stations that could tell those in command when hostile planes were approaching.

GERMANY OVERRUNS EUROPE

POLAND

The German conquest of Poland in Sep- tember 1939 was the first demonstration in war of the new theory of high-speed armoured warfare that had been adopted by the Germans when their rearmament began. Poland was a country all too well suited for such a demonstration. Its frontiers were immensely long—about 3,500 miles (5,633 km) in all; and the stretch of 1,250 miles (2,012 km) adjoining German territory had recently been extended to 1,750 miles (2,816 km) in all by the German occupation of Bohemia-Moravia and of Slovakia, so that Poland's southern flank became exposed to invasion—as the northern flank, facing East Prussia, already was. Western Poland had become a huge salient that lay between Germany's jaws.

When war broke out the Polish Army was able to mobilize about 1,000,000 men, a fairly large number. The Polish Army was woefully outmoded, however, and was almost completely lacking in tanks, armoured personnel carriers, and antitank and antiaircraft guns. Yet many of the Polish military leaders clung to the double belief that their preponderance of horsed cavalry was an important asset and that they could take the offensive against the German mechanized forces. They also tended to discount the effect of Germany's vastly superior air force, which was nearly 10 times as powerful as their own.

The unrealism of such an attitude was repeated in the Polish Army's positions. Approximately one-third of Poland's forces were concentrated in or near the Polish Corridor (in northeastern Poland), where they were perilously exposed to a double envelopment, from East Prussia and the west combined. In the south, facing the main avenues of a German advance, the Polish forces were thinly spread. At the same time, nearly another one-third of Poland's forces were massed in reserve in the north-central part of the country, between Łódź and Warsaw, under the commander in chief, Marshal Edward Rydz-Śmigły. The Poles' forward concentration in general forfeited their chance of fighting a series of delaying actions, since their foot-marching army was unable to retreat to their defensive positions in the rear or to man them before being overrun by the invader's mechanized columns.

The 40-odd infantry divisions employed by the Germans in the invasion counted for much less than their 14 mechanized or partially mechanized divisions. These 14 divisions consisted of six armoured divisions; four light divisions, consisting of motorized infantry (infantry wholly transported by trucks and personnel carriers) with two armoured units; and four motorized divisions. The Germans attacked with about 1,500,000 troops in all. It was the deep and rapid thrusts of these mechanized forces that decided the issue, in conjunction with the overhead pressure of the Luftwaffe, which wrecked the Polish railway system and destroyed most of the Polish Air Force before it could come into action. The Luftwaffe's terror-bombing of Polish cities, bridges, roads, rail lines, and power stations completed the disorganization of the Polish defenses.

The German attack began on Sept. 1, 1939. Against northern Poland, General

The Polish cavalry moves to the front to meet the invading German forces in September of 1939. Popperfoto/Getty Images

Fedor von Bock commanded an army group comprising General Georg von Küchler's 3rd Army, which struck southward from East Prussia, and General Günther von Kluge's 4th Army, which struck eastward across the base of the Corridor. Much stronger in troops and in tanks, however, was the army group in the south under General Gerd von Rundstedt, attacking from Silesia and from the Moravian and Slovakian border. As part of this group, General Johannes Blaskowitz's 8th Army, on the left, was to drive eastward against Łódź. General Wilhelm List's 14th Army, on the right, was to push on toward Kraków and to turn the Poles' Carpathian flank. And General Walter von Reichenau's 10th Army, in the centre, with the bulk of the group's armour, was to deliver the decisive blow with a northwestward thrust into the heart of Poland. By September 3, when Kluge in the north had reached the Vistula and Küchler was approaching the Narew River, Reichenau's armour was already beyond the Warta. Two days later his left wing was well to the rear of Łódź and his right wing at Kielce. By September 8 one of his armoured corps was in the outskirts of Warsaw, having advanced 140 miles (225 km) in the first week of war. Light divisions on Reichenau's right were on the Vistula between Warsaw and Sandomierz by September 9, while List, in the south, was on the San above and below Przemyśl. At the same time, the 3rd Army tanks, led by Guderian, were across the Narew attacking the line of the Bug River, behind Warsaw. All the German armies had made progress in fulfilling their parts in the great enveloping maneuver planned by General Franz Halder, chief of the general staff, and directed by General Walther von Brauchitsch, the commander in chief. The Polish armies were splitting up into uncoordinated fragments, some of which were retreating while others were delivering disjointed attacks on the nearest German columns.

On September 10 the Polish commander in chief, Marshal Edward Rydz-Śmigły, ordered a general retreat to the southeast. The Germans, however, were by that time not only tightening their net around the Polish forces west of the Vistula (in the Łódź area and, still farther west, around Poznań) but also penetrating deeply into eastern Poland. The Polish defense was already reduced to random efforts by isolated bodies of troops when another blow fell: on Sept. 17, 1939, Soviet forces entered Poland from the east. The next day, the Polish government and high command crossed the Romanian frontier on their way into exile. The Warsaw garrison held out against the Germans until September 28, undergoing terror-bombings and artillery barrages that reduced parts of the city to rubble, with no regard for the civilian population. The last considerable fragment of the Polish Army resisted until October 5, and some guerrilla fighting went on into the winter. The Germans took a total of 700,000 prisoners, and about 80,000 Polish soldiers escaped over neutral frontiers. Approximately 70,000 Polish soldiers were killed and more than 130,000 wounded during the battle, whereas the Germans sustained about 45,000 total casualties. Poland was conquered for partition between Germany and the U.S.S.R., the forces of which met and greeted each other on Polish soil. On September 28 another secret German-Soviet protocol modified the arrangements of August: all Lithuania was to be a Soviet sphere of influence, not a German one; but the dividing line in Poland was changed in Germany's favour, being moved eastward to the Bug River.

The Baltic states and the Russo-Finnish War

Profiting quickly from its understanding with Germany, the U.S.S.R. on Oct. 10, 1939, constrained Estonia, Latvia, and Lithuania to admit Soviet garrisons onto their territories. Approached with similar demands, Finland refused to comply, even though the U.S.S.R. offered territorial compensation elsewhere for the cessions that it was requiring for its own strategic reasons. Finland's armed forces amounted to about 200,000 troops in 10 divisions. The Soviets eventually brought about 70 divisions (about 1,000,000 men) to bear

In their attack on Finland, along with about 1,000 tanks. Soviet troops attacked Finland on Nov. 30, 1939.

The invaders succeeded in isolating the little Arctic port of Petsamo in the far north but were ignominiously repulsed on all of the fronts chosen for their advance. On the Karelian Isthmus, the massive reinforced-concrete fortifications of Finland's Mannerheim Line blocked the Soviet forces' direct land route from Leningrad into Finland. The Soviet planners had grossly underestimated the Finns' national will to resist and the natural obstacles constituted by the terrain's numerous lakes and forests.

The western powers exulted overtly over the humiliation of the Soviet Union. One important effect of Finland's early successes was to reinforce the tendency of both Hitler and the western democracies to underestimate the Soviet military capabilities. But in the meantime, the Soviet strategists digested their hard-learned military lessons.

On Feb. 1, 1940, the Red Army launched 14 divisions into a major assault on the Mannerheim Line. The offensive's weight was concentrated along a 10-mile (16-km) sector of the line near Summa, which was pounded by a tremendous artillery bombardment. As the fortifications were pulverized, tanks and sledge-carried infantry advanced to occupy the ground while the Soviet Air Force broke up attempted Finnish counterattacks. After little more than a fortnight of this methodical process, a breach was made through the whole depth of the Mannerheim Line. Once the Soviets had forced a passage on the Karelian Isthmus, Finland's eventual collapse was certain. On March 6 Finland sued for peace, and a week later the Soviet terms were accepted: the Finns had to cede the entire Karelian Isthmus, Viipuri, and their part of the Rybachy Peninsula to the Soviets. The Finns had suffered about 70,000 casualties in the campaign, the Soviets more than 200,000.

GERMAN CONQUESTS IN THE WEST

THE "PHONY WAR"

During their campaign in Poland, the Germans kept only 23 divisions in the west to guard their frontier against the French, who had nearly five times as many divisions mobilized. The French commander in chief, General Maurice-Gustave Gamelin, proposed an advance against Germany through neutral Belgium and The Netherlands, in order to have room to exercise his ponderous military machine. He was overruled, however, and French assaults on the 100-mile (161-km) stretch of available front along the Franco-German frontier had barely dented the German defenses when the collapse of Poland prompted the recall of Gamelin's advanced divisions to defensive positions in the Maginot Line. From October 1939 to March 1940, successive plans were developed for counteraction in the event of a German offensive through Belgium—all of them based on the assumption that the Germans would come across the plain north of Namur, not across the hilly and wooded Ardennes. The Germans would indeed have taken the route foreseen by the French if Hitler's desire for an offensive in November 1939 had not been frustrated, on the one hand, by bad weather and, on the other, by the hesitations of his generals. But in March 1940 the bold suggestion of General Erich von Manstein that an offensive through the Ardennes should, in fact, be practicable for tank forces was adopted by Hitler, despite orthodox military opinion.

After France's failure to interrupt the German conquest of Poland, the western powers and the Germans were so inactive with regard to land operations that journalists began to speak derisively, over the next six months, of the "phony war." At sea, however, the period was somewhat more eventful. German U-boats sank the British aircraft carrier *Courageous* (September 17) and the battleship *Royal Oak* (October 14). The U-boats' main warfare, however, was against merchant shipping: they sank more than 110 vessels in the first four months of the war. Both the Germans and the British, meanwhile, were engaged in extensive mine laying.

In surface warfare at sea, the British were on the whole more fortunate than the Germans. A German pocket battleship in the Atlantic, the *Admiral Graf Spee* sank nine ships before coming to a tragic end. Having sustained and inflicted damage in an engagement with three British cruisers off the Río de la Plata on Dec. 13, 1939, she made off to Montevideo and obtained leave to spend four days there for repairs. In that time,

A German U-boat, or submarine, with some of its crew on deck, circa 1940. Keystone/Hulton Archive/Getty Images

the British mustered reinforcements for the two cruisers still capable of action after the engagement, namely the *Ajax* and the *Achilles*, and brought the *Cumberland* to the scene in time. But, on December 17, when the *Graf Spee* put to sea again, its crew scuttled the ship a little way out of the harbour before the fight could be resumed.

THE INVASION OF NORWAY

Hitler's immediate outlook had been changed by considerations about Scandinavia. Originally he had intended to respect Norway's neutrality. Then rumours leaked out, prematurely, of British designs on Norway—as, in fact, Winston Churchill, first lord of the Admiralty, was arguing that mines should be laid in Norwegian waters to stop the export of Swedish iron ore from Gällivare to Germany through Norway's rail terminus and port of Narvik. The British Cabinet, in response to Churchill, authorized at least the preparation of a plan for a landing at Narvik; and in mid-December 1939 a Norwegian politician, Vidkun Quisling, leader of a pro-Nazi party, was introduced to Hitler. On Jan. 27, 1940, Hitler ordered plans for an invasion of Norway, which he would use if he could no longer respect Norway's neutrality.

British plans for landings on the Norwegian coast in the third week of March 1940 were temporarily postponed. Prime Minister Neville Chamberlain, however, was by that time convinced that some aggressive action ought to be taken.

Paul Reynaud, who succeeded Daladier as France's premier on March 21, was of the same opinion. It was agreed that mines should be laid in Norwegian waters and that the mining should be followed by the landing of troops at four Norwegian ports, Narvik, Trondheim, Bergen, and Stavanger.

Because of Anglo-French arguments, the date of the mining was postponed from April 5 to April 8. The postponement was catastrophic. Hitler had on April 1 ordered the German invasion of Norway to begin on April 9. So, when on April 8 the Norwegian government was preoccupied with earnest protest about the British mine laying, the German expeditions were well on their way.

On April 9, 1940, the major Norwegian ports from Oslo northward to Narvik were occupied by advance detachments of German troops. At the same time, a single parachute battalion (the first ever employed in warfare) took the Oslo and Stavanger airfields, and 800 operational aircraft overawed the Norwegian population. Norwegian resistance at Narvik, at Trondheim, at Bergen, at Stavanger, and at Kristiansand had been overcome very quickly; and Oslo's effective resistance to the seaborne forces was nullified when German troops from the airfield entered the city.

Simultaneously, along with their Norwegian enterprise, the Germans on April 9 occupied Denmark, sending troopships, covered by aircraft, into Copenhagen harbour and marching over the land frontier into Jutland. This

During the German invasion of Norway, several homes in Narvik were burnt to the ground. Fox Photos/Hulton Archive/Getty Images

occupation was obviously necessary for the safety of their communications with Norway.

Allied troops began to land at Narvik on April 14. Shortly afterward, British troops were landed also at Namsos and at Åndalsnes, to attack Trondheim from the north and from the south, respectively. The Germans, however, landed fresh troops in the rear of the British at Namsos and advanced up the Gudbrandsdal from Oslo against the force at Åndalsnes. By this time the Germans had about 25,000 troops in Norway. By May 2, both Namsos and Åndalsnes were evacuated by the British. The Germans at Narvik held out against five times as many British and French troops until May 27. By that time the German offensive in France had progressed to such an extent that the British could no longer afford any commitment in Norway, and the 25,000 Allied troops were evacuated from Narvik 10 days after their victory. The Norwegian king Haakon VII and his government left Norway for Britain at the same time. Hitler garrisoned Norway with about 300,000 troops for the rest of the war. By occupying Norway, Hitler had ensured the protection of Germany's supply of iron ore from Sweden and had obtained naval and air bases with which to strike at Britain if necessary.

What was to happen in Norway became a less important question for the western powers when, on May 10, 1940, they were surprised by Hitler's long-debated stroke against them through the Low Countries.

THE INVASION OF THE LOW COUNTRIES AND FRANCE

France's 800,000-man standing army was thought at the time to be the most powerful in Europe. But the French had not progressed beyond the defensive mentality inherited from World War I, and they relied primarily on their Maginot Line for protection against a German offensive. The Maginot Line was an extremely well-developed chain of fortifications running from the Swiss frontier opposite Basel northward along the left bank of the Rhine and then north-westward no farther than Montmédy, near the Belgian frontier south of the Ardennes Forest. The line consisted of a series of giant pillboxes and other defensive installations constructed in depth, equipped with underground supply and communications facilities, and con-nected by rail lines, with all its heavy guns pointed east at the German frontier. Depending heavily on the line as a defense against German attack, the French had 41 divisions manning it or backing it, whereas only 39 divisions were

watching the long stretch of frontier north of it. This northern frontier stretched from Montmédy through the Ardennes and across Flanders to the English Channel.

In their plan for the invasion of France and the Low Countries, the Germans kept General Wilhelm von Leeb's Army Group C facing the Maginot Line. This tactic was meant to deter the French from diverting forces from the line, while Germany launched Bock's Army Group B into the basin of the Lower Maas River north of Liège and Rundstedt's Army Group A into the Ardennes. Army Group B comprised Küchler's 18th Army, with one armoured division and airborne support, to attack The Netherlands, and Reichenau's 6th, with two armoured divisions, to advance over the Belgian plain. These two armies would have to deal not only with the Dutch and Belgian armies but also with the forces that the Allies, according to their plan, would send into the Low Countries, namely two French armies and nine British divisions. Rundstedt's Army Group A, however, was much stronger, comprising as it did Kluge's 4th Army, List's 12th, and General Ernst Busch's 16th, with General Max-imilian von Weichs's 2nd in reserve, besides a large armoured group under Kleist and a smaller one under General Hermann Hoth. Army Group A amounted to 44 divisions, seven of them armoured, with 27 divisions in reserve. In other words more than 1,500,000 men and more than 1,500 tanks, would strike at the weak hinge of the Allies' wheel into Belgium—that is to say, at two French armies, General Charles Huntziger's 2nd and General André Corap's 9th. Together these armies mustered only 12 infantry and four horsed cavalry divisions and stood, respectively, east and west of Sedan on the least-fortified stretch of the French frontier. Against this weak centre of the Allied line were thus massed nearly two-thirds of Germany's forces in the west and nearly three-quarters of its tank forces.

Küchler's army and the panzer division began their attack on the Netherlands on May 10. The Dutch Army comprised 10 divisions and the equivalent of 10 more in smaller formations, and thus totaled more than 400,000 men. It apparently had a good chance of withstanding the German invasion, since the attacking German army comprised only seven divisions, apart from the airborne forces it would use. The Dutch, however, had a wide front, a very sensitive and loosely settled rear, very few tanks, and no experience of modern warfare. The German attack on The Netherlands began with the capture by parachutists of the bridges at Moerdijk, at Dordrecht, and at Rotterdam and with landings on the airfields around The Hague. On the same day, the weakly held Peel Line, south of the westward-turning arc of the Maas, was penetrated by the German land forces. On May 11 the Dutch defenders fell back westward past Tilburg to Breda, with the consequence that the French 7th Army, under General Henri Giraud, whose leading forces had sped forward

In Focus: Blitzkrieg

Blitzkrieg (German: "lightning war") was a military tactic calculated to create psychological shock and resultant disorganization in enemy forces through the employment of surprise, speed, and superiority in matériel or firepower. Tested by the Germans during the Spanish Civil War in 1938 and against Poland in 1939, the blitzkrieg proved to be a formidable combination of land and air action. The essence of blitzkrieg is the use of mobility, shock, and locally concentrated firepower in a skillfully coordinated attack to paralyze an adversary's capacity to coordinate his own defenses, rather than attempting to physically overcome them, and then to exploit this paralysis by penetrating to his rear areas and disrupting his whole system of communications and administration. The tactics, as employed by the Germans, consisted of a splitting thrust on a narrow front by combat groups using tanks, dive-bombers, and motorized artillery to disrupt the main enemy battle position at the point of attack. Wide sweeps by armoured vehicles followed, creating large pockets of trapped and immobilized enemy forces. These tactics were remarkably economical of both lives and matériel, primarily for the attackers but also, because of the speed and short duration of the campaign, among the victims.

Blitzkrieg tactics were used in the successful German invasions of Belgium, The Netherlands, and France in 1940. German commander Erwin Rommel used them during the desert campaigns in North Africa, as did U.S. General George Patton in the European operations of 1944.

across Belgium over the 140 miles (225 km) to Tilburg, fell back to Breda likewise. The German tanks thus had a clear road to Moerdijk, and by noon on May 12 they were in the outskirts of Rotterdam. North of the Maas, meanwhile, where the bulk of the Dutch defense was concentrated, the Germans achieved a narrow breach of the Geld Valley line on May 12. The Dutch, unable to counterattack, retreated to the "Fortress of Holland" Line protecting Utrecht and Amsterdam. Queen Wilhelmina and her government left the country for England on May 13; and the next day the Dutch commander in chief, General Henri Gerard Winkelman, surrendered to the Germans, who had threatened to bomb Rotterdam and Utrecht, as places in the front line of the fighting, if resistance continued. In fact, Rotterdam was bombed, after the capitulation, by 30 planes through a mistake in the Germans' signal communications.

The news of the German onslaught in the Low Countries, dismaying as it was to the Allies, had one effect that was to be of momentous importance to their fortunes: Chamberlain, whose halfhearted conduct of the war had been bitterly criticized in the House of Commons during the debate of May 7–8 on the campaign in Norway, resigned office in the evening of May 10. He was succeeded as prime minister by Churchill, who formed a coalition government.

For the first phase of the invasion of the Belgian plain north of Liège, Reichenau had four army corps, one armoured corps, and only 500 airborne troops. However, he also had massive cooperation from the German Luftwaffe, whose dive bombers and fighters played a major role in breaking down the Belgian defenses. West of the Maastricht "appendix" of indefensible Dutch territory separating Belgium from Germany, the fortress of Eben Emael, immediately opposite Maastricht, and the line of the Albert Canal constituted the Belgians' foremost defensive position. On May 10 German airborne troops landed in gliders on the top of the fortress and on bridges over the canal. On May 11 the Belgian front was broken. The German tanks continued westward and some of the infantry turned southward to take Liège from the rear, while the Belgians made a general retreat to the Antwerp–Namur, or Dyle, Line. French and British divisions had just arrived on this Dyle Line, and General René Prioux's two tank divisions went out from it to challenge the German advance. After a big battle on May 14, however, Prioux's tanks had to retire to the consolidated Dyle Line. On May 15, notwithstanding a successful defense against a German attack, Gamelin ordered the abandonment of the position, because events farther to the south had made it strategically untenable.

The chances for success of the German offensive against France hinged on Germany's unorthodox decision to advance through the hilly and dense Ardennes Forest, which the French considered to be impassable to tanks. But the Germans did succeed in moving their tank columns through that difficult belt of country by means of an amazing feat of staff work. While the armoured divisions used such roads through the forest as were available, infantry divisions started alongside them by using field and woodland paths and marched so fast across country that the leading ones reached the Meuse River only a day after the armoured divisions had.

The decisive operations in France were those of Rundstedt's Army Group A. Kleist's tanks on May 10 took only three hours to cover the 30 miles (48 km) from the eastern border of independent Luxembourg to the southeastern border of Belgium. On May 11 the French cavalry divisions that had ridden forward into the Ardennes to oppose them were thrown back over the Semois River. By the evening of May 12 the Germans were across the Franco-Belgian frontier and overlooking the Meuse River. The defenses of this sector were rudimentary; it was the least-fortified stretch of the whole French front. Worse still, the defending French 2nd and 9th armies had hardly any antitank guns or antiaircraft artillery with which to slow down the German armoured columns and shoot down their dive-bombers. Such was the folly of the French belief that a German armoured thrust through the Ardennes was unlikely.

On May 13 Kleist's forces achieved a threefold crossing of the Meuse River. At Sedan wave after wave of German dive-bombers swooped on the French defenders of the south bank. The latter could not stand the nerve-racking strain, and the German troops were able to push across the river in rubber boats and on rafts. The tremendous air bombardment was the decisive factor in the crossings. A thousand aircraft supported Kleist's forces, while only a few French aircraft intervened in a gallant but hopeless effort to aid their troops on the ground. Next day, after the tanks had been brought across, Guderian widened the Sedan bridgehead and beat off French counterattacks. On May 15 he broke through the French defenses into open country, turning westward in the direction of the English Channel. On May 16 his forces swept west for nearly 50 miles (80 km). His superiors tried to put on the brake, feeling that such rapid progress was hazardous, but the pace of the German drive upset the French far more, and their collapse spread as Reinhardt's corps joined in the pressure. When more German tanks crossed the Meuse between Givet and Namur, the breach of the French front was 60 miles (97 km) wide.

Driving westward down the empty corridor between the Sambre and the Aisne rivers, Guderian's tanks crossed the Oise River on May 17 and reached Amiens two days later. Giraud, who on May 15 had superseded Corap in command of the French 9th Army, was thus frustrated in his desperate plan of checking the Germans on the Oise. Kleist, meanwhile, by lining the Aisne progressively with tanks until the infantry came up to relieve them, was protecting the southwestern flank of the advance against the danger of a counteroffensive from the south. Indeed, when the Germans, on May 15, were reported to be crossing the Aisne River between Rethel and Laon, Gamelin told Reynaud that he had no reserves in that sector and that Paris might fall within two days' time. Thereupon Reynaud, though he postponed his immediate decision to move the government to Tours, summoned General Maxime Weygand from Syria to take Gamelin's place as commander in chief. Weygand did not arrive until May 19.

Guderian's tanks were at Abbeville on May 20, and on May 22 he turned northward to threaten Calais and Dunkirk, the remaining ports by which the British Expeditionary Force (BEF) could be evacuated. Reinhardt, swinging south of

the British rear at Arras, headed for the same objectives

THE EVACUATION FROM DUNKIRK

For the Allies, all communication between their northern and southern forces was severed by the arc of the westward German advance from the Ardennes to the Somme. The Allied armies in the north, having fallen back from the Dyle Line to the Escaut (Scheldt), were being encircled, and already on May 19 the British commander, Viscount Gort, was considering the withdrawal of the BEF by sea. On May 21, however, to satisfy orders from London for more positive action, he

Following the 1940 German invasion of France and the evacuation of Paris, Parisians flee their city by foot, bicycle, and truck. Hulton Archive/Getty Images

launched an attack from Arras southward against the right flank of the Germans' corridor. But, though it momentarily alarmed the German high command, this small counterstroke lacked the armoured strength necessary for success. Meanwhile, Guderian's tanks had swept up past Boulogne and Calais and were crossing the canal defense line close to Dunkirk when, on May 24, an inexplicable order from Hitler not only stopped their advance but actually called them back to the canal line just as Guderian was expecting to drive into Dunkirk.

Dunkirk was now the only port left available for the withdrawal of the mass of the BEF from Europe, and the British Cabinet at last decided to save what could be saved. The British Admiralty had been collecting every kind of small craft it could find to help in removing the troops, and the British retreat to the coast now became a race to evacuate the troops before the Germans could occupy Dunkirk. Evacuation began on May 26 and became still more urgent the next day, when the Belgians, their right wing and their centre broken by Reichenau's advance, sued for an armistice. On May 27, likewise, bombing by the Luftwaffe put the harbour of Dunkirk out of use. Many of the thousands of men thronging the 10-mile (16-km) stretch of beaches had to be ferried out to sea by petty craft pressed into service by the Royal Navy and manned largely by amateur seamen, though the harbour's damaged breakwater still offered a practicable exit for the majority. By June 4, when the operation came to an end, 198,000 British and 140,000 French and Belgian troops had been saved. However, virtually all of their heavy equipment had to be abandoned, and, of the 41 destroyers participating, six were sunk and 19 others damaged. The men who were saved represented a considerable part of the experienced troops possessed by Great Britain and were an inestimable gain to the Allies. The success of the near-miraculous evacuation from Dunkirk was due, on the one hand, to fighter cover by the Royal Air Force from the English coast and on the other to Hitler's fatal order of May 24 halting Guderian. That order had been made for several reasons. Chiefly, Hermann Göring, head of the Luftwaffe, had mistakenly assured Hitler that his aircraft alone could destroy the Allied troops trapped on the beaches at Dunkirk. And Hitler himself seems to have believed that Great Britain might accept peace terms more readily if its armies were not constrained into humiliating surrender. Three days passed before Brauchitsch, the German Army commander in chief, was able to persuade Hitler to withdraw his orders and allow the German armoured forces to advance on Dunkirk. But they met stronger opposition from the British, who had had time to solidify their defenses, and almost immediately Hitler stopped the German armoured forces again, ordering them instead to move south and prepare for the attack on the Somme–Aisne line.

The campaign in northern France was wound up by Küchler's forces, after

After being cut off by the German army, the British Expeditionary Forces are evacuated from Dunkirk, France. Keystone/Hulton Archive/Getty Images

both Guderian and Reichenau had been ordered southward. Altogether, the Germans had taken more than 1,000,000 prisoners in three weeks, at a cost of 60,000 casualties. Some 220,000 Allied troops, however, were rescued by British ships from France's northwestern ports (Cherbourg, Saint-Malo, Brest, and Saint-Nazaire), thus bringing the total of Allied troops evacuated to about 558,000.

There remained the French armies south of the Germans' Somme–Aisne front. The French had lost 30 divisions in the campaign so far. Weygand still managed to muster 49 divisions, apart from the 17 left to hold the Maginot Line, but against him the Germans had 130 infantry divisions as well as their 10 divisions of tanks. The Germans, after redisposing their units, began a new offensive on June 5 from their positions on the Somme. The French resisted stiffly for two days, but on June 7 the German tanks in the westernmost sector, led by Major General Erwin Rommel, broke through toward Rouen, and on June 9 they were over the Seine. On June 9 the Germans attacked on the Aisne: the infantry forced the crossings, and then Guderian's armour drove through the breach toward Châlons-sur-Marne before turning eastward for the Swiss frontier, thus isolating all the French forces still holding the Maginot Line.

Italy's Entry into the War and the French Armistice

Italy had been unprepared for war when Hitler attacked Poland, but if the Italian leader, Benito Mussolini, was to reap any positive advantages from partnership with Hitler it seemed that Italy would have to abandon its nonbelligerent stance before the western democracies had been defeated by Germany single-handed. The obvious collapse of France convinced Mussolini that the time to implement his Pact of Steel with Hitler had come, and on June 10, 1940, Italy declared war against France and Great Britain. With about 30 divisions available on their Alpine frontier, the Italians delayed their actual attack on southeastern France until June 20, but it achieved little against the local defense. In any case, the issue in France had already been virtually settled by the victory of Italy's German ally.

Meanwhile, Reynaud had left Paris for Cangé, near Tours. Weygand, after speaking frankly and despondently to Churchill at the Allied military headquarters at Briare on June 11, told Reynaud and the other ministers at Cangé on June 12 that the battle for France was lost and that a cessation of hostilities was compulsory. There was little doubt that he was correct in this estimate of the military situation: the French armies were now splitting up into fragments. Reynaud's government was divided

between the advocates of capitulation and those who, with Reynaud, wanted to continue the war from French North Africa. The only decision that it could make was to move itself from Tours to Bordeaux.

The Germans entered Paris on June 14, 1940, and were driving still deeper southward along both the western and eastern edges of France. Two days later they were in the Rhône valley. Meanwhile, Weygand was still pressing for an armistice, backed by all the principal commanders. Reynaud resigned office on June 16, whereupon a new government was formed by Marshal Philippe Pétain, the revered and aged hero of the Battle of Verdun in World War I. In the night of June 16 the French request for an armistice was transmitted to Hitler. While discussion of the terms went on, the German advance went on too. Finally, on June 22, 1940, at Rethondes, the scene of the signing of the Armistice of 1918, the new Franco-German Armistice was signed. The Franco-Italian Armistice was signed on June 24. Both armistices came into effect early on June 25.

The Armistice of June 22 divided France into two zones: one to be under German military occupation and one to be left to the French in full sovereignty. The occupied zone comprised all northern France from the northwestern frontier of Switzerland to the Channel and from the Belgian and German frontiers to the Atlantic, together with a strip extending from the lower Loire southward along the Atlantic coast to the western end of the Pyrenees; the unoccupied zone comprised only two-fifths of France's territory, the southeast. The French Navy and Air Force were to be neutralized, but it was not required that they be handed over to the Germans. The Italians granted very generous terms to the French: the only French territory that they claimed was the small frontier tract that their forces had succeeded in overrunning since June 20. Meanwhile, from June 18, General Charles de Gaulle, whom Reynaud had sent on a military mission to London on June 5, was broadcasting appeals for the continuance of France's war.

The collapse of France in June 1940 posed a severe naval problem to the British, because the powerful French Navy still existed. Strategically, it was of immense importance to the British that these French ships not fall into German hands, since they would have tilted the balance of sea power decidedly in favour of the Axis—the Italian Navy being now also at war with Britain. Mistrustful of promises that the French ships would be used only for "supervision and minesweeping," the British decided to immobilize them. Thus, on July 3, 1940, the British seized all French ships in British-controlled ports, encountering only nominal resistance. But when British ships appeared off Mers el-Kébir, near Oran on the Algerian coast, and demanded that the ships of the important French naval force there either join the Allies or sail out to sea, the French refused to submit. The British eventually opened fire, damaging the battleship *Dunkerque*,

IN FOCUS: FREE FRENCH

The Free French Forces in World War II were formed for the continuation of warfare against Germany after the military collapse of Metropolitan France in the summer of 1940. Led by General Charles de Gaulle, the Free French were eventually able to unify most French resistance forces in their struggle against Germany.

The government of France had been constitutionally transmitted to Marshal Philippe Pétain on June 16, 1940. Pétain had already decided that France must conclude an armistice with Germany. Two days later, a French army officer, General Charles de Gaulle, appealed by radio from London (whence he had fled on June 17) for a French continuation of the war against Germany. On June 28 de Gaulle was recognized by the British as the leader of Free France (as the nascent resistance movement was named), and from his base in London de Gaulle began to build up the Forces Françaises Libres, or Free French Forces. At first these consisted merely of French troops in England, volunteers from the French community resident in England since prewar times, and a few units of the French Navy.

In the autumn of 1940 the French colonial territories of Chad, Cameroun, Moyen-Congo, French Equatorial Africa, and Oubangi-Chari (all in sub-Saharan Africa) rallied to de Gaulle's Free France, and the smaller French colonies in India and in the Pacific soon followed suit. A Free French military expedition in September 1940 to capture the important naval base of Dakar in French West Africa failed, however, and the base remained in the hands of French forces loyal to the national government that Pétain had set up in Vichy.

In 1941 Free French forces participated in British-controlled operations against Italian forces in Libya and Egypt, and that same year they joined the British in defeating the Vichy forces in Syria and Lebanon. In September de Gaulle created the Comité National Français (French National Committee), a Free French government-in-exile that was recognized by the Allied governments.

Despite these gains, the Free French remained a small force until 1942, by which time an underground anti-Nazi Résistance movement had sprung up in France. In his efforts to obtain the support of the Résistance, de Gaulle changed the name of his movement to Forces Françaises Combattantes (Fighting French Forces) and sent his emissary Jean Moulin to France to try to unify all the various Résistance groups in France under de Gaulle's leadership. Moulin came close to accomplishing this in May 1943 with his establishment of the Conseil Nationale de la Résistance (National Council of the Resistance).

French general Charles de Gaulle (1890–1970) delivers a historic speech from London, urging the French people to fight Germany despite the truce between Germany and France. Hulton Archive/Getty Images

The successful Anglo-American invasion of northwestern Africa in November 1942 resulted in the defection of most of the Vichy troops stationed there to the side of the Free French. De Gaulle then entered a power struggle with the Allied-backed commander in chief of the French forces in North Africa, General Henri Giraud. In June 1943 a Comité Français de Libération Nationale (French Committee of National Liberation) was constituted in Algiers, with Giraud and de Gaulle as its joint presidents. But de Gaulle soon outmaneuvered Giraud, whose resignation in the spring of 1944 left de Gaulle in supreme control of the entire French war effort outside of Metropolitan France. More and more Résistance groups were meanwhile acknowledging de Gaulle's leadership.

More than 100,000 Free French troops fought in the Anglo-American campaign in Italy in 1943, and, by the time of the Allied invasion of Normandy in June 1944, the Free French forces had swelled to more than 300,000 regular troops. They were almost wholly American-equipped and supplied. In August 1944 the Free French 1st Army, under General Jean de Lattre de Tassigny, took part in the Allies' invasion of southern France, driving thence northeastward into Alsace before joining in the Western Allies' final thrust into Germany. In August 1944 the Résistance groups, now organized as Forces Françaises de l'Intérieur (French Forces of the Interior), mounted an anti-German insurrection in Paris, and the Free French 2nd Armoured Division under General Jacques-Philippe Leclerc drove into Paris to consummate the liberation. On Aug. 26, 1944, de Gaulle entered Paris in triumph.

destroying the *Bretagne*, and disabling several other vessels. Thereupon, Pétain's government, which on July 1 had installed itself at Vichy, on July 4 severed diplomatic relations with the British. In the eight following days, the constitution of France's Third Republic was abolished and a new French state created, under the supreme authority of Pétain himself. The few French colonies that rallied to General de Gaulle's Free French movement were strategically unimportant.

THE BATTLE OF BRITAIN

With France conquered, Hitler could now turn his forces on Germany's sole remaining enemy: Great Britain, which was protected from the formidable German Army by the waters of the English Channel. On July 16, 1940, Hitler issued a directive ordering the preparation and, if necessary, the execution of a plan for the invasion of Great Britain. But an amphibious invasion of Britain would only be possible, given Britain's large navy, if Germany could establish control of the air in the battle zone. To this end, the Luftwaffe chief, Göring, on August 2 issued the "Eagle Day" directive, laying down a plan of attack in which a few massive blows from the air were to destroy British air power and so open the way for the amphibious invasion, termed

Operation "Sea Lion." Victory in the air battle for the Luftwaffe would indeed have exposed Great Britain to invasion and occupation. The victory by the Royal Air Force (RAF) Fighter Command blocked this possibility and, in fact, created the conditions for Great Britain's survival, for the extension of the war, and for the eventual defeat of Nazi Germany.

The forces engaged in the battle were relatively small. The British disposed some 600 frontline fighters to defend the country. The Germans made available about 1,300 bombers and dive-bombers, and about 900 single-engined and 300 twin-engined fighters. These were based in an arc around England from Norway to

Supermarine Spitfire, Britain's premier fighter plane from 1938 through World War II. Quadrant/Flight

the Cherbourg Peninsula in northern coastal France. The preliminaries of the Battle of Britain occupied June and July 1940, the climax August and September, and the aftermath—the so-called Blitz—the winter of 1940–41. In the campaign, the Luftwaffe had no systematic or consistent plan of action. Sometimes it tried to establish a blockade by the destruction of British shipping and ports. Sometimes, it worked to destroy Britain's Fighter Command by combat and by the bombing of ground installations. And sometimes, it sought direct strategic results by attacks on London and other populous centres of industrial or political significance. The British, on the other hand, had prepared

themselves for the kind of battle that in fact took place. Their radar early warning, the most advanced and the most operationally adapted system in the world, gave Fighter Command adequate notice of where and when to direct their fighter forces to repel German bombing raids. The Spitfire, moreover, though still in short supply, was unsurpassed as an interceptor by any fighter in any other air force.

The British fought not only with the advantage—unusual for them—of superior equipment and undivided aim but also against an enemy divided in object and condemned by circumstance and lack of forethought to fight at a tactical disadvantage. The German bombers lacked

The entrance to a large London hospital, surrounded by debris, after being damaged by a bomb, c. 1940. Keystone/Hulton Archive/Getty Images

the bomb-load capacity to strike permanently devastating blows and also proved, in daylight, to be easily vulnerable to the Spitfires and Hurricanes. Britain's radar, moreover, largely prevented them from exploiting the element of surprise. The German dive-bombers were even more vulnerable to being shot down by British fighters, and long-range fighter cover was only partially available from German fighter aircraft, since the latter were operating at the limit of their flying range.

The German air attacks began on ports and airfields along the English Channel, where convoys were bombed and the air battle was joined. In June and July 1940, as the Germans gradually redeployed their forces, the air battle moved inland over the interior of Britain. On August 8 the intensive phase began, when the Germans launched bombing raids involving up to nearly 1,500 aircraft a day and directed them against the British fighter airfields and radar stations. In four actions, on August 8, 11, 12, and 13, the Germans lost 145 aircraft as against the British loss of 88. By late August the Germans had lost more than 600 aircraft, the RAF only 260, but the RAF was losing badly needed fighters and experienced pilots at too great a rate, and its effectiveness was further hampered by bombing damage done to the radar stations. At the beginning of September the British retaliated by unexpectedly launching a bombing raid on Berlin, which so infuriated Hitler that he ordered the Luftwaffe to shift its attacks from Fighter Command installations to London and other cities.

These assaults on London, Coventry, Liverpool, and other cities went on unabated for several months. But already, by September 15, on which day the British believed, albeit incorrectly, that they had scored their greatest success by destroying 185 German aircraft, Fighter Command had demonstrated to the Luftwaffe that it could not gain air ascendancy over Britain. This was because British fighters were simply shooting down German bombers faster than German industry could produce them. The Battle of Britain was thus won, and the invasion of England was postponed indefinitely by Hitler. The British had lost more than 900 fighters but had shot down about 1,700 German aircraft.

During the following winter, the Luftwaffe maintained a bombing offensive, carrying out night-bombing attacks on Britain's larger cities. By February 1941 the offensive had declined, but in March and April there was a revival, and nearly 10,000 sorties were flown, with heavy attacks made on London. Thereafter German strategic air operations over England withered.

CENTRAL EUROPE AND THE BALKANS

The continued resistance of the British caused Hitler once more to change his timetable. His great design for a campaign against the U.S.S.R. had originally been scheduled to begin about 1943—by which time he should have secured the German position on the rest of the

European continent by a series of "local-ized" campaigns and have reached some sort of compromise with Great Britain. But in July 1940, seeing Great Britain still undefeated and the United States increas-ingly inimical to Germany, he decided that the conquest of the European part of the Soviet Union must be undertaken in May 1941, in order both to demonstrate Germany's invincibility to Great Britain and to deter the United States from intervention in Europe (because the elim-ination of the U.S.S.R. would strengthen the Japanese position in the Far East and in the Pacific). Events in the interval, however, were to make him change his plan once again.

While the invasion of the U.S.S.R. was being prepared, Hitler was much concerned to extend German influence across Slovakia and Hungary into Romania, the oil fields of which he was anxious to secure against Soviet attack. In addition, he believed the military manpower of Romania might be joined to the forces of the German coalition. In May 1940 he obtained an oil and arms pact from Romania. But, when Romania, after being constrained by a Soviet ulti-matum in June to cede Bessarabia and northern Bukovina to the U.S.S.R., requested a German military mission and a German guarantee of its remaining frontiers, Hitler refused to comply until the claims of other states against Romania had been met. Romania was compelled to cede southern Dobruja to Bulgaria on August 21 (an act that was formalized in the Treaty of Craiova on September 7); but its

negotiations with Hungary about Tran-sylvania were broken off on August 23. Since, if war had broken out between Romania and Hungary, the U.S.S.R. might have intervened and won control over the oil wells, Hitler decided to arbitrate immediately. By the Vienna Award of August 30, Germany and Italy assigned northern Transylvania, including the Szekler district, to Hungary, and Germany then guaranteed what was left of Romania. In the face of the Romanian nationalists' outcry against these proceedings, the king, Carol II, transferred his dictatorial powers to General Ion Antonescu on Sept. 4, 1940, and abdicated his crown in favour of his young son Michael two days later. Antonescu had already repeated the request for a German military mission, which arrived in Bucharest on October 12.

Though Hitler had apprised the Italian foreign minister, Galeazzo Ciano, of his intention to send a military mission to Romania, Ciano had not apprised Mussolini. So, since the latter's Balkan ambitions had been continually restrained by Hitler, particularly with regard to Yugoslavia, the sudden news of the mission annoyed him. On Oct. 28, 1940, therefore, having given Hitler only the barest hints of his project, Mussolini launched seven Italian divisions (155,000 men) from Albania into a separate war of his own against Greece.

The result was exasperating for Hitler. His ally's forces were not only halted by the Greeks, a few miles over the border, on Nov. 8, 1940, but were also driven back by General Alexandros Papagos's counteroffensive of November 14, which was to put the Greeks in possession of one-third of Albania by mid-December. Moreover, British troops landed in Crete, and some British aircraft were sent to bases near Athens, whence they might have attacked the Romanian oil fields. Lastly, the success of the Greeks caused Yugoslavia and Bulgaria, who had hitherto been attentive to overtures from the Axis powers, to revert to a strictly neutral policy.

Anticipating Mussolini's appeal for German help in his "separate" or "parallel" war, Hitler in November 1940 drew Hungary, Romania, and Slovakia successively into the Axis, or Tripartite, Pact that Germany, Italy, and Japan had concluded on September 27. He also obtained Romania's assent to the assembling of German troops in the south of Romania for an attack on Greece through Bulgaria. Hungary consented to the transit of these troops through its territory lest Romania take Hungary's place in Germany's favour and so be secured in possession of the Transylvanian lands left to it by the Vienna Award. Bulgaria, however, for fear of Soviet reaction, on the one hand, and of Turkish, on the other (Turkey had massed 28 divisions in Thrace when Italy attacked Greece), delayed its adhesion to the Axis until March 1, 1941. Only thereafter, on March 18, did the Yugoslav regent, Prince Paul, and his ministers Dragiša Cvetkovic and Aleksandar Cincar-Marković agree to Yugoslavia's adhesion to the Axis.

Meanwhile, the German 12th Army had crossed the Danube from Romania into Bulgaria on March 2, 1941. Consequently, in accordance with a Greco-British agreement of February 21, a British expeditionary force of 58,000 men from Egypt landed in Greece on March 7, to occupy the Olympus–Vermion line. Then, on March 27, 1941, two days after the Yugoslav government's signature, in Vienna, of its adhesion to the Axis Pact, a group of Yugoslav Army officers, led by General Dušan Simović, executed a coup d'état in Belgrade, overthrowing the regency in favour of the 17-year-old king Peter II and reversing the former government's policy.

Almost simultaneously with the Belgrade coup d'état, the decisive Battle of Cape Matapan took place between the British and Italian fleets in the Mediterranean, off the Peloponnesian mainland northwest of Crete. Hitherto, Italo-British naval hostilities in the Mediterranean area since June 1940 had comprised only one noteworthy action: the sinking in November at the Italian naval base of Taranto of three battleships by aircraft from the British carrier *Illustrious*. In March 1941, however, some Italian naval forces, including the battleship *Vittorio Veneto*, with several cruisers and destroyers, set out to threaten British convoys to Greece. British forces, including the battleships *Warspite*, *Valiant*, and *Barham* and the aircraft carrier *Formidable*, likewise with cruisers and destroyers, were sent to intercept them. When the forces met in the morning of March 28, off Cape Matapan, the *Vittorio Veneto* opened fire on the lighter British ships but was soon trying to escape from the engagement, for fear of the torpedo aircraft from the *Formidable*. The battle then became a pursuit, which lasted long into the night. Finally, though the severely damaged *Vittorio Veneto* made good its escape, the British sank three Italian cruisers and two destroyers. The Italian Navy made no more surface ventures into the eastern Mediterranean.

The German attack on Greece, scheduled for April 1, 1941, was postponed for a few days when Hitler, because of the Belgrade coup d'état, decided that Yugoslavia was to be destroyed at the same time. While Great Britain's efforts to draw Yugoslavia into the Greco-British defensive system were fruitless, Germany began canvassing allies for its planned invasion of Yugoslavia and Greece. Italy agreed to collaborate in the attack, and Hungary and Bulgaria agreed to send troops to occupy the territories that they coveted as soon as the Germans should have destroyed the Yugoslav state.

On April 6, 1941, the Germans, with 24 divisions and 1,200 tanks, invaded both Yugoslavia (which had 32 divisions) and Greece (which had 15 divisions). The operations were conducted in the same way as Germany's previous blitzkrieg campaigns. While massive air raids struck Belgrade, List's 12th Army drove westward and southward from the Bulgarian frontiers, Kleist's armoured group moved northwestward from Sofia, and Weichs's 2nd Army advanced southward from Austria and from western Hungary. The 12th Army's advance

through Skopje to the Albanian border cut communications between Yugoslavia and Greece in two days. Niš fell to Kleist on April 9, Zagreb to Weichs on April 10, and on April 11 the Italian 2nd Army (comprising 15 divisions) advanced from Istria into Dalmatia. After the fall of Belgrade to the German forces from bases in Romania (April 12), the remnant of the Yugoslav Army—whose only offensive, in northern Albania, had collapsed—was encircled in Bosnia. Its capitulation was signed, in Belgrade, on April 17.

In Greece, meanwhile, the Germans took Salonika (Thessaloníki) on April 9, 1941, and then initiated a drive toward Ioánnina (Yannina), thus severing communication between the bulk of the Greek Army (which was on the Albanian frontier) and its rear. The isolated main body capitulated on April 20, the Greek Army as a whole followed suit on April 22. Two days later the pass of Thermopylae, defended by a British rear guard, was taken by the Germans, who entered Athens on April 27. All mainland Greece and all the Greek Aegean islands except Crete were under German occupation by May 11. The Ionian islands were under Italian control. The remainder of Britain's 50,000-man force in Greece was hastily evacuated with great difficulty after leaving all of their tanks and other heavy equipment behind.

The campaign against Yugoslavia brought 340,000 soldiers of the Yugoslav Army into captivity as German prisoners of war. In the campaign against Greece the Germans took 220,000 Greek and

20,000 British or Commonwealth prisoners of war. The combined German losses in the Balkan campaigns were about 2,500 dead, 6,000 wounded, and 3,000 missing.

German airborne troops began to land in Crete on May 20, 1941, at Máleme, in the Canea-Suda area, at Réthimnon, and at Iráklion. Fighting, on land and on the sea, with heavy losses on both sides, went on for a week before the Allied commander in chief, General Bernard Cyril Freyberg of the New Zealand Expeditionary Force, was authorized to evacuate the island. The last defenders were overwhelmed at Réthimnon on May 31. The prisoners of war taken by the Germans in Crete numbered more than 15,000 British or Commonwealth troops, besides the Greeks taken. In battles around the island, German air attacks sank three light cruisers and six destroyers of the British Mediterranean fleet and damaged three battleships, one aircraft carrier, six light cruisers, and five destroyers.

Both the Yugoslav and the Greek royal governments went into exile on their armies' collapse. The Axis powers were left to dispose as they would of their conquests. Yugoslavia was completely dissolved. Croatia, the independence of which had been proclaimed on April 10, 1941, was expanded to form Great Croatia, which included Srem (Syrmia, the zone between the Sava and the Danube south of the Drava confluence) and Bosnia and Hercegovina. Most of Dalmatia was annexed to Italy, while Montenegro was restored to independence. Yugoslav Macedonia was partitioned between Bulgaria and Albania, and Slovenia was partitioned between Italy and Germany. The Baranya triangle and the Bačka went to Hungary, and finally, the Banat and Serbia were put under German military administration. Of the independent states, Great Croatia, ruled by Ante Pavelić's nationalist Ustaše ("Insurgents"), and Montenegro were Italian spheres of influence, although German troops still occupied the eastern part of Great Croatia. A puppet government was set up by the Germans in Serbia, in August 1941.

While Bulgarian troops occupied eastern Macedonia and most of western Thrace, the rest of mainland Greece, theoretically subject to a puppet government in Athens, was militarily occupied by the Italians except for three zones, namely the Athens district, the Salonika district, and the Dimotika strip of Thrace, which the German conquerors reserved for themselves. The Germans also remained in occupation of Lesbos, Chios, Samos, Melos, and Crete.

THE BATTLE FOR AFRICA AND THE MIDDLE EAST

EGYPT AND CYRENAICA

The contemporary course of events in the Balkans, described above, nullified the first great victory won by British land forces in World War II, which took place in North Africa. When Italy declared war against Great Britain in June 1940, it had nearly 300,000 men under Marshal Rodolfo Graziani in Cyrenaica (present-day Libya), to confront the 36,000 troops whom the British commander in chief in the Middle East, General Sir Archibald Wavell, had in Egypt to protect the North African approaches to the Suez Canal. Between these forces lay the Western Desert, in which the westernmost position actually held by the British was Mersa Matruh (Marsā Maṭīūḥ), 120 miles (193 km) east of the Cyrenaican frontier. The Italians in September 1940 occupied Sīdī Barrānī, 170 miles (274 km) west of Mersa Matruh. But, after settling six divisions into a chain of widely separated camps, they did nothing more for weeks, and during that time Wavell received some reinforcements.

Wavell, whose command included not only Egypt but also the East African fronts against the Italians, decided to strike first in North Africa. On Dec. 7, 1940, some 30,000 men, under Major General Richard Nugent O'Connor, advanced westward, from Mersa Matruh, against 80,000 Italians. But, whereas the Italians at Sīdī Barrānī had only 120 tanks, O'Connor had 275. Having passed by night through a gap in the chain of forts, O'Connor's forces stormed three of the Italian camps, while the 7th Armoured Division was already cutting the Italians' road of retreat along the coast to the west. On December 10 most of the positions closer to Sīdī Barrānī were overrun. On December 11 the reserve tanks made a further enveloping bound to the coast beyond Buqbuq, intercepting a large column of retreating Italians. In three

days the British had taken nearly 40,000 prisoners.

Falling back across the frontier into Cyrenaica, the remnant of the Italian forces from Sīdī Barrānī shut itself up in the fortress of Bardia (Bardīyah), which O'Connor's tanks speedily isolated. On Jan. 3, 1941, the British assault on Bardia began, and three days later the whole garrison of Bardia surrendered—45,000 men. The next fortress to the west, Tobruk (Ṭubruq), was assaulted on January 23 and captured the next day (30,000 more prisoners).

To complete their conquest of Cyrenaica, it remained for the British to take the port of Benghazi. On Feb. 3, 1941, however, O'Connor learned that the Italians were about to abandon Benghazi and to retreat westward down the coast road to Agheila (al-'Uqaylah). Thereupon he boldly ordered the 7th Armoured Division to cross the desert hinterland and intercept the Italian retreat by cutting the coast road well to the east of Agheila. On February 5, after an advance of 170 miles (274 km) in 33 hours, the British were blocking the Italians' line of retreat south of Beda Fomm (Bayḍā' Fumm). In the morning of February 6, as the main Italian columns appeared, a day of battle began. Though the Italians had, altogether, nearly four times as many cruiser tanks as the British, by the following morning 60 Italian tanks had been crippled, 40 more abandoned, and the rest of Graziani's army was surrendering in crowds. The British, only 3,000 strong and having lost only three of their 29 tanks, took 20,000 prisoners, 120 tanks, and 216 guns.

The British, having occupied Benghazi on February 6 and Agheila on February 8, could now have pushed on without hindrance to Tripoli, but the chance was foregone: the Greek government had accepted Churchill's reiterated offer of British troops to be sent to Greece from Egypt, which meant a serious reduction of British strength in North Africa.

The reduction was to have serious consequences, because on February 6, the very day of Beda Fomm, a young general, Erwin Rommel, had been appointed by Hitler to command two German mechanized divisions that were to be sent as soon as possible to help the Italians. Arriving in Tripolitania, Rommel decided to try an offensive with what forces he had. Against the depleted British strength, he was rapidly and brilliantly successful. After occupying Agheila with ease on March 24 and Mersa Bréga (Qasr al-Burayqah) on March 31, he resumed his advance on April 2—despite orders to stand still for two months—with 50 tanks backed by two new Italian divisions. The British evacuated Benghazi the next day and began a precipitate retreat into Egypt, losing great numbers of their tanks on the way (a large force of armour, surrounded at Mechili, had to surrender on April 7). By April 11 all Cyrenaica except Tobruk had been reconquered by Rommel's audacious initiative.

Tobruk, garrisoned mainly by the 9th Australian Division, held out against siege. And Rommel, though he defeated two British attempts to relieve the place (May and June 1941), was obliged to suspend his offensive on the Egyptian frontier, since he had overstretched his supply lines.

EAST AFRICA

Wavell, the success of whose North African strategy had been sacrificed to Churchill's recurrent fantasy of creating a Balkan front against Germany (Greece in 1941 was scarcely less disastrous for the British than the Dardanelles in 1915), nevertheless enjoyed one definitive triumph before Churchill, doubly chagrined at having lost Cyrenaica for Greece's sake and Greece for no advantage at all, removed him, in the summer of 1941, from his command in the Middle East. That triumph was the destruction of Italian East Africa and the elimination, thereby, of any threat to the Suez Canal from the south or to Kenya from the north.

In August 1940 Italian forces mounted a full-scale offensive and overran British Somaliland. Wavell, however, was already assured of the collaboration of the former Ethiopian emperor Haile Selassie in raising the Ethiopians in patriotic revolt against the Italians. And, whereas in June he had disposed only of meagre resources against the 200,000 men and 325 aircraft under the Duca d'Aosta, Amedeo di Savoia, his troops in the Sudan were reinforced by two Indian divisions before the end of the year. After Haile

Italian soldiers surrender to an Australian soldier near Italian Libya, circa 1941. Keystone/
Hulton Archive/Getty Images

Selassie and a British major, Orde Wingate, with two battalions of Ethiopian exiles, had crossed the Sudanese frontier directly into Ethiopia, General William Platt and the Indian divisions invaded Eritrea on Jan. 19, 1941 (the Italians had already abandoned Kassala). Almost simultaneously, British troops from Kenya, under General Alan Cunningham, advanced into Italian Somaliland.

Platt's drive eastward into Eritrea was checked on February 5, at Keren, where the best Italian troops, under General Nicolangelo Carnimeo, put up a stiff defense facilitated by a barrier of cliffs. But when Keren fell on March 26, Platt's

way to Asmara (Asmera), to Massawa (Mitsiwa), and then from Eritrea southward into Ethiopia was comparatively easy. Meanwhile, Cunningham's troops were advancing northward into Ethiopia; and on April 6 they entered the Ethiopian capital, Addis Ababa. Finally, the Duca d'Aosta was caught between Platt's column and Cunningham's. At Amba Alaji, on May 20, he and the main body of his forces surrendered.

IRAQ AND SYRIA

In 1940 Prince ʻAbd al-Ilāh, regent of Iraq for King Fayṣal, had a government divided within itself about the war. He himself and his foreign minister, Nuri as-Said, were pro-British, but his prime minister, Rashid Ali al-Gailani, had pro-German leanings. Having resigned office in January 1941, Rashid Ali on April 3 seized power in Baghdad with help from some army officers and announced that the temporarily absent regent was deposed. The British, ostensibly exercising their right under the Anglo-Iraqi Treaty of 1930 to move troops across Iraqi territory, landed troops at Basra on April 19 and rejected Iraqi demands that these troops be sent on into Palestine before any further landings. Iraqi troops were then concentrated around the British air base at Ḥabbānīyah, west of Baghdad. On May 2 the British commander there opened hostilities, lest the Iraqis should attack first. Having won the upper hand at Ḥabbānīyah and been reinforced from Palestine, the British troops from the air base marched on Baghdad; and on May 30 Rashid Ali and his friends took refuge in Iran. ʿAbd al-Ilāh was reinstated as regent; Nuri became prime minister; and the British military presence remained to uphold them.

German military supplies for Rashid Ali were dispatched too late to be useful to him; but they reached Iraq via Syria, whose high commissioner, General H.-F. Dentz, was a nominee of the Vichy government of France. Lest Syria and Lebanon should fall altogether under Axis control, the British decided to intervene there. Consequently, Free French forces, under General Georges Catroux, with British, Australian, and Indian support, were sent into both countries from Palestine on June 8, 1941. A week later British forces invaded Syria from Iraq. Dentz's forces put up an unexpectedly stiff resistance, particularly against the Free French, but were finally obliged to capitulate: an armistice was signed at Acre on July 14. By an arrangement of July 25 the Free French retained territorial command in Syria and Lebanon subject to strategic control by the British.

PRIMARY SOURCE: FRANKLIN D. ROOSEVELT'S PROPOSAL FOR LEND-LEASE

As Britain's situation in the war grew more desperate, its ability to pay for needed arms and material rapidly diminished. Following his election to a third term in November 1940, President Roosevelt determined to find some means of underwriting an Allied victory over Germany without huge inter-government loans. In mid-December he hit upon the idea of Lend-Lease: the materials of war would be turned over to Allied nations now, and would be paid for at the end of the war in goods and services. In a press conference on December 17, Roosevelt outlined the underlying premises of the Lend-Lease program. A portion of the December 17 press conference is reprinted here. Source: FDR, IX, pp. 604–615.

In the present world situation of course there is absolutely no doubt in the mind of a very overwhelming number of Americans that the best immediate defense of the United States is the success of Great Britain in defending itself; and that, therefore, quite aside from our historic and current interest in the survival of democracy in the world as a whole, · it is equally important, from a selfish point of view of American defense, that we should do everything to help the British Empire to defend itself . . .

Orders from Great Britain are therefore a tremendous asset to American national defense because they automatically create additional facilities. I am talking selfishly, from the American point of view—nothing else. Therefore, from the selfish point of view, that production must be encouraged by us. There are several ways of encouraging it—not just one, as the narrow-minded fellow I have been talking about might assume, and has assumed. He has assumed that the only way was to repeal certain existing statutes, like the Neutrality Act and the old Johnson Act and a few other things like that, and then to lend the money to Great Britain to be spent over here—either lend it through private banking circles, as was done in the earlier days of the previous war, or make it a loan from this government to the British government . . .

It is possible—I will put it that way—for the United States to take over British orders and, because they are essentially the same kind of munitions that we use ourselves, turn them into American orders. We have enough money to do it. And thereupon, as to such portion of them as the military events of the future determine to be right and proper for us to allow to go to the other side, either lease or sell the materials, subject to mortgage, to the people on the other side. That would be on the general theory that it may still prove true that the best defense of Great Britain is the best defense of the United States, and therefore that these materials would be more useful to the defense of the United States if they were used in Great Britain than if they were kept in storage here. . .

Well, let me give you an illustration: Suppose my neighbor's home catches fire, and I have a length of garden hose 400 or 500 feet away. If he can take my garden hose and connect it up with his hydrant, I may help him to put out his fire. Now, what do I do? I don't say to him before that operation, "Neighbor, my garden hose cost me $15; you have to pay me $15 for it." What is the transaction that goes on? I don't want $15—I want my garden hose back after the fire is over. All right. If it goes through the fire all right, intact, without any damage to it, he gives it back to me and thanks me very much for the use of it. But suppose it gets smashed up—holes in it—during the fire; we don't have to have too much formality about it, but I say to him, "I was glad to lend you that hose; I see I can't use it any more, it's all smashed up." He says, "How many feet of it were there?" I tell him, "There were 150 feet of it." He says, "All right, I will replace it." Now, if I get a nice garden hose back, I am in pretty good shape.

In other words, if you lend certain munitions and get the munitions back at the end of the war, if they are intact—haven't been hurt—you are all right; if they have been damaged or have deteriorated or have been lost completely, it seems to me you come out pretty well if you have them replaced by the fellow to whom you have lent them.

Naval Warfare in the West

At the outbreak of World War II, the primary concerns of the British Navy were to defend Great Britain from invasion and to retain command of the ocean trading routes, both in order to protect the passage of essential supplies of food and raw materials for Britain and to deny the trading routes to the Axis powers, thus drawing tight once again the blockade that had proved so successful during World War I. Britain had adequate forces of battleships, aircraft carriers, cruisers, and other ships to fulfill these tasks.

The German Navy's role was to protect Germany's coasts, to defend its sea communications and to attack those of the Allies', and to support land and air operations. These modest goals were in keeping with Germany's position as the dominant land-based power in continental Europe. Germany's main naval weapon during the war was to be the submarine, or U-boat, with which it attacked Allied shipping much as it had in World War I.

German control of the Biscay ports after the fall of France in June 1940 provided the U-boats with bases from which they could infest the Atlantic without having to pass either through the Channel or around the north of the British Isles at the end of every sortie. Thenceforward, so long as naval escorts for outgoing convoys from the British Isles could go only 200 or 300 miles (322–483 km) out to sea before having to turn back to escort incoming convoys, the U-boats had a very wide field for free-ranging activity. And indeed, sinkings rose sharply from 55,580 tons in May 1940 to 352,407 tons in October, achieved mainly by solitary attacks by single U-boats at night. But the beginning of lend-lease and the freeing of British warships after the German invasion threat waned enabled the British to escort their convoys for 400 miles (644 km) by October 1940 and halfway across the Atlantic by April 1941. Since air cover for shipping could also be provided from the British Isles, from Canada, and from Iceland, the Atlantic space left open to the U-boats was reduced by May 1941 to a width of only 300 miles (483 km). Moreover, British surface vessels had the ASDIC (Anti-Submarine Detection Investigation Committee) device to detect submerged U-boats. By the spring of 1941, under the guidance of Admiral Karl Dönitz, the U-boat commanders were changing their tactic of individual operation to one of wolf-pack attacks: groups of U-boats, disposed in long lines, would rally when one of them by radio signaled a sighting and overwhelm the convoy by weight of numbers. Between July and December 1941 the German U-boat strength was raised from 65 to more than 230.

Furthermore, the German surface fleet became more active against Allied seaborne trade. Six armed German raiders disguised as merchantmen, with orders to leave convoys alone and to confine their attacks to unescorted ships, roamed the oceans with practical impunity from the spring of 1940 and had sunk 366,644 tons of shipping by the end of the year. German battleships—the *Admiral Scheer*, the *Admiral Hipper*, the *Scharnhorst*, and the *Gneisenau*—one after another began similar raiding operations, with considerable success, from October 1940. In May 1941 a really modern battleship, the *Bismarck*, and a new cruiser, the *Prinz Eugen*, put out to sea from Germany. The *Bismarck* and the *Prinz Eugen*, however, were located by British reconnaissance in the North Sea near Bergen, and an intensive hunt for them was immediately set in motion. Tracked from a point northwest of Iceland by two British cruisers, the two German ships were engaged on

May 24 by the battle cruiser *Hood* and by the new battleship *Prince of Wales*. Though the *Hood* was sunk, the *Bismarck*'s fuel supply was put out of action, so that its commander, Admiral Günther Lütjens, decided to make for the French coast. Separating from the *Prinz Eugen* (which escaped), the *Bismarck* threw off its pursuers early on May 25 but was sighted again the next day some 660 miles (1,062 km) west of Brest. Paralyzed by torpedo aircraft from the *Ark Royal*, she was bombarded and sunk by the *King George V*, the *Rodney*, and the *Dorsetshire* on May 27.

In the Mediterranean the year 1941 ended with some naval triumphs for the Axis: U-boats torpedoed the *Ark Royal* on

The German battleship Bismarck *fires on a merchant ship in the North Atlantic in 1941. The* Bismarck *would eventually be sunk by the British fleet on May 27, 1941.* Keystone/Hulton Archive/Getty Images

IN FOCUS: GERMANY'S U-BOATS

The Armistice terms of 1918 required Germany to surrender all its U-boats, and the Treaty of Versailles forbade it to possess them in the future. In 1935, however, Adolf Hitler's Germany repudiated the treaty and forcefully negotiated the right to build U-boats. Britain was ill-prepared in 1939 for a resumption of unrestricted submarine warfare, and during the early months of World War II the U-boats, which at that time numbered only 57, again achieved great successes. The first phase, during which the U-boats generally operated singly, ended in March 1941, by which time many merchant ships were sailing in convoy, trained escort groups were becoming available, and aircraft were proving their effectiveness as anti-U-boat weapons. In the next phase the Germans, having acquired air and U-boat bases in Norway and western France, were able to reach much farther out into the Atlantic, and their U-boats began to operate in groups (called wolf packs by the British). One U-boat would shadow a convoy and summon others by radio, and then the group would attack, generally on the surface at night. These tactics succeeded until radar came to the aid of the escorts and until convoys could be given continuous sea and air escort all the way across the Atlantic in both directions. In March 1943, as in April 1917, the Germans nearly succeeded in cutting Britain's Atlantic lifeline, but by May escort carriers and very-long-range reconnaissance bombers became available. After the U-boats lost 41 of their number during that month, they withdrew temporarily from the Atlantic.

In the next phase, U-boats were sent to remote waters where unescorted targets could still be found. Although at first they achieved considerable successes, especially in the Indian Ocean, the Allied strategy of striking at the U-boats' supply vessels and putting all possible shipping into convoys again proved successful. In the final phase the U-boats—then fitted with the snorkel (schnorkel) ventilating tube, which permitted extended underwater travel and greatly reduced the effectiveness of radar—returned to the coastal waters around the British Isles, but they sank few ships and themselves suffered heavy losses.

In World War II Germany built 1,162 U-boats, of which 785 were destroyed and the remainder surrendered (or were scuttled to avoid surrender) at the capitulation. Of the 632 U-boats sunk at sea, Allied surface ships and shore-based aircraft accounted for the great majority (246 and 245 respectively).

German U-boat officers scan the North Sea waters for merchant ships, October 1939. Popperfoto/Getty Images

November 13 and the *Barham* 12 days later. Italian frogmen, entering the harbour of Alexandria, on December 19 crippled the battleships *Queen Elizabeth* and *Valiant*. Two British cruisers and a destroyer were also sunk in Mediterranean waters in December.

Hitler's Geopolitical Strategy

German strategy in World War II is wholly intelligible only if Hitler's far-reaching system of power politics and his anti-Semitic ideology are borne in mind. Since the 1920s his program had been first to win power in Germany proper, next to consolidate Germany's domination over Central Europe, and then to raise Germany to the status of a world power by two stages: (1) the building up of a continental empire embracing all Europe, including the European portion of the Soviet Union, and (2) the attainment for Germany of equal rank with the British Empire, Japan, and the United States—the only world powers to be left after the elimination of France and the U.S.S.R.—through the acquisition of colonies in Africa and the construction of a strong fleet with bases on the Atlantic. In the succeeding generation Hitler foresaw a decisive conflict between Germany and the United States, during which he hoped that Great Britain would be Germany's ally.

The conquest of the European part of the Soviet Union, which in Hitler's calendar was dated approximately for 1943–45, was to be preceded, he thought, by short localized campaigns elsewhere in Europe to provide a strategic shield and to secure Germany's rear for the great expedition of conquest in the East, which was also bound up with the extermination of the Jews. The most important of the localized campaigns would be that against France. While this European program remained unfulfilled, it was imperative to avoid any world war, since only after the German Reich had come to dominate the whole European continent would it have the economic base and the territorial extent that were prerequisite for success in a great war, especially against maritime world powers.

Hitler had always contemplated the overthrow of the Soviet regime, and though he had congratulated himself on the German-Soviet Nonaggression Pact of 1939 as a matter of expediency, anti-Bolshevism had remained his most profound emotional conviction. His feelings had been stirred up afresh by the Soviet occupation of the Baltic states and of Bessarabia and northern Bukovina in June 1940 and by the consequent proximity of Soviet forces to the Romanian oil fields on which Germany depended. Hitler became acutely suspicious of the intentions of the Soviet leader, Joseph Stalin, and he began to feel that he could not afford to wait to complete the subjugation of western Europe before dealing with the Soviet Union. Hitler and his generals had originally scheduled the invasion of the U.S.S.R. for mid-May 1941, but the unforeseen necessity of invading Yugoslavia and Greece in April of that year had forced them to postpone the Soviet campaign to late June. The swiftness of Hitler's Balkan victories enabled him to keep to this revised timetable, but the five weeks' delay shortened the time for carrying out the invasion of the U.S.S.R. and was to prove the more serious because in 1941 the Russian winter would arrive earlier than usual. Nevertheless, Hitler and the heads of the Oberkommando des Heeres (OKH, or German Army High Command), namely the army commander in chief Werner von Brauchitsch and the army general staff chief Franz Halder, were convinced that the Red Army could be defeated in two or three months, and that, by the end of October, the Germans would have conquered the whole European part of Russia and the Ukraine west of a line stretching from Archangel to Astrakhan. The invasion of the Soviet Union was given the code name "Operation Barbarossa."

GERMANY INVADES THE SOVIET UNION

For the campaign against the Soviet Union, the Germans allotted almost 150 divisions containing a total of about 3,000,000 men. Among these were 19 panzer divisions, and in total the "Barbarossa" force had about 3,000 tanks, 7,000 artillery pieces, and 2,500 aircraft. It was in effect the largest and most powerful invasion force in human history. The Germans' strength was further increased by more than 30 divisions of Finnish and Romanian troops.

The Soviet Union had twice or perhaps three times the number of both tanks and aircraft as the Germans had, but their aircraft were mostly obsolete. The Soviet tanks were about equal to those of the Germans, however. A greater hindrance to Hitler's chances of victory was that the German intelligence service underestimated the troop reserves that Stalin could bring up from the depths of the U.S.S.R. The Germans correctly estimated that there were about 150 divisions in the western parts of the U.S.S.R. and reckoned that 50 more might be produced. But the Soviets actually brought up more than 200 fresh divisions by the middle of August, making a total of 360. The consequence was that, though the Germans succeeded in shattering the original Soviet armies by superior technique, they then found their path blocked by fresh ones. The effects of the miscalculations were increased because much of August was wasted while Hitler and his advisers were having long arguments as to what course they should follow after their initial victories. Another factor in the Germans' calculations was purely political, though no less mistaken. They believed that within three to six months of their invasion, the Soviet regime would collapse from lack of domestic support.

The German attack on the Soviet Union was to have an immediate and highly salutary effect on Great Britain's situation. Until then Britain's prospects had appeared hopeless in the eyes of most people except the British themselves. The government's decision to continue the struggle after the fall of France and to reject Hitler's peace offers could spell only slow suicide unless relief came from either the United States or the U.S.S.R. Hitler brought Great Britain relief by turning eastward and invading the Soviet Union just as the strain on Britain was becoming severe.

On June 22, 1941, the German offensive was launched by three army groups under the same commanders as in the invasion of France in 1940. On the left (north), an army group under Leeb struck from East Prussia into the Baltic states toward Leningrad. On the right (south), another army group, under Rundstedt, with an armoured group under Kleist, advanced from southern Poland into the Ukraine against Kiev, whence it was to wheel south-eastward to the coasts of the Black Sea and the Sea of Azov. And in the centre, north of the Pripet Marshes, the main blow was delivered by Bock's army group, with one armoured group under Guderian and another under Hoth, thrusting northeast-ward at Smolensk and Moscow.

The invasion along a 1,800-mile (2,897-km) front took the Soviet leadership completely by surprise and caught the Red Army in an unprepared and partially demobilized state. Piercing the northern border, Guderian's tanks raced 50 miles (80 km) beyond the frontier on the first day of the invasion and were at Minsk, 200 miles (322 km) beyond it, on June 27. At Minsk they converged with Hoth's tanks, which had pierced the opposite flank, but Bock's infantry could not follow up quickly enough to complete the

July 1941: Using a dead horse for cover, a Russian soldier on the Eastern Front takes aim. Popperfoto/Getty Images

encirclement of the Soviet troops in the area. Though 300,000 prisoners were taken in the salient, a large part of the Soviet forces was able to escape to the east. The Soviet armies were clumsily handled and frittered their tank strength away in piecemeal action like that of the French in 1940. But the isolated Soviet troops fought with a stubbornness that the French had not shown, and their resistance imposed a brake by continuing to block road centres long after the German tide had swept past them. The result was similar when Guderian's tanks, having crossed the Dnepr River on July 10, entered Smolensk six days later and converged with Hoth's thrust through Vitebsk: 200,000 Soviet prisoners were taken. Some Soviet forces were withdrawn from the trap to the line of the Desna, and a large pocket of resistance lay behind the German armour. By mid-July, moreover, a series of rainstorms were turning the sandy Russian roads into clogging mud, over which the wheeled vehicles of the German transport behind the tanks could make only very slow progress. The Germans also began to be hampered by the scorched earth policy adopted by the retreating Soviets. The Soviet troops burned crops, destroyed bridges, and evacuated factories in the face of the German advance. Entire steel and munitions plants in the westernmost portions of the U.S.S.R. were dismantled and shipped by rail to the east, where they were put back into production. The Soviets also destroyed or evacuated most of their rolling stock (railroad cars), thus depriving the Germans of the use of the Soviet rail system. Soviet railroad track was of a different gauge than German track and German rolling stock was consequently useless on it.

Nevertheless, by mid-July the Germans had advanced more than 400 miles (644 km) and were only 200 miles (322 km) from Moscow. They still had ample time to make decisive gains before the onset of winter, but they lost the opportunity, primarily because of arguments throughout August between Hitler and the OKH about the destination of the next thrusts thence: whereas the OKH proposed Moscow as the main objective, Hitler wanted the major effort to be directed southeastward, through the Ukraine and the Donets Basin into the Caucasus, with a minor swing northwestward against Leningrad (to converge with Leeb's army group).

In the Ukraine, meanwhile, Rundstedt and Kleist had made short work of the foremost Soviet defenses, stronger though the latter had been. A new Soviet front south of Kiev was broken by the end of July. In the next fortnight the Germans swept down to the Black Sea mouths of the Bug and Dnepr rivers—to converge with Romania's simultaneous offensive. Kleist was then ordered to wheel northward from the Ukraine and Guderian southward from Smolensk, for a pincer movement around the Soviet forces behind Kiev. By the end of September the claws of the encircling movement had caught 520,000 men. These gigantic encirclements were partly the fault of inept Soviet high commanders and partly the fault of Stalin, who as commander in chief stubbornly overrode the advice of his generals and ordered his armies to stand and fight instead of allowing them to retreat eastward and regroup in preparation for a counteroffensive.

Winter was approaching, and Hitler stopped Leeb's northward drive on the outskirts of Leningrad. He ordered Rundstedt and Kleist, however, to press on from the Dnepr toward the Don and the Caucasus; and Bock was to resume the advance on Moscow.

Bock's renewed advance on Moscow began on Oct. 2, 1941. Its prospects looked bright when Bock's armies brought off a great encirclement around Vyazma, where 600,000 more Soviet troops were captured. That left the Germans momentarily with an almost clear path to Moscow. But the Vyazma battle had not been completed until late October. The German troops were tired, and the country became a morass as the weather got worse. In addition, fresh Soviet forces appeared in the path as they plodded slowly forward. Some of the German generals wanted to break off the offensive and to take up a suitable winter line. But Bock wanted to press on, believing that the Soviets were on the verge of collapse, while Brauchitsch and Halder tended to agree with his view. As that also accorded with Hitler's desire, he made no objection. The temptation of Moscow, now so close in front of their eyes, was too great for any of the topmost leaders to resist. On December 2 a further

effort was launched, and some German detachments penetrated into the suburbs of Moscow; but the advance as a whole was held up in the forests covering the capital. The stemming of this last phase of the great German offensive was partly due to the effects of the Russian winter, whose subzero temperatures were the most severe in several decades. In October and November a wave of frostbite cases had decimated the ill-clad German troops, for whom provisions of winter clothing had not been made, while the icy cold paralyzed the Germans' mechanized transport, tanks, artillery, and aircraft. The Soviets, by contrast, were well clad and tended to fight more effectively in winter than did the Germans. By this time German casualties had mounted to levels that were unheard of in the campaigns against France and the Balkans. By November the Germans had suffered about 730,000 casualties.

In the south, Kleist had already reached Rostov-on-Don, gateway to the Caucasus, on November 22, but had exhausted his tanks' fuel in doing so. Rundstedt, seeing the place to be untenable, wanted to evacuate it but was overruled by Hitler. A Soviet counteroffensive recaptured Rostov on November 28, and Rundstedt was relieved of his command four days later. The Germans, however, managed to establish a front on the Mius River—as Rundstedt had recommended.

As the German drive against Moscow slackened, the Soviet commander on the Moscow front, General Georgy

Overcome by exhaustion, a German soldier on the Eastern Front sleeps in a muddy trench, circa 1942. Keystone/Hulton Archive/Getty Images

Konstantinovich Zhukov, on December 6 inaugurated the first great counter-offensive with strokes against Bock's right in the Elets (Yelets) and Tula sectors south of Moscow and against his centre in the Klin and Kalinin sectors to the northwest. Levies of Siberian troops, who were extremely effective fighters in cold weather, were used for these offensives. There followed a blow at the German left, in the Velikie Luki sector. The counteroffensive, which was sustained throughout the winter of 1941–42, soon took the form of a triple convergence toward Smolensk.

These Soviet counteroffensives tumbled back the exhausted Germans, lapped around their flanks, and produced a critical situation. From generals downward, the invaders were filled with ghastly thoughts of Napoleon's retreat from Moscow. In that emergency Hitler forbade any retreat beyond the shortest possible local withdrawals. His decision exposed his troops to awful sufferings in their advanced positions facing Moscow, for they had neither the clothing nor the equipment for a Russian winter campaign. But if they had once started a general retreat it might easily have degenerated into a panic-stricken rout.

The Red Army's winter counteroffensive continued for more than three months after its December launching, though with diminishing progress. By March 1942 it had advanced more than 150 miles (241 km) in some sectors. But the Germans maintained their hold on the main bastions of their winter front—such towns as Schlüsselburg, Novgorod, Rzhev, Vyazma, Bryansk, Orël (Oryol), Kursk, Kharkov, and Taganrog—despite the fact that the Soviets had often advanced many miles beyond these bastions, which were in effect cut off. In retrospect, it became clear that Hitler's veto on any extensive withdrawal worked out in such a way as to restore the confidence of the German troops and probably saved them from a widespread collapse. Nevertheless, they paid a heavy price indirectly for that rigid defense. One immediate handicap was that the strength of the Luftwaffe was drained in the prolonged effort to maintain supplies by air, under winter conditions, to the garrisons of these more or less isolated bastion towns. The tremendous strain of that winter campaign, on armies that had not been prepared for it, had other serious effects. Before the winter ended, many German divisions were reduced to barely a third of their original strength, and they were never fully built up again.

The German plan of campaign had begun to miscarry in August 1941, and its failure was patent when the Soviet counteroffensive started. Nevertheless, having dismissed Brauchitsch and appointed himself army commander in chief in December, Hitler persisted in overruling the tentative opposition of the general staff to his strategy.

The first three months of the German-Soviet conflict produced cautious rapprochements between the U.S.S.R. and Great Britain and between the U.S.S.R. and the United States. The Anglo-Soviet agreement of July 12, 1941, pledged the signatory powers to assist one another and to abstain from making any separate peace with Germany. On Aug. 25, 1941, British and Soviet forces jointly invaded Iran, to forestall the establishment of a German base there and to divide the country into spheres of occupation for the duration of the war. Then late in September—at a conference in Moscow—Soviet, British, and U.S. representatives formulated the monthly quantities of supplies, including aircraft, tanks, and raw materials, that Great Britain and the United States should try to furnish to the Soviet Union.

The critical situation on the Eastern Front did not deter Hitler from declaring Germany to be at war with the United States on Dec. 11, 1941, after the Japanese attack on the U.S., British, and Dutch positions in the Pacific and in the Far East. This extension of hostilities did not immediately commit the German land forces to any new theatre but at the same time had the merit of entitling the German Navy to intensify the war at sea.

THE WAR IN EAST ASIA AND THE PACIFIC

CHINA

In 1931–32, as you may recall, the Japanese had invaded Manchuria (Northeast China) and, after overcoming ineffective Chinese resistance there, had created the Japanese controlled puppet state of Manchukuo. In the following years the Nationalist government of China, headed by Chiang

IN FOCUS: EIGHTH ROUTE ARMY

The Eighth Route Army was the larger of the two major Chinese Communist forces that fought the Japanese from 1937 to 1945. The Eighth Route Army also engaged in political and propaganda work, helping to increase Communist support among the populace. The army grew from 30,000 troops in July 1937 to 156,000 in 1938 and 400,000 in 1940. Reduced to about 300,000 by the fierce fighting between 1941 and 1944, its size almost doubled to a total of 600,000 men in 1945.

Formed in 1937 at the time of the second United Front (the anti-Japanese alliance between the Chinese Nationalists under Chiang Kai-shek and the Chinese Communists), the Eighth Route Army was headed by Mao Zedong's old comrade in arms Zhu De but was placed under the overall direction of the Nationalist government. In 1938 the Eighth Route Army was reorganized as the Eighteenth Army Group under the Nationalist commander Yan Xishan. In practice, however, the army remained under Zhu De's control and operated independently of the Nationalists, especially after 1941, when relations between the Communists and Nationalists had deteriorated.

Following the end of World War II, the Eighteenth Army Group was incorporated into the new People's Liberation Army. Units from the former Eighth Route Army were active in the 1948 capture of Manchuria (Northeast Provinces) from the Nationalists, which placed the Communist forces in a position to take North China and turn the civil war in their favour.

Kai-shek, temporized in the face of Japanese military and diplomatic pressures and instead waged an internal war against the Chinese Communists, led by Mao Zedong, who were based in Shaanxi Province in north-central China. Meanwhile, the Japanese began a military buildup in North China proper, which in turn stimulated the formation of a unified resistance by the Nationalists and the Communists.

Overt hostilities between Japan and China began after the Marco Polo Bridge incident of July 7, 1937, when shots were exchanged between Chinese and Japanese troops on the outskirts of Beijing. Open fighting broke out in that area, and in late July the Japanese captured the Beijing-Tianjin area. Thereupon full-scale hostilities began between the two nations. The Japanese landed near Shanghai, at the mouth of the Yangtze River, and took Shanghai in November and the Chinese capital, Nanjing, in December 1937. Chiang Kai-shek moved his government to Hankou (one of the Wuhan cities), which lay 435 miles (700 km) west of Shanghai along the Yangtze. The Japanese also pushed southward and westward from the Beijing area into Hebei and Shanxi provinces. In 1938 the Japanese launched several ambitious military campaigns that brought them deep into the heart of central China. They advanced to the northeast and west from Nanjing, taking Suzhou and occupying the Wuhan cities. The Nationalists were forced to move their government to Chongqing in Sichuan Province, about 500 miles (805 km) west of the Wuhan cities. The Japanese also occupied Guangzhou and several other coastal cities in South China in 1938.

Nationalist Chinese resistance to these Japanese advances was ineffective,

In Focus: Flying Tigers

The Flying Tigers were American volunteer pilots recruited by Claire L. Chennault, a retired U.S. Army captain, to fight the Japanese in Burma (Myanmar) and China during 1941–42, at a time when Japan's control over China's ports and transportation system had almost cut off China's Nationalist government from the outside world. Facing chronic shortages of fuel, parts, and pilots, this small company of air fighters nevertheless scored victory after victory over the far larger and better-equipped Japanese air force. They flew supplies, provided air cover for the Burma Road, succeeded in protecting the Chinese capital of Chongqing, and fought the Japanese over south-western and other parts of China. Surprise, mobility, precision flying, and unorthodox tactics enabled the Tigers to outwit the Japanese and inflict considerable damage on their air and ground forces. On July 4, 1942, members of the unit who wished were absorbed into the U.S. 10th Air Force and became the nucleus of the China Air Task Force (reorganized in March 1943 as the 14th Air Force), still under the command of Chennault, who was later promoted to brigadier general (1942) and major general (1943).

primarily because the Nationalist leadership was still more interested in holding their forces in reserve for a future struggle with the Communists than in repelling the Japanese. By contrast, the Communists, from their base in north-central China, began an increasingly effective guerrilla war against the Japanese troops in Manchuria and North China. The Japanese needed large numbers of troops to maintain their hold on the immense Chinese territories and populations they controlled. Of the 51 infantry divisions making up the Japanese Army in 1941, 38 of them, comprising about 750,000 men, were stationed in China (including Manchuria).

JAPANESE POLICY BEFORE THE ATTACK ON PEARL HARBOR

When war broke out in Europe in September 1939, the Japanese, despite a series of victorious battles, had still not brought their war in China to an end. On the one hand, the Japanese strategists had made no plans to cope with the guerrilla warfare pursued by the Chinese. On the other, the Japanese commanders in the field often disregarded the orders of the supreme command at the Imperial headquarters and occupied more Chinese territory than they had been ordered to take. Half of the Japanese Army was thus still tied down in China when the commitment of Great Britain and France to war against Germany opened up the prospect of wider conquests for Japan in

Southeast Asia and in the Pacific. Japan's military ventures in China proper were consequently restricted rather more severely henceforth.

The German victories over The Netherlands and France in the summer of 1940 further encouraged the Japanese premier, Prince Konoe, to look southward at those defeated powers' colonies and also, of course, at the British and U.S. positions in the Far East. The island archipelago of the Dutch East Indies (now Indonesia) along with French Indochina and British-held Malaya contained raw materials (tin, rubber, petroleum) that were essential to Japan's industrial economy, and if Japan could seize these regions and incorporate them into the empire, it could make itself virtually self-sufficient economically and thus become the dominant power in the Pacific Ocean. Since Great Britain, single-handedly, was confronting the might of the Axis in Europe, the Japanese strategists had to reckon, primarily, with the opposition of the United States to their plans for territorial aggrandizement. When Japanese troops entered northern Indochina in September 1940 (in pursuance of an agreement extorted in August from the Vichy government of France), the United States uttered a protest. Germany and Italy, by contrast, recognized Japan as the leading power in the Far East by concluding with it the Tripartite, or Axis, Pact of Sept. 27, 1940. Negotiated by Japanese foreign minister Matsuoka Yosuke, the pact pledged its signatories to come to one another's help in the event of an attack "by a power not already engaged in war." Japan also concluded a neutrality pact with the U.S.S.R. on April 13, 1941.

On July 2, 1941, the Imperial Conference decided to press the Japanese advance southward even at the risk of war with Great Britain and the United States. This policy was pursued even when Matsuoka was relieved of office a fortnight later. On July 26, in pursuance of a new agreement with Vichy France, Japanese forces began to occupy bases in southern Indochina.

This time the United States reacted vigorously, not only freezing Japanese assets under U.S. control but also imposing an embargo on supplies of oil to Japan. Dismay at the embargo drove the Japanese naval command, which had hitherto been more moderate than the army, into collusion with the army's extremism. When negotiations with the Dutch of Indonesia for an alternative supply of oil produced no satisfaction, the Imperial Conference on September 6, at the high command's insistence, decided that war must be undertaken against the United States and Great Britain unless an understanding with the United States could be reached in a few weeks' time.

General Tōjō Hideki, who succeeded Konoe as premier in mid-October 1941, continued the already desperate talks. The United States, however, persisted in making demands that Japan could not concede: renunciation of the Tripartite Pact (which would have left Japan diplomatically isolated); the withdrawal of Japanese troops from China and from Southeast Asia (a humiliating retreat from an overt commitment of four years' standing); and an open-door regime for trade in China. When Cordell Hull, the U.S. secretary of state, on Nov. 26, 1941, sent an abrupt note to the Japanese bluntly requiring them to evacuate China and Indochina and to recognize no Chinese regime other than that of Chiang Kai-shek, the Japanese could see no point in continuing the talks.

Since peace with the United States seemed impossible, Japan set in motion its plans for war, which would now necessarily be waged not only against the United States but also against Great Britain (the existing war effort of which depended on U.S. support and the Far Eastern colonies of which lay within the orbit of the projected Japanese expansion) and against the Dutch East Indies (the oil of which was essential to Japanese enterprises, even apart from geopolitical considerations).

The evolving Japanese military strategy was based on the peculiar geography of the Pacific Ocean and on the relative weakness and unpreparedness of the Allied military presence in that ocean. The western half of the Pacific is dotted with many islands, large and small, while the eastern half of the ocean is, with the exception of the Hawaiian Islands, almost devoid of landmasses (and hence of usable bases). The British, French, American, and Dutch military forces in the entire Pacific region west of Hawaii amounted to only about 350,000 troops, most of them lacking combat experience and being of disparate nationalities. Allied air power in the Pacific was weak and consisted mostly of obsolete planes. If the Japanese, with their large, well-equipped armies that had been battle-hardened in China, could quickly launch coordinated attacks from their existing bases on certain Japanese-mandated Pacific islands, on Formosa (Taiwan), and from Japan itself, they could overwhelm the Allied forces, over-run the entire western Pacific Ocean as well as Southeast Asia, and then develop those areas' resources to their own military-industrial advantage. If successful in their campaigns, the Japanese planned to establish a strongly fortified defensive perimeter extending from Burma in the west to the southern rim of the Dutch East Indies and northern New Guinea in the south and sweeping around to the Gilbert and Marshall islands in the southeast and east. The Japanese believed that any American and British counter-offensives against this perimeter could be repelled, after which those nations would eventually seek a negotiated peace that would allow Japan to keep its newly won empire.

Until the end of 1940 the Japanese strategists had assumed that any new war to be waged would be against a single enemy. When it became clear, in 1941, that the British and the Dutch as well as the Americans must be attacked, a new and daring war plan was successfully sponsored by the commander in chief of the Combined Fleet, Admiral Yamamoto Isoroku.

Yamamoto's plan prescribed two operations, together involving the whole strength of his navy, which was composed of the following ships: 10 battleships, six regular aircraft carriers, four auxiliary carriers, 18 heavy cruisers, 20 light cruisers, 112 destroyers, 65 submarines, and 2,274 combat planes. The first operation, to which all six regular aircraft carriers, two battleships, three cruisers, and 11 destroyers were allocated, was to be a surprise attack, scheduled for December 7 (December 8 by Japanese time), on the main U.S. Pacific Fleet in its base at Pearl Harbor in the Hawaiian Islands. The rest of the Japanese Navy was to support the army in the "Southern Operation." Eleven infantry divisions and seven tank regiments, assisted by 795 combat planes, were to undertake two drives, one from Formosa through the Philippines, the other from French Indochina and Hainan Island through Malaya. Both drives were meant to converge on the Dutch East Indies, with a view to the capture of Java as the culmination of a campaign of 150 days—during which, moreover, Wake Island, Guam, the Gilbert Islands, and Burma should also have been secured as outer bastions, besides Hong Kong.

PEARL HARBOR AND JAPANESE EXPANSION

In accordance with Yamamoto's plan, the aircraft carrier strike force commanded by Admiral Nagumo Chuichi sailed eastward undetected by any U.S. reconnaissance until it had reached a point 275 miles (443 km) north of Hawaii. From there, on Sunday, Dec. 7, 1941, a total of about 360 aircraft, composed of dive-bombers, torpedo bombers, and a few fighters, was launched in two waves in the early morning at the giant U.S. naval base at Pearl Harbor. The base at that time was accommodating 70 U.S. fighting ships, 24 auxiliaries, and some 300 planes. The Americans were taken completely by surprise, and all eight battleships in the harbour were hit (though six were eventually repaired and returned to service); three cruisers, three destroyers, a mine-layer, and other vessels were damaged; more than 180 aircraft were destroyed and others damaged (most while parked at airfields); and more than 2,330 troops were killed and over 1,140 wounded. Japanese losses were comparatively small. The Japanese attack failed in one crucial respect, however. The Pacific Fleet's three aircraft carriers were at sea at the time of the attack and escaped harm, and these were to become the nucleus of the United States' incipient naval defense in the Pacific. Pearl Harbor's shore installations and oil-storage facilities also escaped damage. The Pearl Harbor attack, unannounced beforehand by the Japanese as it was, unified the American public and swept away any remaining support for American neutrality in the war. On December 8 the U.S. Congress

PRIMARY SOURCE: FRANKLIN D. ROOSEVELT'S REQUEST FOR A DECLARATION OF WAR

On Dec. 7, 1941, Japan attacked Pearl Harbor in Hawaii. The next day, President Franklin Roosevelt went before Congress to ask for a declaration of war against Japan. The message of December 8 is reprinted below. Source: Congressional Record, Washington, 77 Cong., 1 Sess., pp. 9519–9520. Congressional Record Appendix, Washington, 77 Cong., 1 Sess., pp. A5509–5511. Record, App., 77 Cong., 1 Sess., pp. A5509–A5511.

Yesterday, December 7, 1941—a date which will live in infamy—the United States of America was suddenly and deliberately attacked by naval and air forces of the Empire of Japan.

The United States was at peace with that nation, and, at the solicitation of Japan, was still in conversation with its government and its emperor looking toward the maintenance of peace in the Pacific. Indeed, one hour after Japanese air squadrons had commenced bombing in Oahu, the Japanese ambassador to the United States and his colleague delivered to the secretary of state a formal reply to a recent American message. While this reply stated that it seemed useless to continue the existing diplomatic negotiations, it contained no threat or hint of war or armed attack.

It will be recorded that the distance of Hawaii from Japan makes it obvious that the attack was deliberately planned many days or even weeks ago. During the intervening time the

American President Franklin Roosevelt addresses the United States Congress on Dec. 8, 1941. MPI/Hulton Archive/ Getty Images

Japanese government has deliberately sought to deceive the United States by false statements and expressions of hope for continued peace.

The attack yesterday on the Hawaiian Islands has caused severe damage to American naval and military forces. Very many American lives have been lost. In addition, American ships have been reported torpedoed on the high seas between San Francisco and Honolulu.

Yesterday the Japanese government also launched an attack against Malaya.

Last night Japanese forces attacked Hong Kong.

Last night Japanese forces attacked Guam.

Last night Japanese forces attacked the Philippine Islands.

Last night the Japanese attacked Wake Island.

This morning the Japanese attacked Midway Island.

Japan has, therefore, undertaken a surprise offensive extending throughout the Pacific area. The facts of yesterday speak for themselves. The people of the United States have already formed their opinions and well understand the implications to the very life and safety of our nation.

As commander in chief of the Army and Navy I have directed that all measures be taken for our defense.

Always will we remember the character of the onslaught against us. No matter how long it may take us to overcome this premeditated invasion, the American people, in their righteous might, will win through to absolute victory. I believe I interpret the will of the Congress and of the people when I assert that we will not only defend ourselves to the uttermost but will make very certain that this form of treachery shall never endanger us again.

Hostilities exist. There is no blinking at the fact that our people, our territory, and our interests are in grave danger.

With confidence in our armed forces—with the unbounded determination of our people—we will gain the inevitable triumph so help us God.

I ask that the Congress declare that since the unprovoked and dastardly attack by Japan on Sunday, December 7, a state of war has existed between the United States and the Japanese Empire.

declared war on Japan with only one dissenting vote.

On the day of the attack, December 8 by local time, Formosa-based Japanese bombers struck Clark and Iba airfields in the Philippines, destroying more than 50 percent of the U.S. Army's Far East aircraft. Two days later, further raids destroyed not only more U.S. fighters but also Cavite Naval Yard, likewise in the Philippines. Part of the U.S. Asiatic Fleet, however, had already gone south in November. The surviving major ships and bomber aircraft, which were vulnerable for lack of fighter protection, were withdrawn in the next fortnight to safety in bases in Java and Australia.

Japanese forces began to land on the island of Luzon in the Philippines on December 10. The main assault, consisting of the bulk of one division, was made at Lingayen Gulf, 100 miles (161 km) north-northwest of Manila, on December 22, and a second large landing took place south of Manila two days later. Manila itself fell unopposed to the Japanese on Jan. 2, 1942, but by that time the U.S. and Filipino forces under General Douglas MacArthur were ready to hold Bataan Peninsula (across the bay from Manila) and Corregidor Island (in the bay). The Japanese attack on Bataan was halted initially, but it was reinforced in the following eight weeks. MacArthur was

The USS Arizona *sinks in a cloud of smoke after the Imperial Japanese Navy attacked Pearl Harbor on December 7, 1941.* Hulton Archive/Getty Images

ordered to Australia on March 11, leaving Bataan's defense to Lieutenant General Jonathan M. Wainwright. The latter and his men surrendered on April 9. Corregidor fell in the night of May 5–6, and the southern Philippines capitulated three days later.

Japanese bombers had already destroyed British air power at Hong Kong on Dec. 8, 1941, and the British and Canadian defenders surrendered to the ground attack from the Kowloon Peninsula (the nearest mainland) on December 25. To secure their flank while pushing southward into Malaya, the Japanese also occupied Bangkok on December 9 and Victoria Point in southernmost Burma on December 16. The Japanese landings in Malaya, from December 8 onward, accompanied as they were by air strikes, overwhelmed the small Australian and Indian forces. The British battleship *Prince of Wales* and the battle cruiser *Repulse*, sailing from Singapore to cut Japanese communications, were sunk by Japanese aircraft on December 10. By the end of January 1942, two Japanese divisions, with air and armoured support, had occupied all Malaya except Singapore Island. In Burma, meanwhile, other Japanese troops had taken Moulmein and were approaching Rangoon and Mandalay.

On the eastern perimeter of the war zone, the Japanese had bombed Wake Island on December 8, attempted to

Women firefighters in action after the Japanese attack on Pearl Harbor. Three Lions/Hulton Archive/Getty Images

capture it on December 11, and achieved a landing on December 23, quickly subduing the garrison. Guam had already fallen on December 10. Having also occupied Makin and Tarawa in the Gilbert Islands in the first days of the war, the Japanese successfully attacked Rabaul, the strategic base on New Britain (now part of Papua New Guinea), on Jan. 23, 1942.

A unified American–British–Dutch–Australian Command, ABDACOM, under Wavell, responsible for holding Malaya, Sumatra, Java, and the approaches to Australia, became operative on Jan. 15, 1942; but the Japanese had already begun their advance on the oil-rich Dutch East Indies. They occupied Kuching (December 17), Brunei Bay (January 6), and Jesselton (January 11), on the northern coast of Borneo, as well as Tarakan Island (off northeastern Borneo) and points on Celebes. Balikpapan (on Borneo's east coast) and Kendari (in southeastern Celebes) fell to the Japanese on Jan. 24, 1942, Amboina on February 4, Makasar City (in southwestern Celebes) on February 8, and Bandjarmasin (in southern Borneo) on February 16. Bali was invaded on February 18, and by February 24 the Japanese were also in possession of Timor.

The Fall of Singapore

On Feb. 8 and 9, 1942, three Japanese divisions landed on Singapore Island. On February 15 they forced the 90,000-strong British, Australian, and Indian garrison there, under Lieutenant General A.E. Percival, to surrender. Singapore was the major British base in the Pacific and had been regarded as unassailable due to its strong seaward defenses. The Japanese took it with comparative ease by advancing down the Malay Peninsula and then assaulting the base's landward side, which the British had left inadequately defended. On February 13, moreover, Japanese paratroopers had landed at Palembang in

In Focus: Battle of Wake Island

Wake Island, a small atoll in the central Pacific that was the site of a half-completed U.S. air and submarine base, was attacked by 36 Japanese bombers at noon on Dec. 8, 1941 (Wake time; December 7, Hawaiian time), a few hours after the Pearl Harbor attack. A Japanese naval task force that included cruisers and destroyers appeared on December 11 but was repulsed with considerable loss by the coastal-defense guns and aircraft. Thereafter, however, the Japanese had the atoll under almost continuous air attack, and a U.S. relief force failed to reach the area before the Japanese returned on December 23 with a much more powerful force and in five hours forced the surrender of the island forces under U.S. Navy Commander Winfield Scott Cunningham. Altogether 1,616 Americans were captured, and most of them were evacuated to China and Japan. The Japanese fortified the atoll heavily, but repeated attacks by U.S. aircraft during the remainder of the war devastated it completely. The Japanese garrison surrendered the atoll on Sept. 4, 1945.

In Focus: Bataan Death March

Following the Japanese capture of the Philippines in the early stages of World War II, some 90,000 to 100,000 American and Filipino prisoners of war, including wounded soldiers, began a forced march under brutal conditions. Starting out from Mariveles, on the southern end of the Bataan Peninsula, on April 9, 1942, they were force-marched 55 miles (88 km) to San Fernando, then taken by rail to Capas, from where they walked the final 8 miles (13 km) to Camp O'Donnell. They were starved and mistreated, often kicked or beaten on their way, and many who fell were bayoneted. Only 54,000 reached the camp; 7,000–10,000 died on the way and the rest escaped to the jungle.

After the war, the Japanese commander of the invasion forces in the Philippines, Lieutenant General Homma Masaharu, was charged with responsibility for the death march and was tried by a U.S. military commission in Manila in January–February 1946. Convicted, he was executed on April 3.

Sumatra, which fell to an amphibious assault three days later.

When ABDACOM was dissolved on Feb. 25, 1942, only Java remained to complete the Japanese program of conquest. The Allies' desperate attempt to intercept the Japanese invasion fleet was defeated in the seven-hour Battle of the Java Sea on February 27, in which five Allied warships were lost and only one Japanese destroyer damaged. The Japanese landed at three points on Java on February 28 and rapidly expanded their beachheads. On March 9 the 20,000 Allied troops in Java surrendered. In the Indian Ocean, the Japanese captured the Andaman Islands on March 23, and began a series of attacks on British shipping. After the failure of ABDACOM, the U.S.–British Combined Chiefs of Staff placed the Pacific under the U.S. Joint Chiefs' strategic direction. MacArthur became supreme commander of the Southwest Pacific Area, which comprised the Dutch East Indies (less Sumatra), the Philippines, Australia, the Bismarck Archipelago, and the Solomons; and Admiral Chester W. Nimitz became commander in chief of the Pacific Ocean Areas, which comprised virtually every area not under MacArthur. Their missions were to hold the U.S.–Australia line of communications, to contain the Japanese within the Pacific, to support the defense of North America, and to prepare for major amphibious counteroffensives.

Japan's initial war plans were realized with the capture of Java. But despite their military triumphs, the Japanese saw no indication that the Allies were ready for a negotiated peace. On the contrary, it seemed evident that an Allied counterstroke was in the making. The U.S. Pacific Fleet bombed the Marshall Islands on Feb. 1, 1942, Wake Island on February 23, and Marcus Island (between Wake and Japan) on March 1. These moves, together with the bombing of Rabaul on February 23 and the establishment of bases in Australia and a line of communications across the South Pacific, made the Japanese decide to expand so as to cut the Allied line of communications to Australia. They planned to occupy New Caledonia, the Fiji Islands, and Samoa and also to seize eastern New Guinea, whence they would threaten Australia from an air base to be established at Port Moresby. They planned also to capture Midway Island in the North Pacific and to establish air bases in the Aleutians. In pursuance of this new program, Japanese troops occupied Lae and Salamaua in New Guinea and Buka in the Solomon Islands in March 1942 and Bougainville in the Solomons and the Admiralty Islands (north of New Guinea) early in April.

Something to raise the Allies' morale was achieved on April 18, 1942, when 16 U.S. bombers raided Tokyo—though they did little real damage except to the Japanese government's prestige. Far more important were the consequences of the U.S. intelligence services' detection of Japanese plans to seize Port Moresby and Tulagi (in the southern Solomons). Had these two places fallen, Japanese aircraft could have dominated the Coral Sea. In the event, after U.S. aircraft on

The smoking remains of the Japanese heavy cruiser Mikuma, *after the Battle of Midway, an important Allied victory in the Pacific campaign.* Time & Life Pictures/Getty Images

May 3, 1942, had interfered with the Japanese landing on Tulagi, U.S. naval units, with aircraft, challenged the Japanese ships on their circuitous detour from Rabaul to Port Moresby. On May 5 and 6 the opposing carrier groups sought each other out, and the four-day Battle of the Coral Sea ensued. On May 7 planes from the Japanese carriers sank a U.S. destroyer and an oil tanker, but U.S. planes sank the Japanese light carrier *Shoho* and a cruiser. The next day, though Japanese aircraft sank the U.S. carrier *Lexington* and damaged the carrier *Yorktown*, the large Japanese carrier *Shokaku* had to retire crippled. Finally, the Japanese lost so many planes in the battle that their enterprise against Port Moresby had to be abandoned.

Despite the mixed results of the Battle of the Coral Sea, the Japanese continued with their plan to seize Midway Island. Seeking a naval showdown with the remaining ships of the U.S. Pacific Fleet and counting on their own numerical superiority to secure a victory, the Japanese mustered four heavy and three light aircraft carriers, two seaplane carriers, 11 battleships, 15 cruisers, 44 destroyers, 15 submarines, and miscellaneous small vessels. The U.S. Pacific Fleet had only three heavy carriers, eight cruisers, 18 destroyers, and 19 submarines, though there were some 115 aircraft in support

IN FOCUS: THE AGE OF THE AIRCRAFT CARRIER

Early in World War II the primary instrument for delivering naval combat power became the aircraft carrier. The reason was range: aircraft could deliver a concerted attack at 200 miles (322 km) or more, whereas battleships could do so only at 20 miles (32 km) or less. While in the 1920s and '30s aircraft could not lift enough destruction to supersede the battleship, by the end of that decade, engines were carrying adequate payloads, dive-bomber and torpedo-plane designs had matured, carrier arresting gear and associated flight-deck handling facilities were up to their tasks, and proficient strike tactics had been well practiced. U.S. and Japanese naval aviators were pacesetters in these developments.

The question remained: could the enemy be found at the outer limits of aircraft range? The ability to attack fixed targets such as the Panama Canal or Pearl Harbor, and to achieve surprise in doing so, had been amply demonstrated in naval exercises as well as in battle, but finding, reporting, and closing on ships at sea was a greater challenge. Without detracting from the courage and skill of aviators, it may be said that effective scouting was the dominant tactical problem of carrier warfare and had utmost influence on the outcomes of the crucial carrier battles of the Pacific Theatre in 1942: the Coral Sea (May 4–8), Midway (June 3–6), the Eastern Solomons (August 23–25), and the Santa Cruz Islands (October 26). In those closely matched battles the quality of U.S. and Japanese aviators and their planes was virtually on a par. When the United States won, it did so by superior scouting and screening, owing in large measure to air-search radar and to the advantage of having broken the Japanese code.

The command and control structure polished by the U.S. Navy during the war was the third vital component, after scouting and the delivery of firepower. The U.S. Combat Information Center centralized radar information and voice radio communications. By 1944 the tactical doctrine of coordinating fighter air defenses, along with the now much strengthened antiaircraft firepower on ships of the fleet, was so effective that in the Battle of the Philippine Sea (June 19–21, 1944) more than 90 percent of 450 Japanese aircraft were wiped out in a fruitless attack on Admiral Raymond Spruance's 5th Fleet.

The new tactical formation was circular, with carriers in the centre defended by an antiaircraft and antisubmarine screen composed of their own aircraft plus battleships, cruisers, and destroyers. For offensive purposes, a circle allowed a rapid simultaneous turn by all ships in a task group in order to launch and recover aircraft. For antiaircraft defense, the circle was shrunk in diameter as tightly as possible so that each screening ship, by defending itself, helped defend its neighbour.

The new battle paradigm called for a pulse of combat power to be delivered in a shock attack by one or more air wings. Despite every intention, though, air strikes against alerted defenses were rarely delivered as compactly as practiced, nor were they as decisive tactically as naval aviators had expected. In the five big carrier battles, one attacking air wing took out an average of only one enemy carrier. Since it took more than two hours to launch, marshal, and deliver an air strike, it was difficult to attack before an enemy counterstrike was in the air. Successful command at sea depended as never before on effective scouting and communication, because in order to win a decisive battle, in World War II as in all of naval history, it was necessary to attack effectively first.

World War II marked a shift in naval strategy. Battles at sea, of course, played a role in some of the decisive victories of the war, but attacks from sea to shore were also crucial in securing control of the seas. World War II also marked the end of a traditional tactical maxim, "Ships do not fight forts." After the U.S. repeatedly and successfully took the war against entire airfields, this maxim was suspended for the duration of the war. These, among other developments, marked World War II as the birthplace of the age of the aircraft carrier.

of it. The Americans, however, had the incomparable advantage of knowing the intentions of the Japanese in advance, thanks to the U.S. intelligence services' having broken the Japanese Navy's code and deciphered key radio transmissions. In the ensuing Battle of Midway, the Japanese ships destined to take Midway Island were attacked while still 500 miles (805 km) from their target by U.S. bombers on June 3. The Japanese carriers were still able to launch their aircraft against Midway early on June 4, but in the ensuing battle, waves of carrier- and Midway-based U.S. bombers sank all four of the Japanese heavy carriers and one heavy cruiser. Appalled by this disaster, the Japanese began to retreat in the night of June 4–5. Though the U.S. carrier *Yorktown* was sunk by torpedo on June 6, Midway was saved from invasion. In the Aleutians, the Japanese bombed Dutch

Harbor effectively and on June 7 occupied Attu and Kiska.

The Battle of Midway was probably the turning point of the war in the Pacific, for Japan lost its first-line carrier strength and most of its navy's best trained pilots. Henceforth, the naval strengths of the Japanese and of the Allies were virtually equal. Having lost the strategic initiative, Japan canceled its plans to invade New Caledonia, Fiji, and Samoa.

THE CHINESE FRONT AND BURMA

Japan's entry into war against the western Allies had its repercussions in China. Chiang Kai-shek's government on Dec. 9, 1941, formally declared war not only against Japan (a formality long overdue) but also, with political rather than military intent, against Germany and Italy. Three Chinese armies were rushed to the Burmese frontier, since the Burma Road was the only land route whereby the western Allies could send supplies to the Nationalist Chinese government. On Jan. 3, 1942, Chiang was recognized as supreme Allied commander for the China theatre of war. A U.S. general, Joseph W. Stilwell, was sent to him to be his chief of staff. In the first eight weeks after Pearl Harbor, however, the major achievement of the Chinese was the definitive repulse, on Jan. 15, 1942, of a long-sustained Japanese drive against Changsha, on the Guangzhou–Hankou railway.

Thereafter, Chiang and Stilwell were largely preoccupied by efforts to check the Japanese advance into Burma. By mid-March 1942 two Chinese armies, under Stilwell's command, had crossed the Burmese frontier. But before the end of the month the Chinese force defending Toungoo, in central Burma between Rangoon and Mandalay, was nearly annihilated by the more soldierly Japanese. British and Indian units in Burma fared scarcely better, being driven

IN FOCUS: DOOLITTLE RAID

On April 18, 1942, American aviator and army general James Doolittle led an air raid on Tokyo and other Japanese cities four months after the Japanese attack on Pearl Harbor. Doolittle commanded the bombing mission that began on the deck of the aircraft carrier Hornet. *Sixteen B-25s struck Tokyo, Yokohama, and other Japanese cities. The planes then proceeded westward, and most of the crews arrived safely behind friendly lines on the Chinese mainland. While the raid did little damage, it greatly bolstered U.S. morale and caused the Japanese to shift precious resources to air defense.*

Doolittle, made a brigadier general after the raid, received the Congressional Medal of Honor for his actions and soon was promoted to major general. He continued to lead air operations during the war, on the European, North African, and Pacific fronts, winning promotion to lieutenant general in 1944. He commanded the 8th Air Force in its attacks on Germany during 1944–45.

into retreat by the enemy's numerical superiority both in the air and on the ground. On April 29 the Japanese took Lashio, the Burma Road's southern terminus, thus cutting the supply line to China and turning the Allies' northern flank. Under continued pressure, the British and Indian forces in the following month fell back through Kalewa to Imphāl (across the Indian border), while most of the Chinese retreated across the Salween River into China. By the end of 1942 all of Burma was in Japanese hands, China was effectively isolated (except by air), and India was exposed to the danger of a Japanese invasion through Burma.

Since the U.S. bombers that raided Tokyo on April 18 flew on to Chinese airfields, particularly to those in Zhejiang (the coastal province south of Shanghai), the Japanese reacted by launching a powerful offensive to seize those airfields. By the end of July they had generally achieved their objectives.

CHAPTER 3

AXIS HIGH TIDE, 1941–42

NORTH AFRICA

ALLIED STRATEGY AND CONTROVERSIES

In the year following the collapse of France in June 1940, British strategists, relying as they could on supplies from the nonbelligerent United States, were concerned first with home defense, second with the security of the British positions in the Middle East, and third with the development of a war of attrition against the Axis powers, pending the buildup of adequate forces for an invasion of the European continent. For the United States, President Roosevelt's advisers, from November 1940, based their strategic plans on the "Europe first" principle: that is to say, if the United States became engaged in war simultaneously against Germany, Italy, and Japan, merely defensive operations should be conducted in the Pacific (to protect at least the Alaska–Hawaii–Panama triangle) while an offensive was being mounted in Europe.

Japan's entry into the war terminated the nonbelligerency of the United States. The three weeks' conference, named Arcadia, that Roosevelt, Churchill, and their advisers opened in Washington, D.C., on Dec. 22, 1941, reassured the British about U.S. maintenance of the "Europe first" principle and also produced two plans. One of these plans was a tentative one, code-named "Sledgehammer," for the buildup of an offensive force in Great Britain, in case it should be decided to invade France. The other, code-named "Super-Gymnast," would combine a British landing behind the German forces in Libya (already planned under the code name "Gymnast") with a U.S. landing near Casablanca on the Atlantic coast of Morocco. The same conference furthermore created the machinery of the Combined Chiefs of Staff, where the British Chiefs of Staff Committee was to be linked continuously, through delegates in Washington, D.C., with the newly established U.S. Joint Chiefs of Staff Organization, so that all aspects of the war could be studied in concert. It was on Jan. 1, 1942, during the Arcadia Conference, that the Declaration of the United Nations was signed in Washington, D.C., as a collective statement of the Allies' war aims in sequel to the Atlantic Charter.

Meanwhile, Churchill became anxious to do something to help the embattled Soviets—who were clamouring for the United States and Britain to invade continental Europe so as to take some of the German pressure off the Eastern Front. Roosevelt was no less conscious than Churchill of the fact that the Soviet Union was bearing by far the greatest burden of the war against Germany. This consideration inclined him to listen to the arguments of his Joint Chiefs of Staff Organization for a change of plan. After some hesitation, he sent his confidant Harry Hopkins and his army chief of staff General George C. Marshall to London in April 1942 to suggest the scrapping of

"Super-Gymnast" in favour of "Bolero," namely the concentration of forces in Great Britain for a landing in Europe (perhaps at Brest or at Cherbourg) in the autumn. Then "Roundup," an invasion of France by 30 U.S. and 18 British divisions, could follow in April 1943. The British agreed but soon began to doubt the practicability of mounting an amphibious invasion of France at such an early date.

Attempts to conclude an Anglo-Soviet political agreement were renewed without result, but a 20-year Anglo-Soviet alliance was signed on May 26, 1942; and, though Churchill warned Molotov not to expect an early second front in Europe, Molotov seemed gratified by what he was told about Anglo-U.S. plans.

Visiting Roosevelt again in the latter part of June 1942, Churchill at Hyde Park, N.Y., and in Washington, D.C., pressed for a revised and enlarged joint operation in North Africa before the end of the year, instead of a buildup for the invasion of France. But the U.S. Joint Chiefs resolutely upheld the latter plan. After further debate and disagreement, in July the U.S. Joint Chiefs yielded at last to British obstinacy in favour of a North African enterprise: it was decided that "Torch," as this combined Anglo-U.S. operation came to be called, should begin the following autumn.

Already, on July 17, 1942, Churchill had had to notify Stalin that convoys of Allied supplies to northern Russia must be suspended because of German submarine activity on the Arctic sea route (on June 2 a convoy from Iceland had lost 23 out of 34 vessels). Consequently, it was more awkward to inform Stalin that there would be no second front in Europe before 1943. In mid-August 1942, when Churchill went to Moscow to break the news, Stalin raged against the retreat from the plan for a second front in Europe but had to admit the military logic of "Torch."

LIBYA AND EGYPT

In the Western Desert, a major offensive against Rommel's front was undertaken on Nov. 18, 1941, by the British 8th Army, commanded by Cunningham under the command in chief of Wavell's successor in the Middle East, General Sir Claude Auchinleck. The offensive was routed. General Neil Methuen Ritchie took Cunningham's place on November 25, still more tanks were brought up, and a fortnight's resumed pressure constrained Rommel to evacuate Cyrenaica and to retreat to Agedabia. There, however, Rommel was at last, albeit meagrely, reinforced. After repulsing a British attack on December 26, he prepared a counter-offensive. When the British still imagined his forces to be hopelessly crippled, he attacked on Jan. 21, 1942, and, by a series of strokes, drove the 8th Army back to the Gazala Bir Hakeim line, just west of Tobruk.

Both sides were subsequently further reinforced. Then, on the night of May 26–27, Rommel passed around Ritchie's southern flank with his three German divisions and two Italian ones, leaving only four Italian divisions to face the Gazala line. Though at first Rommel did some damage to the British tanks as they came into action piecemeal from a weak position, he failed to break through to the coast behind Gazala. In a single day one third of Rommel's tank force was lost; and, after another unsuccessful effort to reach the coast, he decided, on May 29, to take up a defensive position.

The new German position, aptly known as the Cauldron, seemed indeed to be perilously exposed. Throughout the first days of June the British attacked it continually from the air and from the ground, imagining that Rommel's armour was caught at last. The British tanks, however, persisted in making direct assaults in small groups against the Cauldron and were beaten off with very heavy losses. Rommel, meanwhile, secured his rear and his line of supply by overwhelming several isolated British positions to the south.

Whereas in May 1942 the British had had 700 tanks, with 200 more in reserve, against Rommel's 525, by June 10 their present armoured strength was reduced, through their wasteful tactics against the Cauldron, to 170, and most of the reserve was exhausted. Suddenly then, on June 11, Rommel struck eastward, to catch most of the remaining British armour in the converging fire of two panzer divisions. By nightfall on June 13 the British had barely 70 tanks left, and Rommel, with some 150 still fit for action, was master of the battlefield.

The British on June 14 began a precipitate retreat from the Gazala line toward the Egyptian frontier. A garrison of 33,000 men, however, with an immense quantity of material, was left behind in Tobruk—on the retention of which Churchill characteristically and most unfortunately insisted in successive telegrams from London. Rommel's prompt reduction of Tobruk, achieved on June 21, 1942, was felt by Great Britain as a national disaster second only to the loss of Singapore; and 80 percent of the transport with which Rommel chased the remnant of the 8th Army eastward consisted of captured British vehicles.

At this point Auchinleck relieved Ritchie of his command and in a realistic and soldierly way ordered a general British retreat back to the Alamein area. By June 30 the German tanks were pressing against the British positions between el-Alamein (al-ʿAlamayn) and the Qattara Depression, some 60 miles (97 km) west of Alexandria, after an advance of more than 350 miles (563 km) from Gazala. Hitler and Mussolini could expect that within a matter of days Rommel would be the master of Egypt.

The ensuing First Battle of el-Alamein, which lasted throughout July 1942, marked the end of the German hopes of a rapid victory. Rommel's troops, having come so far and so fast, were exhausted. Their first assaults failed to break the defense rallied by Auchinleck, and they were also subjected to disconcerting counterstrokes. At this point, the respite that Rommel had to grant to his men gave Auchinleck time to bring up reinforcements. By the end of July Rommel knew that it was he rather than Auchinleck who was now on the defensive.

Auchinleck had saved Egypt by halting Rommel's invasion, but his counterattacks had not driven it back. Early in August, when Churchill arrived in Cairo to review the situation, Auchinleck insisted on postponing the resumption of the offensive until September, so that his new forces could be properly acclimatized and trained for desert warfare. Impatient of this delay, Churchill removed Auchinleck from the command in chief in the Middle East and gave the post to General Sir Harold Alexander, while the command of the 8th Army was transferred eventually (after the sudden death of Churchill's first nominee) to General Bernard Law Montgomery. Paradoxically, Montgomery postponed the resumption of the offensive even longer than Auchinleck had desired.

While the British in the course of August raised their strength in armour at the front to some 700 tanks, Rommel received only meagre reinforcement in the shape of infantry. He had, however, about 200 gun-armed German tanks and also 240 Italian tanks (of an obsolete model). With this armament, in the night of Aug. 30–31, 1942, he launched a fresh attack, intending to capture by surprise the minefields on the southern sector of the British front and then to drive eastward with his armour for some 30 miles (48 km) before wheeling north into the 8th Army's supply area on the coast. In the event, the minefields proved unexpectedly deep, and by daybreak Rommel's spearhead was only eight miles (13 km) beyond them. Delayed on their eastward drive and already under attack from the air, the two German panzer divisions of the

Afrika Korps had to make their wheel to the north at a much shorter distance from the breach than Rommel had planned. Their assault thus ran mainly into the position held by the British 22nd Armoured Brigade, to the southwest of the ridge 'Alam al-Halfa.' Shortage of fuel on the German side and reinforced defense on the British, together with intensification of the British bombing, spelled the defeat of the offensive, and Rommel on September 2 decided to make a gradual withdrawal.

GERMANY CAPTURES CAUCASUS OIL FIELDS IN SOUTHERN RUSSIA

The German plan to launch another great summer offensive crystallized in the early months of 1942. Hitler's decision was influenced by his economists, who mistakenly told him that Germany could not continue the war unless it obtained petroleum supplies from the Caucasus. Hitler was the more responsive to such arguments because they coincided with his belief that another German offensive would so drain the Soviet Union's manpower that the U.S.S.R. would be unable to continue the war. His thinking was shared by his generals, who had been awed by the prodigality with which the Soviets squandered their troops in the fighting of 1941 and the spring of 1942. By this time at least 4,000,000 Soviet troops had been killed, wounded, or captured, while German casualties totaled only 1,150,000.

In the early summer of 1942 the German southern line ran from Orël southward east of Kursk, through

IN FOCUS: DESERT RATS

The British Seventh Armoured Division, commonly known as the Desert Rats, were a group of British soldiers who helped defeat the Germans in North Africa during World War II. The Desert Rats, led by General Allen Francis Harding, were especially noted for a hard-fought, three-month campaign against the more experienced German Afrika Korps, led by General Erwin Rommel ("The Desert Fox").

The term "Rats of Tobruk," a moniker applied by the Nazi propagandist broadcaster William Joyce ("Lord Haw-Haw"), referred more generally to any of the Allied troops (including Australian, British, and Polish units) who defended Tobruk, Libya.

The 7th British Armoured Division— called the Desert Rats—sitting on a field gun prior to the fall of Tobruk during the North African campaign in 1942. Hulton Archive/Getty Images

Belgorod, and east of Kharkov down to the loop of the Soviet salient opposite Izyum, beyond which it veered southeastward to Taganrog, on the northern coast of the Sea of Azov. Before the Germans were ready for their principal offensive, the Red Army in May started a drive against Kharkov. This premature effort actually served the Germans' purposes, since it not only pre-empted the Soviet reserves but also provoked an immediate counterstroke against its southern flank, where the Germans broke into the salient and reached the Donets River near Izyum. The Germans cap-tured 240,000 Soviet prisoners in the encirclement that fol-lowed. In May also the Germans drove the Soviet defenders of the Kerch Peninsula out of the Crimea. On June 3 the Germans began an assault against Sevastopol, which, however, held out for a month.

The Germans' crossing of the Donets near Izyum on June 10, 1942, was the prelude to their summer offensive, which was launched at last on June 28. Field Marshal Max-imilian von Weichs's Army Group B, from the Kursk–Belgorod sector of the front, struck toward the middle Don River opposite Voronezh, whence General Friedrich Paulus's 6th

Army was to wheel southeastward against Stalingrad (Volgograd). List's Army Group A, from the front south of Kharkov, with Kleist's 1st Panzer Army, struck toward the lower Don to take Rostov and to thrust thence northeastward against Stalingrad as well as southward into the

German Field Marshal Erwin Rommel, commander of the Afrika Korps. Considered to be the most skilled commander of desert warfare, Rommel earned the nickname "The Desert Fox." Keystone/Hulton Archive/Getty Images

vast oil fields of Caucasia. Army Group B swept rapidly across a 100-mile (161 km) stretch of plain to the Don and captured Voronezh on July 6. The 1st Panzer Army drove 250 miles (402 km) from its starting line and captured Rostov on July 23. Once his forces had reached Rostov, Hitler decided to split his troops so that they could both invade the rest of the Caucasus and take the important industrial city of Stalingrad on the Volga River, 220 miles (354 km) northeast of Rostov. This decision was to have fatal consequences for the Germans, since they lacked the resources to successfully take and hold both of these objectives.

Maikop (Maykup), the great oil centre 200 miles (322 km) south of Rostov, fell to Kleist's right-hand column on August 9, and Pyatigorsk, 150 miles (241 km) east of Maikop, fell to his centre on the same day, while the projected thrust against Stalingrad, in the opposite direction from Rostov, was being developed. Shortage of fuel, however, slowed the pace of Kleist's subsequent southeastward progress through the Caucasian mountains. And, after forcing a passage over the Terek River near Mozdok early in September, he was halted definitively just south of that river. From the end of October 1942 the Caucasian front was stabilized. Yet the titanic struggle for Stalingrad, draining manpower that might have won victory for the Germans in Caucasia, was to rage on, fatefully, for three more months. Already, however, it was evident that Hitler's new offensive had fallen short of its objectives, and the scapegoat this time was Halder, who was superseded by Kurt Zeitzler as chief of the army general staff.

CHAPTER 4

THE TIDE TURNS 1942–43

JAPANESE RETREAT BEGINS

ALLIES RETAKE SOUTHEAST ASIAN ISLANDS

On July 2, 1942, the U.S. Joint Chiefs of Staff ordered limited offensives in three stages to recapture the New Britain–New Ireland–Solomons–eastern New Guinea area. First, they ordered the seizure of Tulagi and of the Santa Cruz Islands, with adjacent positions. The second stage involved the occupation of the central and northern Solomons and of the northeast coast of New Guinea. The third stage was to seize Rabaul and other points in the Bismarck Archipelago.

On July 6 the Japanese landed troops on Guadalcanal, one of the southern Solomons, and began to construct an air base. The Allied high command, fearing further Japanese advances southeastward, sped into the area to dislodge the enemy and to obtain a base for later advances toward Japan's main base in the theatre, Rabaul. The U.S. 1st Marine Division poured ashore on August 7 and secured Guadalcanal's airfield, Tulagi's harbour, and neighbouring islands by dusk on August 8—the Pacific war's first major Allied offensive. During the night of August 8–9, Japanese cruisers and destroyers, attempting to hold Guadalcanal, sank four U.S. cruisers, themselves sustaining one cruiser sunk and one damaged and later sunk. On August 23–25, in the Battle of the Eastern

Solomons, the Japanese lost a light carrier, a destroyer, and a submarine and sustained damage to a cruiser and to a seaplane carrier but sank an Allied destroyer and crippled a cruiser. On August 31 another U.S. carrier was disabled, and on September 15 Japanese submarines sank the carrier *Wasp* and damaged a battleship. The sea battles of Cape Esperance and of the Santa Cruz Islands—in which two Japanese cruisers and two destroyers were sunk and three carriers and two destroyers damaged in return for the loss of one U.S. carrier and two destroyers, besides damage to six other Allied ships—thwarted an attempt to reinforce further the Japanese ground troops, whose attack proved a failure (October 20–29).

Earlier, before Allied plans to secure eastern New Guinea had been implemented, the Japanese had landed near Gona on the north coast of Papua (the southeastern extremity of the great island) on July 24, 1942, in an attempt to reach Port Moresby overland, via the Kokoda Trail. Advanced Japanese units from the north, despite Australian opposition, had reached a ridge 32 miles (51 km) from Port Moresby by mid-September. Then, however, they had to withdraw

In Focus: Battle of Guadalcanal

On Aug. 7, 1942, in the Allies' first major offensive in the Pacific, 6,000 U.S. Marines landed on Guadalcanal and seized the airfield, surprising the island's 2,000 Japanese defenders. Both sides then began landing reinforcements by sea, and bitter fighting ensued in the island's jungles. More than 6,000 Japanese troops reinforced their Guadalcanal garrison, attacking the Marines' beachhead on August 20-21 and on September 12-14. On September 18 some U.S. reinforcements arrived, and mid-October saw about 22,000 Japanese ranged against 23,000 U.S. troops.

After October, Allied strength was built up. Another Japanese attempt at counter-reinforcement led to the naval Battle of Guadalcanal, fought on November 13-15. The battle cost Japan two battleships, three destroyers, one cruiser, two submarines, and 11 transports. The Allies (now under Admiral William F. Halsey) had two cruisers and seven destroyers sunk and one battleship and one cruiser damaged. Only 4,000 Japanese troops out of 12,500 managed to reach land, without equipment. On November 30 eight Japanese destroyers, attempting to land more troops, were beaten off in the Battle of Tassafaronga, losing one destroyer sunk and one crippled, at an Allied cost of one cruiser sunk and three damaged.

By Jan. 5, 1943, Guadalcanal's Allied garrison totaled 44,000, against 22,500 Japanese. The Japanese decided to evacuate the position, carrying away 12,000 men in early February in daring destroyer runs. In ground warfare Japanese losses were more than 24,000 for the Guadalcanal campaign, Allied losses about 1,600 killed and 4,250 wounded (figures that ignore the higher number of casualties from disease). On February 21, U.S. infantry began occupying the Russell Islands, to support advances on Rabaul.

exhausted to Gona and to nearby Buna, where there were some 7,500 Japanese assembled by November 18. The next day U.S. infantry attacked them there. Each side was subsequently reinforced; but the Australians took Gona on December 9 and the Americans Buna village on December 14. Buna government station fell to the Allies on Jan. 2, 1943, Sanananda on January 18, and all Japanese resistance in Papua ceased on January 22.

The retaking of Guadalcanal and Papua ended the Japanese drive south, and communications with Australia and New Zealand were now secure. Altogether, Papua cost Japan nearly 12,000 killed and 350 captured. Allied losses were 3,300 killed and 5,500 wounded. Allied air forces had played a particularly important role, interdicting Japanese supply lines and transporting Allied supplies and reinforcements.

Japan, having lost Guadalcanal, fought henceforth defensively, with worsening prospects. Its final effort to reinforce the Lae–Salamaua position in New Guinea from the stronghold of Rabaul was a disaster: in the Battle of the Bismarck Sea, on March 2–4, 1943, the Japanese lost four destroyers and eight transports, and only 1,000 of the 7,000 troops reached their destination. On March 25 the Japanese Army and Navy high commands agreed on a policy of strengthening the defense of strategic points and of counterattacking wherever possible, priority being given to the defense of the remaining Japanese positions in New Guinea, with secondary emphasis on the Solomon Islands. In the

following three weeks, however, the Allies improved their own position in New Guinea, and Japanese intervention was confined to air attacks. Before the end of April, moreover, the Japanese Navy sustained a disaster: the guiding genius of the Japanese war effort, Yamamoto, was sent late in March to command the forces based on Rabaul but was killed in an American air ambush on a flight to Bougainville.

Developments of the Allies' war against Japan also took place outside the southwest Pacific area. British forces in the summer of 1942 invaded Vichy French-held Madagascar. A renewed British offensive in September 1942 overran the island. Hostilities ceased on November 5, and a Free French administration of Madagascar took office on Jan. 8, 1943. In the North Pacific, meanwhile, the United States had decided to expel the Japanese from the Aleutians. Having landed forces on Adak in August 1942, they began air attacks against Kiska and Attu from Adak the next month and from Amchitka also in the following January, while a naval blockade prevented the Japanese from reinforcing their garrisons. Finally, U.S. troops, bypassing Kiska, invaded Attu on May 11, 1943—to kill most of the island's 2,300 defenders in three weeks of fighting. The Japanese then evacuated Kiska. Bases in the Aleutians thenceforth facilitated the Allies' bombing of the Kuril Islands.

Burma

On the Burmese front the Allies found they could do little to dislodge the

Japanese from their occupation of that country, and what little the Allies did attempt proved abortive. Brigadier General Orde Wingate's "Chindits," which were long-range penetration groups depending on supplies from the air, crossed the Chindwin River in February 1943 and were initially successful in severing Japanese communications on the railroad between Mandalay and Myitkyina. But the Chindits soon found themselves in unfavourable terrain and in grave danger of encirclement, and so they made their way back to India.

In May 1943, however, the Allies reorganized their system of command for Southeast Asia. Vice Admiral Lord Louis Mountbatten was appointed supreme commander of the South East Asia Command (SEAC), and Stilwell was appointed deputy to Mountbatten. Stilwell at the same time was chief of staff to Chiang Kai-shek. The British–Indian forces destined for Burma meanwhile constituted the 14th Army, under Lieutenant General William Slim, whose operational control Stilwell agreed to accept. Shortly afterward, Auchinleck

During a sandstorm on the battlefield at el-Alamein on Oct. 25, 1942, two soldiers belonging to the Commonwealth and Allied forces take aim at a surrendering German soldier. AFP/ Getty Images

succeeded Wavell as commander in chief in India.

BATTLE OF EL-ALAMEIN AND ROMMEL'S RETREAT

While Churchill was still chafing in London about his generals' delay in resuming the offensive in Egypt, Montgomery waited for seven weeks after "Alam al-Halfa" in order to be sure of success. He finally chose to begin his attack in the night of Oct. 23–24, 1942, when there would be moonlight for the clearing of gaps in the German minefields.

By mid-October the British 8th Army had 230,000 men and 1,230 gun-armed tanks ready for action, while the German-Italian forces numbered only 80,000 men, with only 210 tanks of comparable quality ready; and in air support the British enjoyed a superiority of 1,500 to 350. Allied air and submarine attacks on the Axis supply lines across the Mediterranean, moreover, had prevented Rommel's army from receiving adequate replenishments of fuel, ammunition, and food. Rommel himself, who had been ill before "Alam al-Halfa," was convalescing in Austria.

The British launched their infantry attack at el-Alamein at 10:00 PM on Oct. 23, 1942, but found the German minefields harder to clear than they had foreseen. Two days later, however, some of those tanks were deploying six miles (10 km) beyond the original front. When Rommel, ordered back to Africa by Hitler, reached the front in the evening of October 25,

half of the Germans' available armour was already destroyed. Nevertheless, the impetus of the British onslaught was stopped the next day, when German antitank guns took a heavy toll of armour trying to deepen the westward penetration. In the night of October 28 Montgomery turned the offensive northward from the wedge, but this drive likewise miscarried. In the first week of their offensive the British lost four times as many tanks as the Germans but still had 800 available against the latter's remaining 90.

When Montgomery switched the British line of attack back to its original direction, early on Nov. 2, 1942, Rommel was no longer strong enough to withstand him. After expensive resistance throughout the daytime, he ordered a retreat to Fūka (Fūkah). In the afternoon of November 3 the retreat was fatally countermanded by Hitler, who insisted that the Alamein position be held. The 36 hours wasted in obeying this long-distance instruction cost Rommel his chance of making a stand at Fūka. When he resumed his retreat, he had to race much farther back to escape successive British attempts to intercept him on the coast road by scythelike sweeps from the south. A fortnight after resuming his withdrawal from el-Alamein, Rommel was 700 miles (1,126 km) to the west, at the traditional backstop of Agheila. As the British took their time to mount their attacks, he fell back farther by stages: after three weeks, 200 miles (322 km) to Buerat (al-Bu'ayrāt); after three more weeks, in mid-January

General Bernard Montgomery, commander of the Allied forces in the Western Desert campaign, is pictured here in the turret of a tank during the Allied advance on el-Alamein, circa 1942. Popperfoto/Getty Images

1943, the whole distance of 350 miles (563 km) past Tripoli to the Mareth Line within the frontiers of Tunisia. By that time the Axis position in Tunisia was being battered from the west, through the execution of "Torch."

BATTLE OF STALINGRAD AND THE GERMAN RETREAT

The German 4th Panzer Army, after being diverted to the south to help Kleist's attack on Rostov late in July 1942, was redirected toward Stalingrad a fortnight later. Stalingrad was a large industrial city producing armaments and tractors;

it stretched for 30 miles (48 km) along the banks of the Volga River. By the end of August the 4th Army's northeastward advance against the city was converging with the eastward advance of the 6th Army, under General Friedrich Paulus, with 330,000 of the German Army's finest troops. The Red Army, however, put up the most determined resistance, yielding ground only very slowly and at a high cost as the 6th Army approached Stalingrad. On August 23 a German spearhead penetrated the city's northern suburbs, and the Luftwaffe rained incendiary bombs that destroyed most of the city's wooden housing. The Soviet 62nd Army was pushed back into Stalingrad proper, where, under the command of General Vasily I. Chuikov, it made a determined stand. Meanwhile, the Germans' concentration on Stalingrad was increasingly draining reserves from their flank cover, which was already strained by having to stretch so far—400 miles (644 km) on the left (north), as far as Voronezh, and 400 miles again on the right (south), as far as the Terek River. By mid-September the Germans had pushed the Soviet forces in Stalingrad back until the latter occupied only a nine-mile-long (14 km) strip of the city along the Volga, and this strip was only two or three miles (3–5 km) wide. The Soviets had to supply their troops by barge and boat across the Volga from the other bank. At this point Stalingrad became the scene of some of the fiercest and most concentrated fighting of the war. Streets, blocks, and individual buildings were fought over by many small units of troops and often changed hands again and again. The city's remaining buildings were pounded into rubble by the unrelenting close combat. The most critical moment came on October 14, when the Soviet defenders had their backs so close to the Volga that the few remaining supply crossings of the river came under German machine-gun fire. The Germans, however, were growing dispirited by heavy losses, by fatigue, and by the approach of winter.

A huge Soviet counteroffensive, planned by generals G.K. Zhukov, A.M. Vasilevsky, and Nikolay Nikolayevich Voronov, was launched on Nov. 19–20, 1942, in two spearheads, north and south of the German salient whose tip was at Stalingrad. The twin pincers of this counteroffensive struck the flanks of the German salient at points about 50 miles (80 km) north and 50 miles (80 km) south of Stalingrad and were designed to isolate the 250,000 remaining men of the German 6th and 4th armies in the city. The attacks quickly penetrated deep into the flanks, and by November 23 the two prongs of the attack had linked up about 60 miles (96 km) west of Stalingrad. The encirclement of the two German armies in Stalingrad was complete. The German high command urged Hitler to allow Paulus and his forces to break out of the encirclement and rejoin the main German forces west of the city, but Hitler would not contemplate a retreat from the Volga River and ordered Paulus to "stand and fight." With winter setting in and food and medical supplies dwindling, Paulus' forces grew weaker. In mid-December Hitler allowed one of the most talented German commanders, Field Marshal Erich von Manstein, to form a special army corps to rescue Paulus's forces by fighting its way eastward, but Hitler refused to let Paulus fight his way westward at the same time in order to link up with Manstein. This fatal decision doomed Paulus's forces, since the main German forces now simply lacked the reserves needed to break through the Soviet encirclement single-handedly. Hitler exhorted the trapped German forces to fight to the death. But on Jan. 31, 1943, Paulus surrendered, and 91,000 frozen, starving men (all that was left of the 6th and 4th armies) and 24 generals surrendered with him.

Besides being the greatest battle of the war, Stalingrad proved to be the turning point of the military struggle between Germany and the Soviet Union. The battle used up precious German reserves, destroyed two entire armies, and humiliated the prestigious German war machine. It also marked the increasing skill and professionalism of a group of younger Soviet generals who had emerged as capable commanders, chief among whom was Zhukov.

Meanwhile, early in January 1943, only just in time, Hitler acknowledged that the encirclement of the Germans in Stalingrad would lead to an even worse disaster unless he extricated his forces from the Caucasus. Kleist was therefore ordered to retreat, while his northern flank of 600 miles (966 km) was still protected by the desperate resistance of the encircled Paulus. Kleist's forces were making their way back across the Don at Rostov when Paulus at last surrendered. Had Paulus surrendered three weeks earlier (after seven weeks of isolation), Kleist's escape would have been impossible.

Even west of Rostov there were threats to Kleist's line of retreat. In January, two Soviet armies, the one under

German troops attack a Russian tank during the Battle of Stalingrad in 1942. Haynes Archive/Popperfoto/Getty Images

General Nikolay Fyodorovich Vatutin, the other under General Filipp Ivanovich Golikov, had crossed the Don upstream from Serafimovich and were thrusting southwestward to the Donets between Kamensk and Kharkov. Vatutin's forces, having crossed the Donets at Izyum, took Lozovaya Junction on February 11, Golikov's took Kharkov five days later. Farther to the north, a third Soviet army, under General Ivan Danilovich Chernyakhovsky, had initiated a drive westward from Voronezh on February 2 and had retaken Kursk on February 8. Thus, the Germans had to retreat from all the territory they had taken in their great summer offensive in 1942. The Caucasus returned to Soviet hands.

A sudden thaw supervened to hamper the Red Army's transport of supplies and reinforcements across the swollen courses of the great rivers. With the momentum of the Soviet counteroffensive thus slowed, the Germans made good their retreat to the Dnepr along the easier routes of the Black Sea littoral and were able, before the end of February 1943, to mount a counteroffensive of their own.

ALLIED INVASION OF NORTHWEST AFRICA

When the U.S. and British strategists had decided on "Torch" (Allied landings on the western coast of North Africa) late in July 1942, it remained to settle the practical details of the operation. The purpose of "Torch" was to hem Rommel's forces in

between U.S. troops on the west and British troops to the east. After considerable discussion, it was finally agreed that landings, under the supreme command of Major General Dwight D. Eisenhower, should be made on November 8. The landings would take place at three places in the vicinity of Casablanca on the Atlantic coast of Morocco and on beaches near Oran and near Algiers itself on the Mediterranean coast of Algeria. The amphibious landings would involve a total of about 110,000 troops, most of them Americans.

The conciliation of the French on whose colonial territory the landings would be made was a more delicate matter. All of French North Africa was still loyal to the Vichy government of Marshal Pétain, with which the United States, unlike Great Britain, was still formally maintaining diplomatic relations. Thus, the French commander in chief in Algeria, General Alphonse Juin, and his counterpart in Morocco, General Charles-Auguste Noguès, were subordinate to the supreme commander of all Vichy's forces, namely Admiral Jean-François Darlan. American diplomats and generals tried to gain these officers' collaboration with the Allies in the landings, for it was vital to try to avoid a situation in which Vichy French troops put up armed resistance to the landings at the beaches.

The U.S.-British landings at Algiers began on November 8 and were met by little French resistance. The simultaneous landings near Oran met stiffer resistance, and on November 9 the whole U.S. plan of operations was dislocated by a French counterattack on the Arzew beachhead. Around Casablanca the U.S. landings were accomplished without difficulty, but resistance developed when the invaders tried to expand their beachheads. On November 10, however, the fighting was called off. The next day the French authorities in Morocco concluded an armistice with the Americans.

The landing in Algiers, meanwhile, was complicated by the fact that Darlan himself was in the city at the time. The situation was muddled, with some French troops loyal to Pétain while others backed de Gaulle and the anti-Vichy French general whom the Allies were sponsoring in North Africa, Henri Giraud.

On Nov. 11, 1942, in reaction to the Allied landings, German and Italian forces overran southern France, the metropolitan territory hitherto under Pétain's immediate authority. This event helped induce Noguès and the other French commanders in Algeria to assent to Darlan's proposals for a working agreement with the Allies, including recognition of Giraud as military commander in chief of the French forces. Concluded on November 13, the agreement was promptly endorsed by Eisenhower. French West Africa, including Senegal, with the port of Dakar, likewise followed Darlan's lead. The Germans, however, by mining the exit from the harbour of Toulon, forestalled plans for the escape of the main French fleet from metropolitan France to North Africa: on November 27, the French crews scuttled their ships to avoid capture. On Dec. 24, 1942, Darlan was assassinated; both Royalist and Gaullist circles in North Africa had steadfastly objected to him on political grounds. Giraud thereupon took his place, for a time, as French high commissioner in North Africa.

ALLIES RETAKE TUNISIA

Axis troops had begun to arrive in Tunisia as early as Nov. 9, 1942, and were reinforced in the following fortnight until they numbered about 20,000 combat troops (which were subsequently heavily reinforced by air). Thus, when the British general Kenneth Anderson, designated to command the invasion of Tunisia from the west with the Allied 1st Army, started his offensive on November 25, the defense was unexpectedly strong. By December 5 the 1st Army's advance was checked a dozen miles (19 km) from Tunis and from Bizerte. Further reinforcements enabled Colonel General Jürgen von Arnim, who assumed the command in chief of the Axis defense in Tunisia on December 9, to expand his two bridgeheads in Tunisia until they were merged into one. Germany and Italy had won the race for Tunis but were henceforth to succumb to the lure of retaining their prize regardless of the greater need of conserving their strength for the defense of Europe.

After Rommel had fallen back from Libya to the Mareth Line in mid-January 1943, two German armies, Arnim's and

Rommel's, were holding the north and the south of the eastern littoral both against Anderson's 1st Army attacking from the west and against Montgomery's 8th from the southeast. Rommel judged that a counterstroke should be delivered first against the Allies in the west. Accordingly, on February 14 the Axis forces delivered a major attack against U.S. forces between the Fā'iḍ Pass in the north and Gafsa in the south. West of Fā'iḍ, the 21st Panzer Division, under General Heinz Ziegler, destroyed 100 U.S. tanks and drove the Americans back 50 miles (80 km). In the Kasserine Pass, however, the Allies put up some stiffer opposition.

When on February 19 Rommel received authority to continue his attack, he was ordered to advance not against Tébessa but northward from Kasserine against Thala—where, in fact, Alexander was expecting him. Having overcome the stubborn U.S. resistance in the Kasserine Pass on February 20, the Germans entered Thala the next day, only to be expelled a few hours later by Alexander's reserve troops. His chance having been forfeited, Rommel began a gradual withdrawal on February 22.

The delays ensuing from the frustration of Rommel's stroke against the 1st Army reduced the effectiveness of his stroke against the 8th. Whereas on Feb. 26, 1943, Montgomery had had only one division facing the Mareth Line, he quadrupled his strength in the following week, massing 400 tanks and 500 anti-tank guns. Rommel's attack, on March 6, was brought to an early halt, and 50 German tanks were lost. A sick man and a disappointed soldier, Rommel relinquished his command.

The Allied 1st Army resumed the offensive on March 17, with attacks by the U.S. II Corps, under General George Patton, on the roads through the mountains. The aim was to cut the Afrika Korps' line of retreat up the coast to Tunis; but these attacks were checked by the Germans in the passes. In the night of March 20–21, however, the British 8th Army launched a frontal assault on the Mareth Line, combined with an outflanking movement by the New Zealand Corps toward el-Hamma (al-Ḥāmmah) in the Germans' rear. A few days later, seeing the frontal assault to have failed, Montgomery switched the main weight of his attack to the flank. Threatened with encirclement, the Germans decided to abandon the Mareth Line, which the 8th Army occupied on March 28. The German defenses at el-Hamma held out long enough to enable the rest of the Afrika Korps to retreat without much loss to a new line on the Wādī al-'Akārīt, north of Gabès. The new line, however, was breached by the 8th Army on April 6; and, meanwhile, the Americans were also advancing on the Axis troops' rear from Gafsa. By the following morning the Afrika Korps was retreating rapidly northward along the littoral toward Tunis, and by April 11 it had joined hands with Arnim's forces for the defense of a 100-mile (161-km) perimeter stretching around Tunis and Bizerte (Banzart).

Thanks to the rapidity of the Afrika Korps' retreat from Wādī al-'Akārīt, the German high command had an opportunity to withdraw its forces from the rump of Tunisia to Sicily, but it chose instead to defend the indefensible rump. The defenders indeed withstood the converging assaults that the 8th and 1st armies delivered against the perimeter from April 20 to April 23. On May 6, however, a concentrated attack by Allied artillery, aircraft, infantry, and tanks was launched on the two-mile (3 km) front of the Medjerda (Majardah) Valley leading to Tunis. On May 7 the city fell to the leading British armoured forces, while the Americans and the French almost simultaneously captured Bizerte. At the same time, the Germans' line of retreat into the Cap Bon Peninsula was severed by an armoured division's swift turn southeastward from Tunis. A general collapse of the German resistance followed, the Allies taking more than 250,000 prisoners, including 125,000 German troops and Arnim himself. North Africa had been cleared of Axis forces and was now completely in Allied hands. Its capture insured the safety of Allied shipping and naval movements throughout the Mediterranean, and North Africa would serve as a base for future Allied operations against Italy itself.

IN FOCUS: CASABLANCA AND TRIDENT CONFERENCES

U.S. President Franklin D. Roosevelt and British Prime Minister Winston Churchill, together with their respective military chiefs and aides, met in Casablanca, Morocco, on Jan. 12–23, 1943, to plan future global military strategy for the western Allies during World War II. Though invited, Soviet leader Joseph Stalin declined to attend.

The work of the conference was primarily military—deciding on the invasion of Sicily (after completion of the North African campaign) rather than an immediate invasion of western Europe, apportioning forces for the Pacific theatre and outlining major lines of attack in the Far East, and agreeing on the concentrated bombing of Germany. Roosevelt and Churchill also found time to discuss nuclear bomb research, to consider competing claims between Henri Giraud and Charles de Gaulle for the leadership of the French war effort against the Axis powers, and, most important of all, to demand an "unconditional surrender" from Germany, Italy, and Japan.

Only four months after Casablanca it became necessary to hold another Anglo-U.S. conference. In mid-May 1943, Roosevelt, Churchill, and their advisers met, in Washington, D.C., for the conference code-named Trident. There the Sicilian project was effectively confirmed, and the date May 1, 1944, was prescribed—definitively in the U.S view, provisionally in the British—for the landing of 29 divisions in France; but the question whether the conquest of Sicily should be followed, as the British proposed, by an invasion of Italy was left unsettled.

114 | World War II: People, Politics, and Power

COMMAND OF SEA AND SKY IN THE WEST

U-BOATS AND CONVOYS

The year 1942 was, on the whole, a favourable one for the German U-boats. First, the U.S. entry into the war entitled them to infest the U.S. coast of the North Atlantic; and it was not until the middle of the year that the Allies' introduction of the convoy system from the Caribbean northward constrained the raiders to go so far afield as the waters between Brazil and West Africa. Second, U-tankers were developed; i.e., large converted U-boats equipped to provide fuel, torpedoes, and other supplies to U-boats operating in remote waters. In the course of 1942, the U-boats sank more than 6,266,000 tons of shipping. Since in the same period their operational strength rose from 91 to 212, it seemed conceivable that they might soon score their desired target of 800,000 tons of sinkings per month.

March 1943 saw the climax of the U-boats' good fortune. Their strength rose to 240, and they sank in that single month 627,377 tons of shipping. In addition, in the greatest convoy battle of the war, when 20 of them attacked two convoys merged into one, they sank 21 ships (141,000 tons) out of 77 with the loss of only one of their own number. The anticlimax followed, thanks to five developments of the Allies' counteraction. "Support groups" were reintroduced. Aircraft carriers became progressively available for escorts. More and more

long-range Liberator aircraft began to cover the convoys offshore. Ships were equipped with a radar set of very short wavelength, the probing of which was undetectable to the U-boats. And a regular offensive against U-boats on their transit routes was launched from the air (56 were destroyed in April–May 1943). The U-boats sank 327,943 tons in April, 264,852 in May, only 95,753 in June 1943. For the rest of the war monthly totals were less than 100,000 tons except in July and September 1943 and in March 1944.

Late in 1944 the U-boats were equipped with the snorkel breathing tube, which provided them with the necessary oxygen to recharge their batteries under water and so converted them from submersible torpedo boats into almost complete submarines virtually undetectable to radar. About the same time a new model of U-boat, with greater underwater speed and endurance, came into operation. These improvements came too late, however, because the Allies' surface and air resources for the protection of the convoys were already overwhelming.

CARPET AND INCENDIARY BOMBING OF GERMAN CITIES

Early in 1942 the RAF bomber command, headed by Sir Arthur Harris, began an intensification of the Allies' growing strategic air offensive against Germany. These attacks, which were aimed against factories, rail depots, dockyards, bridges, and dams and against cities and towns themselves, were intended to both destroy

IN FOCUS: BATTLE OF THE ATLANTIC

For the Allied Powers, the Battle of the Atlantic had three objectives: blockade of the Axis Powers in Europe, security of Allied sea movements, and the freedom to project military power across the seas. The Axis, in turn, hoped to frustrate the Allied imperative of moving men and equipment across the oceans. For British Prime Minister Winston Churchill, the Battle of the Atlantic represented Germany's best chance to defeat the Western Powers.

The first phase of the battle for the Atlantic lasted from the autumn of 1939 until the fall of France in June 1940. During this period, the Anglo-French coalition drove German merchant shipping from the Atlantic and maintained a fairly effective long-range blockade. The battle took a radically different turn following the Axis conquest of the Low Countries, the fall of France, and Italy's entry into the war on the Axis side in May–June 1940. Britain lost French naval support at the very moment when its own sea power was seriously crippled by losses incurred in the retreat from Norway and the evacuation from Dunkirk. The sea and air power of Italy, reinforced by German units, imperiled and eventually barred the direct route through the Mediterranean Sea to the Suez Canal, forcing British shipping to use the long alternative route around the Cape of Good Hope. This cut the total cargo-carrying capacity of the British merchant marine almost in half at the very moment when German acquisition of naval and air bases on the English Channel and on the west coast of France foreshadowed more destructive attacks on shipping in northern waters.

At this critical juncture, the United States, though still technically a nonbelligerent, assumed a more active role in the battle for the Atlantic. Through the provisions of the Lend-Lease Act, the United States turned over 50 World War I destroyers to Great Britain, which helped to make good previous naval losses. In return, the United States received 99-year leases for ship and airplane bases in Newfoundland, Bermuda, and numerous points in the Caribbean. U.S. units were also deployed in Iceland and Greenland.

Early in 1942, after the United States had become a full belligerent, the Axis opened a large-scale submarine offensive against coastal shipping in American waters. German U-boats also operated in considerable force along the south Atlantic ship lanes to India and the Middle East. The Allied campaign (1942–43) to reopen the Mediterranean depended almost entirely upon seaborne supply shipped through submarine-infested waters. Allied convoys approaching the British Isles, as well as those bound for the Russian ports of Murmansk and Archangelsk, had to battle their way through savage air and undersea attacks. It was publicly estimated at the close of 1942 that Allied shipping losses, chiefly from planes and U-boats, exceeded those suffered during the worst period of 1917 during World War I. And a considerable weight of Allied naval power had to be kept constantly available in northern waters in case Germany's formidable surface raiders, especially the super battleship Tirpitz, should break into the Atlantic shipping lanes as the Bismarck had done briefly in 1941.

In 1942 and early 1943 the ever-tightening Allied blockade of Axis Europe began to show perceptible progress in combating the Axis war on shipping. With more and better equipment, the convoy system was strengthened and extended. Unprecedented shipbuilding, especially in the

United States, caught up and began to forge ahead of losses, though the latter still remained dangerously high. Bombing raids on Axis ports and industrial centres progressively impaired Germany's capacity to build and service submarines and aircraft. The occupation of virtually all West African ports, including the French naval bases at Casablanca and Dakar, denied to Axis raiders their last possible havens in southern waters. By these and other means, the Atlantic Allies thwarted Axis efforts to halt the passage of American armies and material to Europe and North Africa, to prevent supplies reaching Britain and the Soviet Union, and to break up the blockade of Axis Europe.

The battle's decisive stage was early 1943, when the Allies gained a mastery over Germany's submarines that translated into significant reductions in shipping losses. By the time of the Normandy Invasion in June 1944, the Battle of the Atlantic was essentially over, and the western powers exercised control of Atlantic sea-lanes. Though German U-boats continued to operate in the Atlantic almost until the end of the war, they were ineffective against Allied convoys and were systematically sunk almost as fast as they made it out to sea.

Germany's war industries and to deprive its civilian population of their housing, thus sapping their will to continue the war. The characteristic feature of the new program was its emphasis on area bombing, or carpet bombing, in which the centres of towns would be the points of aim for nocturnal raids.

Already in March 1942 an exceptionally destructive bombing raid, using the Germans' own incendiary method, had been made on Lübeck. Intensive attacks were also made on Essen (site of the Krupp munitions works) and other Ruhr towns. In the night of May 30–31 more than 1,000 bombers were dispatched against Cologne, where they did heavy damage to one-third of that city's built-up area. Such operations, however, became highly expensive to the bomber command, particularly because of the defense put up by the German night fighter force. Interrupted

for two months during which the bombers concentrated their attention on U-boat bases on the Bay of Biscay, the air offensive against Germany was resumed in March 1943. In the following 12 months, moreover, its resources were to be increased formidably, so that by March 1944 the bomber command's average daily operational strength had risen to 974 from about 500 in 1942. These numbers helped the RAF to concentrate effectively against major industrial targets, such as those in the Ruhr. The phases of the resumed offensive were: (1) the Battle of the Ruhr, from March to July 1943, comprising 18,506 sorties and costing 872 aircraft shot down and 2,126 damaged, its most memorable operation being that of the night of May 16–17, when the Möhne Dam in the Ruhr Basin and the Eder Dam in the Weser Basin were breached, (2) the Battle of Hamburg, from July to November

1943, comprising 17,021 sorties and costing 695 bombers lost and 1,123 damaged but, nevertheless, thanks in part to the new Window antiradar and "H$_2$S" radar devices, achieving an unprecedented measure of devastation, since four out of its 33 major actions, with a little help from minor attacks, killed about 40,000 people and drove nearly 1,000,000 from their homes, and (3) the Battle of Berlin, from November 1943 to March 1944, comprising 20,224 sorties but costing 1,047 bombers lost and 1,682 returned damaged and achieving, on the whole, less devastation than the Battle of Hamburg.

The U.S. 8th Air Force, based in Great Britain, also took part in the strategic offensive against Germany from January 1943. Its bombers, Flying Fortresses and Liberators, attacked industrial targets in daylight. They proved, however, to be very vulnerable to German fighter attack whenever they went beyond the range of their own escort of fighters—that is to say, farther than the distance from Norfolk to Aachen. The raid against the important ball-bearing factory at Schweinfurt, for instance, on Oct. 14, 1943, lost 60 out of the 291 bombers participating, and 138 of those that returned were damaged. Not until December 1943 was the P-51B (Mustang III) brought into operation with the 8th Air Force—a long-range fighter that portended a change in the balance of air power. The Germans, meanwhile, continued to increase their production of aircraft and, in particular, of their highly successful fighters.

EXTERMINATION AND SLAVE LABOUR IN GERMAN-OCCUPIED EUROPE

Hitler's anti-Semitic ideology and his brutal conception of power politics caused him to pursue certain aims in those European countries conquered by the Germans in the period 1939–42. Hitler intended that those western and northern European areas in which civil administrations were installed—The Netherlands and Norway—would at some later date become part of the German Reich, or nation. Those countries left by Germany under military administration (which originally had been imposed everywhere), such as France and Serbia, would eventually be included more loosely in a German-dominated European bloc. Poland and the Soviet Union, on the other hand, were to be a colonial area for German settlement and economic exploitation.

Without regard to these distinctions, the SS, the elite corps of the Nazi Party, possessed exceptional powers throughout German-dominated Europe and in the course of time came to perform more and more executive functions, even in those countries under military administration. Similarly, the powers that Hitler gave to his chief labour commissioner, Fritz Sauckel, for the compulsory enrollment of foreign workers into the German armaments industry were soon applied to the whole of German-dominated Europe and ultimately turned 7,500,000 people into forced or slave labourers.

After being liberated by the U.S. Armored Division of the 1st U.S. army, a Russian slave labourer points at a former Nazi guard who beat the prisoners. Harold M. Roberts/Hulton Archive/Getty Images

Above all, however, there was the Final Solution of the "Jewish question" as ordered by Hitler, which meant the physical extermination of the Jewish people throughout Europe wherever German rule was in force or where German influence was decisive.

The German occupation authorities' attempts to eradicate resistance in most cases merely fanned the flames, due to the Germans' use of indiscriminate reprisals against civilians. It is generally agreed that by 1944 the Germans had earned the overwhelming antipathy of most of the people in the occupied nations of Europe. It should be noted, however, that the German occupation was in general far harsher in eastern Europe and the Balkans than in western Europe. In the Soviet Union, Poland, Yugoslavia, and Greece, a process of guerrilla warfare by organized Resistance movements and Nazi reprisals began in 1941 and rose to a crescendo in 1943–44 as the fury of Nazi racism resulted in a war of annihilation upon the Slavic peoples.

THE EASTERN FRONT AND THE BATTLE OF KURSK

The German counteroffensive of February 1943 threw back the Soviet forces that had been advancing toward the Dnepr River on the Izyum sector of the front, and by mid-March the Germans had retaken Kharkov and Belgorod and reestablished a front on the Donets River. Hitler also authorized the German forces to fall back, in March, from their advanced positions facing Moscow to a straighter line in front of Smolensk and Orël. Finally, there was the existence of the large Soviet bulge, or salient, around Kursk, between Orël and Belgorod, which extended for about 150 miles (241 km) from north to south and protruded 100 miles (161 km) into the German lines. This salient irresistibly tempted Hitler and Zeitzler into undertaking a new and extremely ambitious offensive instead of remaining content to hold their newly shortened front.

Hitler concentrated all efforts on this offensive without regard to the risk that an unsuccessful attack would leave him without reserves to maintain any subsequent defense of his long front. The Germans' increasing difficulty in building up their forces with fresh drafts of men and equipment was reflected in the increased delay that year in opening the summer offensive. Three months' pause followed the close of the winter campaign.

By contrast, the Red Army had improved much since 1942, both in quality and in quantity. The flow of new equipment had greatly increased, as had the number of new divisions, and its numerical superiority over the Germans was now about 4 to 1. Better still, its leadership had improved with experience: generals and junior commanders alike had become more skilled tacticians. That could already be discerned in the summer of 1943, when the Soviets waited to let the Germans lead off and commit themselves deeply to an offensive, and so stood well-poised to exploit the Germans' loss of balance in lunging.

The German offensive against the Kursk salient was launched on July 5, 1943, and into it Hitler threw 20 infantry divisions and 17 armoured divisions having a total of about 3,000 tanks. But the German tank columns got entangled in the deep minefields that the Soviets had laid, forewarned by the long preparation of the offensive. The Germans advanced only 10–30 miles (16–48 km), and no large bag of Soviet prisoners was taken, since the Red Army had withdrawn their main forces from the salient before the German attack began. After a week of effort the German armoured divisions were seriously reduced by the well prepared Soviet anti-tank defenses in the salient. On July 12, as the Germans began to pull out, the Soviets launched a counteroffensive upon the German positions in the salient and met with great success, taking Orël on August 5. By this time the Germans had lost 2,900 tanks and 70,000 men in the Battle of Kursk, which was the largest tank battle in history. The Soviets continued to advance steadily, taking Belgorod and then Kharkov. In September the Soviet advance was accelerated, and by the end of the month the Germans in the Ukraine had been driven back to the Dnepr.

THE ALLIES COUNTERATTACK IN THE SOUTHWEST AND SOUTH PACIFIC

A Pacific military conference held in Washington, D.C., in March 1943 produced a new schedule of operations calling for the development of some counterattacks against the Japanese. The reduction of the threat from the large Japanese naval base at Rabaul, by encirclement if not by the capture of that stronghold, was a primary objective for MacArthur.

Between June 22 and June 30, 1943, two U.S. regiments invaded Woodlark and Kiriwina islands (northeast of the tip of Papua), whence aircraft could range over not only the Coral Sea but also the approaches to Rabaul and to the Solomons. At the same time, U.S. and Australian units advanced from Buna along the coast of New Guinea toward Lae and Salamaua, while other Australian forces simultaneously advanced from Wau in the hinterland. In the night of June 29–30, U.S. forces secured Nassau Bay as a base for further advances against the same positions.

U.S. landings on New Georgia and on Rendova in the Solomons, however, also made in the night of June 29–30, provoked the Japanese into strong counteraction. Between July 5 and July 16, in the battles of Kula Gulf and of Kolombangara, the Allies lost one cruiser and two destroyers and had three more cruisers crippled. In addition, the Japanese, though they lost a cruiser and two destroyers, were able to land considerable reinforcements (from New Britain). Only substantial counter-reinforcement secured the New Georgia group of islands for the Allies, who, moreover, began on August 15 to extend their operation to the island of Vella Lavella also. In the last two months of the struggle, which ended with the Japanese evacuation of Vella Lavella on October 7, the Japanese sank an Allied destroyer and crippled two more but lost a further six of their own. Moreover, their attempt to defend the Solomon Islands cost them 10,000 lives, as against the Americans' 1,150 killed and 4,100 wounded.

Meanwhile, U.S. planes on August 17–18 had attacked Japanese bases at Wewak (on the New Guinea coast far to the west of Lae) and destroyed more than 200 aircraft there. On September 4 an Australian division landed near Lae, and the next day U.S. paratroops dropped at Nadzab, above Lae on the Markham River, where they were soon joined by an Australian airborne division. Salamaua fell to the Allies on September 12, Lae on September 16, and Finschhafen, on the Huon Peninsula behind Lae, on October 2. On Sept. 30, 1943, the Japanese made a new policy decision: a last defense line was to be established from western New Guinea and the Carolines to the Marianas by spring 1944, to be held at all costs, and also to be used as a base for counterattacks.

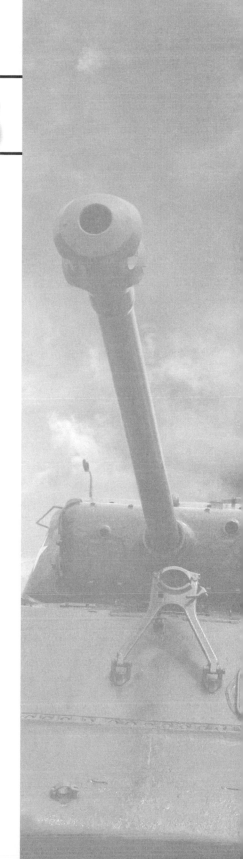

CHAPTER 5

ALLIES TRIUMPHANT, 1944–45

ITALY COLLAPSES

SICILY AND THE FALL OF MUSSOLINI

Hitler's greatest strategic disadvantage in opposing the Allies' imminent reentry into Europe lay in the immense stretch of Germany's conquests; from the west coast of France to the east coast of Greece. It was difficult for him to gauge where the Allies would strike next. The Allies' greatest strategic advantage lay in the wide choice of alternative objectives and in the powers of distraction they enjoyed through their superior sea power. Hitler, while always having to guard against a cross-Channel invasion from England's shores, had cause to fear that the Anglo-American armies in North Africa might land anywhere on his southern front between Spain and Greece.

Having failed to save its forces in Tunisia, the Axis had only 10 Italian divisions of various sorts and two German panzer units stationed on the island of Sicily at midsummer 1943. The Allies, meanwhile, were preparing to throw some 478,000 men into the island—150,000 of them in the first three days of the invasion. Under the supreme command of Alexander, Montgomery's British 8th Army and Patton's U.S. 7th Army were to be landed on two stretches of beach 40 miles long (64 km), 20 miles (32 km) distant from one another, the British in the southeast of the island, the Americans in the south. The Allies' air superiority in the Mediterranean theatre was so great by this time—more than 4,000 aircraft against some 1,500 German and Italian ones—that the Axis bombers had been withdrawn from Sicily in June to bases in north-central Italy.

On July 10 Allied seaborne troops landed on Sicily. The coastal defenses, manned largely by Sicilians unwilling to turn their homeland into a battlefield for the Germans' sake, collapsed rapidly enough. The British forces had cleared the whole southeastern part of the island in the first three days of the invasion. The Allies' drive toward Messina then took the form of a circuitous movement by the British around Mount Etna in combination with an eastward drive by the Americans, who took Palermo, on the western half of the northern coast, on July 22. Meanwhile, the German armoured strength in Sicily had been reinforced.

After the successive disasters sustained by the Axis in Africa, many of the Italian leaders were desperately anxious to make peace with the Allies. The invasion of Sicily, representing an immediate threat to the Italian mainland, prompted them to action. On the night of July 24–25, 1943, when Mussolini revealed to the Fascist Grand Council that the Germans were thinking of evacuating the southern half of Italy, the majority of the council voted for a resolution against him, and he resigned his powers. On July 25 the king, Victor Emmanuel III, ordered the arrest of Mussolini and entrusted Marshal Pietro Badoglio with the formation of a new government. The new government entered into secret negotiations with the Allies, despite the presence of sizable German forces in Italy.

A few days after the fall of Mussolini, Field Marshal Albert Kesselring, the German commander in chief in Italy, decided that the Axis troops in Sicily must be evacuated. The local Italian commander thought so too. While rear-guard actions held up the Allies at Adrano (on the western face of Mount Etna) and at Randazzo (to the north), 40,000 Germans and 60,000 Italian troops were safely withdrawn across the Strait of Messina to the mainland, mostly in the week ending on Aug. 16, 1943—the day before the Allies' entry into Messina.

The Allies sustained about 22,800 casualties in their conquest of Sicily. The Axis powers suffered about 165,000 casualties, of whom 30,000 were Germans.

The success of the Sicilian operation and the fall of Mussolini converted the American military and political leadership into supporters of a campaign in Italy. Furthermore, Lieutenant General Sir Frederick Morgan, who after Casablanca had been designated chief of staff to the Supreme Allied Commander (COSSAC), produced a detailed and realistic plan for the long-envisaged invasion of France from Great Britain, thus enabling the U.S. strategists to calculate more precisely how much of the Allies' resources were needed for that purpose and how much could be spared for operations in the

(From left, seated) *Canadian Prime Minister W.L. Mackenzie King, U.S. President Franklin D. Roosevelt, and British Prime Minister Winston Churchill at an Allied conference in Quebec, 1943.* Encyclopædia Britannica, Inc.

Mediterranean and for the Pacific. With regard to the Pacific, plans sponsored by Admiral Nimitz for operations against the Gilbert and Marshall islands apart from the enterprise against Rabaul were approved early in August 1943.

THE ALLIES' INVASION OF ITALY AND THE ITALIAN VOLTE-FACE

From Sicily, the Allies had a wide choice of directions for their next offensive. Calabria, the "toe" of Italy, was the nearest

and most obvious possible destination, the "shin" was also vulnerable, and the "heel" was also very attractive. The two army corps of Montgomery's 8th Army crossed the Strait of Messina and landed on the "toe" of Italy on Sept. 3, 1943. Though the initial resistance was practically negligible, they made only very slow progress, as the terrain, with only two good roads running up the coasts of the great Calabrian "toe" prevented the deployment of large forces. On the day of the landing, however, the Italian

IN FOCUS: THE QUEBEC CONFERENCES

The new turn of strategic thought following the successful invasion of Sicily necessitated a new Anglo-U.S. conference between U.S. President Franklin D. Roosevelt and British Prime Minister Winston Churchill, which took place in Quebec, Aug. 11-24, 1943, and was code-named "Quadrant." After vigorous debate, the question of the timing of Operation Overlord (the planned Normandy Invasion) was eventually left open, but it was agreed that the strength of the assault force should exceed the original estimate by 25 percent, that the cross-Channel landing should be supported by a landing in southern France, and that a U.S. officer should be in command of "Overlord." It was also decided that a new Southeast Asia theatre of war should be organized, under British command.

Differences between U.S. and British strategists about the coordination of the Italian campaign with Operation Overlord were not resolved and had to be settled at meetings in Moscow, Tehrān, and Cairo later that year. Roosevelt and Churchill met again at Quebec the following year—the Octagon Conference, Sept. 11-16, 1944. The decision made there to advance against Germany on two western fronts, instead of pursuing a concerted drive on Berlin, was criticized in the postwar period because it allowed the Soviet army to take possession of the German capital. This second Quebec Conference also resulted in a revised timetable to invade the Philippines, thus resulting in the Battle of Leyte Gulf in October 1944 and the subsequent struggle for Okinawa in late spring 1945.

government at last agreed to the Allies' secret terms for a capitulation. It was understood that Italy would be treated with leniency in direct proportion to the part that it would take, as soon as possible, in the war against Germany. The capitulation was announced on September 8.

The landing on the "shin" of Italy, at Salerno, just south of Naples, was begun on September 9, by the mixed U.S.–British 5th Army, under General Mark Clark. Transported by 700 ships, 55,000 men made the initial assault, and 115,000 more followed up. At first they were faced only by the German 16th Panzer Division. But Kesselring, though he had only eight weak divisions to defend all

southern and central Italy, had had time to plan since the fall of Mussolini and had been expecting a blow at the "shin." His counterstroke made the success of the Salerno landing precarious for six days, and it was not until October 1 that the 5th Army entered Naples.

By contrast, the much smaller landing on the "heel" of Italy, which had been made on September 2 (the day preceding the invasion of the "toe"), took the Germans by surprise. Notwithstanding the paucity of its strength in men and in equipment, the expedition captured two good ports, Taranto and Brindisi, in a very short time; but it lacked the resources to advance promptly. Nearly a fortnight passed before

Allied troops come ashore during the Salerno landings in southern Italy in September 1943.
Keystone/Hulton Archive/Getty Images

another small force was landed at Bari, the next considerable port north of Brindisi, to push thence unopposed into Foggia.

It was the threat to their rear from the "heel" of Italy and from Foggia that had induced the Germans to fall back from their positions defending Naples against the 5th Army. When the Italian government, in pursuance of a Badoglio-Eisenhower agreement of September 29, declared war against Germany on Oct. 13, 1943, Kesselring was already receiving

reinforcements and consolidating the German hold on central and northern Italy. The 5th Army was checked temporarily on the Volturno River, only 20 miles (32 km) north of Naples, then more lastingly on the Garigliano River, while the 8th Army, having made its way from Calabria up the Adriatic coast, was likewise held on the Sangro River. Autumn and midwinter passed without the Allies making any notable impression on the Germans' Gustav Line, which ran for 100

IN FOCUS: TUSKEGEE AIRMEN

In response to pressure from the National Association for the Advancement of Colored People (NAACP), the black press, and others, the U.S. War Department in January 1941 formed the first African American flying unit in the U.S. military. The all-black 99th Pursuit Squadron of the U.S. Army Air Corps (later the U.S. Army Air Forces) was trained using single-engine planes at the segregated Tuskegee Army Air Field at Tuskegee, Ala. The base opened on July 19, and the first class of Tuskegee Airmen, as they became known, graduated the following March. Lieutenant Colonel Benjamin Oliver Davis, Jr., became the squadron's commander.

The Tuskegee Airmen received further training in French Morocco, before their first mission, on June 2, 1943, a strafing attack on Pantelleria Island, an Italian island in the Mediterranean Sea. Later that year the Army activated three more squadrons that, joined in 1944 by the 99th, constituted the 332nd Fighter Group. It fought in the European theatre and was noted as the Army Air Forces' only escort group that did not lose a bomber to enemy planes.

The Tuskegee airfield program expanded to train pilots and crew to operate two-engine B-25 medium bombers. These men became part of the second black flying group, the 477th Bombardment Group. Shortages of crew members, technicians, and equipment troubled the 477th, and before it could be deployed overseas, World War II ended. Altogether 992 pilots graduated from the Tuskegee airfield courses; they flew 1,578 missions and 15,533 sorties, destroyed 261 enemy aircraft, and won more than 850 medals.

miles (161 km) from the mouth of the Garigliano through Cassino and over the Apennines to the mouth of the Sangro.

THE WESTERN ALLIES AND STALIN

Relations between the western Allies and the U.S.S.R. were still delicate. Besides their inability to satisfy Soviet demands for convoys of supplies and for an early invasion of France, the Americans and the British were embarrassed by the discrepancy between their political war aims and Stalin's.

The longest-standing difference was about Poland. While Poles were still fighting on the Allies' side and acknowledging the authority of General Władysław Sikorski's London-based Polish government in exile, Stalin was trying to get the Allies to consent to the U.S.S.R.'s retention, after the war, of all the territory taken from Poland by virtue of the German–Soviet pacts of 1939. On Jan. 16, 1943, the Soviet government announced that Poles from the border territories in dispute were being treated as Soviet citizens and drafted into the Red Army. On April 25, the Soviet government severed relations with the London Poles, and Moscow subsequently began to build up its own puppet government for postwar Poland.

Besides the quarrel over Poland, the western Allies and the U.S.S.R. were also at variance with regard to the postwar fate of other European states still under German domination. But the Americans and the British were really more interested in maintaining the Soviet war effort against Germany than in insisting, at the risk of offense to Stalin, on the detailed application of their own loudly but vaguely enunciated war aims.

Sextant, the conference of Nov. 22–27, 1943, for which Churchill, Roosevelt, and Chiang Kai-shek met in Cairo, was, on Roosevelt's insistence, devoted mainly to discussing plans for a British–U.S.–Chinese operation in northern Burma. Little was produced by Sextant except the Cairo Declaration, published on December 1, a further statement of war aims. It prescribed inter alia that Japan was to surrender all Pacific islands acquired since 1914, to retrocede Manchuria, Formosa, and the Pescadores to China, and to give up all other territory "taken by violence and greed"; and, in

(Left to right) *Soviet leader Joseph Stalin, U.S. President Franklin D. Roosevelt, and British Prime Minister Winston Churchill at the Tehrān Conference, December 1943.* Encyclopædia Britannica, Inc.

addition, it was stipulated that Korea was in due course to become independent.

From Cairo, Roosevelt and Churchill went to Tehrān, to meet Stalin at the Eureka conference of November 28–December 1. Stalin renewed the Soviet promise of military intervention against Japan, but he primarily wanted an assurance that "Overlord" (the invasion of France) would indeed take place in 1944. Reassured about this by Roosevelt, he declared that the Red Army would attack simultaneously on the Eastern Front. On the political plane, Stalin now demanded the Baltic coast of East Prussia for the U.S.S.R. as well as the territories annexed in 1939–40. The main communique of the conference was accompanied by a joint declaration guaranteeing the postwar restoration of Iran. Returning to Cairo, Roosevelt and Churchill spent six more days, December 2–7, in staff talks to compose their differences on strategy. They finally agreed that "Overlord" (with Eisenhower in command) should have first claim on resources.

GERMAN TROOP DEPLOYMENT

The Western Front

From late 1942 German strategy, every feature of which was determined by Hitler, was solely aimed at protecting the still very large area under German control—most of Europe and part of North Africa—against a future Soviet onslaught on the Eastern Front and against future Anglo-U.S. offensives on the southern and western fronts. The Germans' vague hopes that the Allies would shrink from such costly tasks or that the "unnatural" coalition of western capitalism and Soviet Communism would break up before achieving victory were disappointed. And so Hitler, in accordance with his dictum that "Germany shall either be a world power or not be at all," consciously resolved to preside over the downfall of the German nation. He gave inflexible orders whereby whole armies were made to stand their ground

In focus: Cairo and Tehrān Conferences

At the first Cairo Conference, Nov. 22–26, 1943, British Prime Minister Winston Churchill and U.S. President Franklin D. Roosevelt discussed plans for the prosecution of the Normandy Invasion. With Chinese leader Chiang Kai-shek, they issued a declaration of the goal of stripping Japan of all the territories it had seized since 1914 and restoring Korea to independence. Upon conclusion of the first Cairo Conference, and the Tehrān Conference with Soviet leader Joseph Stalin, the two Western leaders then returned to Cairo for the second Cairo Conference (December 2–7). There they tried without success to persuade President İsmet İnönü of Turkey to bring his country into the war on the side of the Allied powers. At this meeting Roosevelt also informed Churchill of his choice of General Dwight D. Eisenhower as supreme commander of the Normandy Invasion.

in tactically hopeless positions and were forbidden to surrender under any circumstances. The initial success of this strategy in preventing a German rout during the Soviet winter counteroffensive of 1941–42 had blinded Hitler to its impracticability in the very different military circumstances on the Eastern Front by 1943, by which time the Germans simply lacked sufficient numbers of troops to defend an extremely long front against much more numerous Soviet forces. (By December 1943 the 3,000,000 German troops there were opposed by about 5,500,000 Soviet troops.)

From late 1943 on, Hitler's strategy was to strengthen the German forces in western Europe at the expense of those on the Eastern Front. In view of the danger of the great Anglo-U.S. invasion of western Europe that seemed imminent by early 1944, the loss of some part of his eastern conquests evidently seemed to Hitler to be less serious. Hitler continued to insist on the primacy of the war in the west after the start of the Allied invasion of northern France in June 1944, and while his armies made strenuous efforts to contain the Allied bridgehead in Normandy for the next two months, Hitler accepted the annihilation of the German Army Group Centre on the Eastern Front by the Soviet summer offensive (from June 1944), which brought the Red Army in a few weeks' time to the Vistula River and the borders of East Prussia. But the Western Front likewise crumbled in a few weeks, whereupon the Allies advanced to Germany's western borders.

THE EASTERN FRONT

By the end of the first week of October 1943, the Red Army had established several bridgeheads on the right bank of the Dnepr River. Then, while General N.F. Vatutin's drive against Kiev was engaging the Germans' attention, General Ivan Stepanovich Konev suddenly pushed so far forward from the Kremenchug bridgehead (more than halfway downstream between Kiev and Dnepropetrovsk) that the German forces within the great bend of the Dnepr to the south would have been isolated if Manstein had not stemmed the Soviet advance just in time to extricate them. By early November the Red Army had reached the mouth of the Dnepr also, and the Germans in the Crimea were isolated. Kiev, too, fell to Vatutin on November 6, Zhitomir, 80 miles (129 km) to the west, and Korosten, north of Zhitomir, fell in the next 12 days. Farther north, however, the Germans, who had already fallen back from Smolensk to a line covering the upper Dnepr, repelled with little difficulty five rather predictable Soviet thrusts toward Minsk in the last quarter of 1943.

Vatutin's forces from the Zhitomir-Korosten sector advanced westward across the prewar Polish frontier on Jan. 4, 1944. Though another German flank attack slowed them down, they had reached Lutsk, 100 miles (161 km) farther west, a month later. Vatutin's left wing, meanwhile, wheeled southward to converge with Konev's right, so that 10

German divisions were encircled near Korsun, on the Dnepr line south of Kiev. Vainly trying to save those 10 divisions, the Germans had to abandon Nikopol, in the Dnepr bend far to the south, with its valuable manganese mines.

March 1944 saw a triple thrust by the Red Army: Zhukov, succeeding to Vatutin's command, drove southwest toward Tarnopol, to outflank the Germans on the upper stretches of the southern Bug River. General Rodion Yakovlevich Malinovsky, in the south, advanced across the mouth of the latter river from that of the Dnepr; and between them Konev, striking over the central stretch of the Bug, reached the Dnestr, 70 miles (113 km) ahead, and succeeded in crossing it. When Zhukov had crossed the upper Prut River and Konev was threatening Iaşi on the Moldavian stretch of the river, the Carpathian Mountains were the only natural barrier remaining between the Red Army and the Hungarian Plain. German troops occupied Hungary on March 20, since Hitler suspected that the Hungarian regent, Admiral Miklós Horthy, might not resist the Red Army to the utmost.

Germany launched a counterstroke from the Lwów area of southern Poland against Zhukov's extended flank early in April. This attack not only put an end to the latter's overhasty pressure on the Tatar (Yablonitsky) Pass through the Carpathians but also made possible the withdrawal of some of the German forces endangered by the Red Army's March

operation. Konev, too, was halted in front of Iaşi; but his left swung southward down the Dnestr to converge with Malinovsky's drive on Odessa. That great port fell to the Red Army on April 10. On May 9 the Germans in the Crimea abandoned Sevastopol, caught as they were between Soviet pincers from the mainland north of the isthmus and from the east across the Strait of Kerch.

At the northern end of the Eastern Front, a Soviet offensive in January 1944 had been followed by an orderly German retreat from the fringes of the long-besieged Leningrad area to a shorter line exploiting the great lakes farther to the south. The retreat was beneficial to the Germans but sacrificed their land link with the Finns, who now found themselves no better off than they had been in 1939–40. Finland in February 1944 sought an armistice from the U.S.S.R., but the latter's terms proved unacceptable.

THE WAR IN THE PACIFIC AND EAST ASIA

Considering that it might be necessary for them to invade Japan proper, the Allies drew up new plans in mid-1943. The main offensive, it was decided, should be from the south and from the southeast, through the Philippines and through Micronesia (rather than from the Aleutians in the North Pacific or from the Asian mainland). While occupation of the Philippines would disrupt Japanese communications with the East Indian

IN FOCUS: SIEGE OF LENINGRAD

The Siege of Leningrad, also called the 900-day siege, began Sept. 8, 1941, as German and Finnish armed forces surrounded the city during World War II. The siege, which actually lasted 872 days, was lifted Jan. 27, 1944.

After Nazi Germany invaded the Soviet Union in June 1941, German armies by early September had approached Leningrad from the west and south while their Finnish allies approached to the north down the Karelian Isthmus. Leningrad's entire able-bodied population was mobilized to build antitank fortifications along the city's perimeter in support of the city's 200,000 Red Army defenders. Leningrad's defenses soon stabilized, but by early November it had been almost completely encircled, with all its vital rail and other supply lines to the Soviet interior cut off.

The ensuing German blockade and siege claimed 650,000 Leningrader lives in 1942 alone, mostly from starvation, exposure, disease, and shelling from distant German artillery. Sparse food and fuel supplies reached the city by barge in the summer and by truck and ice-borne sled in winter across Lake Ladoga. These supplies kept the city's arms factories operating and its two million inhabitants barely alive in 1942, while one million more of its children, sick, and elderly were being evacuated. Starvation-level food rationing was eased by new vegetable gardens that covered most open ground in the city by 1943.

Soviet offensives in early 1943 ruptured the German encirclement and allowed more copious supplies to reach Leningrad along the shores of Lake Ladoga. In January 1944 a successful Soviet offensive drove the Germans westward from the city's outskirts, ending the siege. The Soviet government awarded the Order of Lenin to Leningrad in 1945 and bestowed the title Hero City of the Soviet Union on it in 1965, thus paying tribute to the city's successful endurance of one of the most grueling and memorable sieges in history.

isles west of New Guinea and with Malaya, the conquest of Micronesia, from the Gilberts by way of the Marshalls and Carolines to the Marianas, would not only offer the possibility of drawing the Japanese into a naval showdown but also win bases for heavy air raids on the Japanese mainland prior to invasion.

For the approach to the Philippines, it was prerequisite, on the one hand, to complete the encirclement of Rabaul, thereby nullifying the threat from the Japanese positions in the Solomon Islands and in the Bismarck Archipelago (New Britain, New Ireland, etc.) and, on the other, to reduce the Japanese hold on western New Guinea. Great emphasis, however, was put on the advance across the central Pacific through Micronesia, to be begun via the Gilberts.

THE ENCIRCLEMENT OF RABAUL

Allied moves to isolate the large Japanese garrison on Rabaul proceeded by land and air. The encirclement of Rabaul by

IN FOCUS: TOKYO ROSE

(b. July 4, 1916, Los Angeles, Calif., U.S.—d. Sept. 26, 2006, Chicago, Ill.), Ikuko (Iva) Toguri, a Japanese American woman, was the most famous of a group of English-speaking women who made propaganda radio broadcasts under the name of Tokyo Rose for the Japanese government to U.S. troops during World War II. After the war, Toguri was convicted of treason and served six years in a U.S. prison. She was later pardoned by President Gerald R. Ford.

Toguri grew up in Los Angeles and graduated from the University of California, Los Angeles (UCLA), in 1941. Her aunt's illness in July 1941 sent Toguri, a U.S. citizen, to Japan, where she was stranded when Pearl Harbor was bombed by the Japanese and the United States entered World War II. She was considered an enemy alien in Japan. In November 1943 she began radio announcing for "Zero Hour," an English-language propaganda program beamed at U.S. troops. Toguri, now married to Felipe d'Aquino, was one of 13 women announcers, all native speakers of American English, who were collectively known as Tokyo Rose. When the war ended, Toguri d'Aquino was interviewed by American journalists and was subsequently indicted, charged with treason for giving aid and comfort to the enemy in time of war. When she returned to the United States in 1947, an outcry arose, demanding her trial, which began on July 5, 1949. On September 29 she was found guilty and was sentenced to 10 years in a federal penitentiary and a fine of $10,000. She served six years and was released in 1956, her sentence having been reduced for good behaviour.

Later, mitigating information came to light. In Tokyo, she had refused to become a Japanese citizen. Eventually, she found a job at Radio Tokyo. There she met an Australian and an American who were prisoners of war. These men had been ordered to write English-language broadcast material to demoralize Allied servicemen. Secretly, they were attempting to subvert the entire operation. D'Aquino was recruited to announce for them and made her first broadcast in November 1943. Much later, President Ford became convinced that she had been wrongly accused and convicted, and in January 1977 he pardoned her.

land began during October and November 1943 with the capture by New Zealand troops of the Treasury Islands in the Solomons and was accompanied on November 1 by a U.S. landing at Empress Augusta Bay on the west of Bougainville. U.S. reinforcements subsequently repulsed Japanese counterattacks in December, when they sank two destroyers, and in March 1944, when they killed almost 6,000 men. What remained of the Japanese garrison on Bougainville was no longer capable of fighting, though it did not surrender until the end of the war.

Continuing the approach to Rabaul, U.S. troops landed on December 15 at Arawe on the southwestern coast of New Britain, thereby distracting Japanese attention from Cape Gloucester, on the northwestern coast, where a major landing was made on December 26. By Jan. 16, 1944, the airstrip at Cape Gloucester had been captured and defense lines set up. Talasea, halfway to Rabaul, fell in March 1944. The conquest of western New Britain secured Allied control of the Vitiaz and Dampier straits between that island and New Guinea.

By constructing air bases on each island that they captured, the Allies systematically blocked any westward movement that the Japanese might have made. New Zealand troops took the Green Islands southeast of New Guinea on February 15, and U.S. forces invaded Los Negros in the Admiralty Islands on February 29 and captured Manus on March 9.

With the fall of the Emirau Islands on March 20, the Allies' stranglehold on Rabaul and Kavieng was practically complete, so that they could thenceforth disregard the 100,000 Japanese immobilized there.

WESTERN NEW GUINEA

Before they could push northward to the Philippines, the Allies had to subdue Japanese-held western New Guinea. U.S. troops took Saidor, on the Huon Peninsula, on Jan. 2, 1944, and established an air base there. The Australians took Sio, to the east of Saidor, on January 16. Then reinforcements were landed at Mindiri, west of Saidor, on March 5, and Australian infantry began to move westward up the coast, to take Bogadjim, Madang, and Alexishafen.

Bypassing Hansa Bay (which was eventually captured on June 15) and

Wewak, whither the Japanese had retreated, the Allies, on April 22, 1944, made two simultaneous landings at Hollandia: having in the past weeks already destroyed 300 Japanese planes, they captured the airfields there in four days' time. In the following months Hollandia was converted into a major base and command post for the Southwest Pacific area. The Allies also took Aitape, on the coast east of Hollandia, and held it against counterattacks by more than 200,000 Wewak-based Japanese during July and August. Biak, the isle guarding the entrance to Geelvink Bay, west of Hollandia, was invaded by U.S. troops on May 27, 1944. The Japanese defense of it was maintained until early August. Though westernmost New Guinea fell likewise to the Allies in August 1944, the Japanese garrison at Wewak held out until May 10, 1945.

THE CENTRAL PACIFIC

Though the U.S. Joint Chiefs of Staff envisaged no major offensive westward across the Pacific toward Formosa until mid-1944, they nevertheless decided to launch a limited offensive in the central Pacific in 1943, hoping thereby both to speed the pace of the war and to draw the Japanese away from other areas. Accordingly, Nimitz's central Pacific forces invaded the Gilbert Islands on Nov. 23, 1943. Makin fell easily, but well-fortified Japanese defenses on Tarawa cost the U.S. Marines 1,000 killed and

2,300 wounded. Japanese losses in the Gilberts totaled about 8,500 men.

Having been forced to cede the Gilberts, the Japanese elected next to defend the Marshalls, in order both to absorb Allied forces and to strain the latters' extended lines of supply. Nimitz subjected Kwajalein Atoll, which he chose first to attack, to so heavy a preliminary bombardment that the U.S. infantry could land on it on Jan. 31, 1944; and U.S. forces moved on to Enewetak on February 17.

In support of the landings on the Marshalls, the U.S. fleet on Feb. 17, 1944, started a series of day and night attacks against the Japanese base at Truk in the Caroline Islands, where they destroyed some 300 aircraft and 200,000 tons of merchant shipping. Henceforth, the Allies could confidently ignore Truk and bypass it.

The Allies' next objective, for which they required more than 500 ships and 125,000 troops, was to invade the Mariana Islands, lying 1,000 miles (1,609 km) from Enewetak and 3,500 miles (5,633 km) from Pearl Harbor. Against this threat, after the destruction at Truk, the Japanese hastily drew up a new defense plan, "Operation A," relying on their

July 16, 1944: An American Marine machine gun crew fires on Japanese forces during the Battle of Saipan in the Northern Mariana Islands. Keystone/Hulton Archive/Getty Images

remaining 1,055 land-based aircraft in the Marianas, in the Carolines, and in western New Guinea and on timely and decisive intervention by a sea force, which should include nine aircraft carriers with 450 aircraft. But in the spring of 1944 the Japanese air strength was still further depleted, and, moreover, on March 31 the sponsor of the plan, Admiral Koga Mineichi (Yamamoto's successor), and his staff were killed in an air disaster. When, on June 15, two U.S. Marine divisions went ashore on Saipan Island in the Marianas, the 30,000 Japanese defenders put up so fierce a resistance that an army division was needed to reinforce the Marines. Using the same defensive tactics as on other small islands, the Japanese had fortified themselves in underground caves and bunkers that afforded protection from American artillery and naval bombardment. Notwithstanding this, the Japanese defenders were gradually compressed into smaller and smaller pockets, and they themselves ended most organized resistance with a suicidal counterattack on July 7, the largest of its kind during the war.

The loss of Saipan was such a disaster for Japan that when the news was announced in Tokyo the prime minister, Tōjō Hideki, and his entire Cabinet resigned. To realists in the Japanese high command, the loss of the Marianas spelled the ultimate loss of the war, but no one dared say so. Tōjō's Cabinet was succeeded by that of General Koiso Kuniaki, which was pledged to carrying on the fight with renewed vigour.

Air power enthusiasts have called the conquest of Saipan "the turning point of the war in the Pacific," for it enabled the United States to establish air bases there for the big B-29 bombers, which had been developed for the specific purpose of bombing Japan. The first flight of 100 B-29s took off from Saipan on Nov. 24, 1944, and bombed Tokyo, the first bombing raid on the Japanese capital since 1942.

THE BURMESE FRONTIER AND CHINA

For the dry season of 1943–44 both the Japanese and the Allies were resolved on offensives in Southeast Asia. On the Japanese side, Lieutenant General Kawabe Masakazu planned a major Japanese advance across the Chindwin River, on the central front, in order to occupy the plain of Imphāl and to establish a firm defensive line in eastern Assam. The Allies, for their part, planned a number of thrusts into Burma. Stilwell's NCAC forces, including his three Chinese divisions and "Merrill's Marauders" (U.S. troops trained by Wingate on Chindit lines), were to advance against Mogaung and Myitkyina, while Slim's 14th Army was to launch its XV Corps southeastward into Arakan and its IV Corps eastward to the Chindwin. Because the Japanese had habitually got the better of advanced British forces by outflanking them, Slim formulated a new tactic to ensure that his units would stand against attack in the forthcoming

IN FOCUS: BATTLE OF THE PHILIPPINE SEA

While the Japanese were still resisting on Saipan, the Japanese Combined Fleet, under Admiral Ozawa Jisaburō, was approaching from Philippine and East Indian anchorages. This was in accordance with "Operation A," to challenge the U.S. 5th Fleet, under Admiral Raymond Spruance. Ozawa, with only nine aircraft carriers against 15 for the United States, was obviously inferior in naval power, but he counted heavily on help from land-based aircraft on Guam, Rota, and Yap. The encounter, which took place west of the Marianas and is known as the Battle of the Philippine Sea, has been called the greatest carrier battle of the war. It began on June 19, 1944, when Ozawa sent 430 planes in four waves against Spruance's ships.

The result for the Japanese was a disaster. In the first day of the battle the Japanese lost more than 200 planes and two regular carriers; and, as their fleet retired northward toward safe harbour at Okinawa, it lost another carrier and nearly 100 more planes. Having already achieved a great victory, Spruance decided late on the second day not to press his attack further, a controversial decision to this day. During the two days of battle, U.S. losses totaled 130 aircraft and some damage to ships.

The poor showing by the Japanese has been attributed to many factors, but two may be singled out for special mention: pilots and their aircraft. Some Japanese pilots went into action with as little as three months of training, whereas many U.S. pilots had spent two full years in training. Japanese planes were highly maneuverable and had a longer range than U.S. planes, but they were inferior in several respects, particularly in their inadequate armour protection and lack of self-sealing fuel tanks. U.S. submarines also played an important but less publicized role in providing U.S. commanders with intelligence of enemy movements and in sinking Japanese ships.

campaign, even if they should be isolated. They were to know that, when ordered to stand, they could certainly count both on supplies from the air and on his use of reserve troops to turn the situation against the Japanese attackers.

On the southern wing of the Burmese front, the XV Corps's Arakan operation, launched in November 1943, had achieved most of its objectives by the end of January 1944. When the Japanese counter-attack surrounded one Indian division and part of another, Slim's new tactic was brought into play, and the Japanese found themselves crushed between the encircled Indians and the relieving forces.

The Japanese crossing of the Chindwin into Assam, on the central Burmese front, when the fighting in Arakan was dying down, played into Slim's hands, since he could now profit from the Allies' superiority in aircraft and in tanks. The Japanese were able to approach Imphāl and to surround Kohīma, but the British forces protecting these towns were reinforced with several Indian divisions that were taken from the now-secure Arakan front. With air support, Slim's reinforced forces now defended Imphāl against multiple Japanese thrusts and outflanking movements until, in mid-May 1944, he was able to launch two of his divisions into an offensive eastward, while still containing the last bold effort of the Japanese to capture Imphāl. By June 22 the 14th Army had averted the Japanese menace to Assam and won the initiative for its own advance into Burma. The Battle of Imphāl–Kohīma cost the British and Indian forces 17,587 casualties (12,600 of them sustained at Imphāl), and the Japanese forces 30,500 dead (including 8,400 from disease) and 30,000 wounded.

On the northern Burmese front, Stilwell's forces were already approaching Mogaung and Myitkyina before the southern crisis of Imphāl–Kohīma. The subsidiary Chindit operation against Indaw was going well ahead when, on March 24, 1944, Wingate himself was killed in an air crash. Meanwhile, Chiang Kai-shek was constrained by U.S. threats of a suspension of lend-lease to finally authorize some action by the 12 divisions of his Yunnan Army, which on May 12, 1944, with air support, began to cross the Salween River westward in the direction of Myitkyina, Bhamo, and Lashio. Myitkyina airfield was taken by Stilwell's forces, with "Merrill's Marauders," on May 17. Mogaung was taken by the Chindits on June 26, and finally Myitkyina itself was taken by Stilwell's Chinese divisions on August 3. All of northwest and much of northern Burma was now in Allied hands.

In China proper, a Japanese attack toward Changsha, begun on May 27, won control not only of a further stretch of the north–south axis of the Beijing-Hankou railroad but also of several of the airfields from which the Americans had been bombing the Japanese in China and were intending to bomb them in Japan.

DRIVING THE GERMANS OUT OF ITALY

The Allies' northward advance up the Italian peninsula to Rome was still blocked by Kesselring's Gustav Line, which was hinged on Monte Cassino. To bypass that line, the Allies landed some 50,000 seaborne troops, with 5,000 vehicles, at Anzio, only 33 miles (53 km) south of Rome, on Jan. 22, 1944. The landing surprised the Germans and met, at first, with very little opposition. But, instead of driving on over the Alban Hills to Rome at once, the force at Anzio spent so much time consolidating its position there that Kesselring was able, with his reserves, to develop a powerful counteroffensive against it on February 3. The beachhead was thereby reduced to a very shallow dimension, while the defenses at Monte Cassino held out unimpaired against a new assault by Clark's 5th Army.

For a final effort against the Gustav Line, Alexander decided to shift most of the 8th Army, now commanded by Major General Sir Oliver Leese, from the Adriatic flank of the peninsula to the west, where it was to strengthen the 5th Army's pressure around Monte Cassino and on the approaches to the valley of the Liri (headstream of the Garigliano). The combined attack, which was started in the night of May 11–12, 1944, succeeded in breaching the German defenses at a number of points between Cassino and the coast. Thanks to this victory, the Americans could push forward up the coast, while the British entered the valley and outflanked Monte Cassino, which fell to a Polish corps of the 8th Army on May 18. Five days later, the Allies' force at Anzio struck out against the investing Germans (whose strength had been diminished in order to reinforce the Gustav Line). By May 26 it had achieved a breakthrough. When the 8th Army's Canadian Corps penetrated the last German defenses in the Liri Valley, the whole Gustav Line began to collapse.

Concentrating all available strength on his left wing, Alexander pressed up from the south to effect a junction with the troops thrusting northward from Anzio. The Germans in the Alban Hills could not withstand the massive attack. On June 5, 1944, the Allies entered Rome. The propaganda value of their occupying the Eternal City, Mussolini's former capital, was offset, however, by an unforeseen strategical reality: Kesselring's forces retreated not in the expected rout but gradually, to the line of the Arno River. Florence, 160 miles (257 km) north of Rome, did not fall to the Allies until August 13. By that time the Germans had made ready yet another chain of defenses, the Gothic Line, running from the Tyrrhenian coast midway between Pisa and La Spezia, over the Apennines in a reversed S curve, to the Adriatic coast between Pesaro and Rimini.

Alexander might have made more headway against Kesselring's new front if some of his forces had not been subtracted, in August 1944, for the American-sponsored but eventually unnecessary invasion of southern France ("Operation Anvil," finally renamed "Dragoon" [see below]). As it was, the 8th Army, switched back from the west to the Adriatic coast, achieved only an indecisive breakthrough toward Rimini. After this September offensive, the autumn rains set in, to make even more difficult Alexander's indirect movements, against Kesselring's resolute opposition, toward the mouth of the Po River.

THE LIBERATION OF EUROPE

THE NORMANDY INVASION AND GERMAN RETREAT

The German Army high command had long been expecting an Allied invasion of northern France but had no means of knowing where precisely the stroke would come. While Rundstedt, commander in chief in the west, thought that the landings would be made between Calais and Dieppe (at the narrowest width of the Channel between England and France), Hitler prophetically indicated the central and more westerly stretches of the coast of Normandy as the site of the attack. Rommel, who was in charge of the forces on France's Channel coast, finally came around to Hitler's opinion. The fortifications of those stretches were consequently improved, but Rundstedt and Rommel still took different views about the way in which the invasion should be met. While Rundstedt recommended a massive counterattack on the invaders after their landing, Rommel, fearing that Allied air supremacy might interfere fatally with the adequate massing of the German forces for such a counterattack, advocated instead immediate action on the beaches against any

attempted landing. The Germans had 59 divisions spread over western Europe from the Low Countries to the Atlantic and Mediterranean coasts of France, but approximately half of this number was static, and the remainder included only 10 armoured or motorized divisions.

Postponed from May, the western Allies' "Operation Overlord," their long-debated invasion of northern France, took place on June 6, 1944—the war's most celebrated D-Day—when 156,000 men were landed on the beaches of Normandy between the Orne estuary and

U.S. assault troops land on Omaha Beach during the invasion of Normandy in June of 1944. Keystone/Hulton Archive/Getty Images

the southeastern end of the Cotentin Peninsula: 83,000 British and Canadian troops on the eastern beaches, 73,000 Americans on the western. Under Eisenhower's supreme direction and Montgomery's immediate command, invading forces initially comprised the Canadian 1st Army (Lieutenant General Henry Duncan Graham Crerar); the British 2nd Army (Lieutenant General Sir Miles Dempsey); and the British 1st and 6th airborne divisions, the U.S. 1st Army, and the U.S. 82nd and 101st airborne divisions (all under Lieutenant General Omar N. Bradley).

By 9:00 AM on D-Day the coastal defenses were generally breached, but Caen, which had been scheduled to fall on D-Day and was the hinge of an Allied advance, held out until July 9, the one panzer division already available there on June 6 having been joined the next day by a second. Though the heavy fighting at Caen attracted most of the German reserves, the U.S. forces in the westernmost sector of the front likewise met a very stubborn resistance. But when they had taken the port of Cherbourg on June 26 and proceeded to clear the rest of the Cotentin, they could turn southward to take Saint-Lô on July 18.

The Allies could not have made such rapid progress in northern France if their air forces had not been able to interfere decisively with the movement of the German reserves. Allied aircraft destroyed most of the bridges over the Seine River to the east and over the Loire to the south. The German reserves thus had to make long detours in order to reach the Normandy battle zone and were so constantly harassed on the march by Allied strafing that they suffered endless delays and only arrived in driblets. And even where reserves could have been brought up, their movement was sometimes inhibited by hesitation and dissension on the Germans' own side. Hitler, though he had rightly predicted the zone of the Allies' landings, came to mistakenly believe, after D-Day, that a second and larger invasion was to be attempted east of the Seine and so was reluctant to allow reserves to be moved westward over that river. He also forbade the German forces already engaged in Normandy to retreat in time to make an orderly withdrawal to new defenses.

Rundstedt, meanwhile, was slow in obtaining Hitler's authority for the movement of the general reserve's SS panzer corps from its position north of Paris to the front. And Rommel, though he made prompt use of the forces at hand, had been absent from his headquarters on D-Day itself, when a forecast of rough weather had seemed to make a cross-Channel invasion unlikely. Subsequently, Rundstedt's urgent plea for permission to retreat provoked Hitler, on July 3, to appoint Kluge as commander in chief in the west in Rundstedt's place. In addition, Rommel was badly hurt on July 17, when his car crashed under attack from Allied planes.

Meanwhile, on July 31, 1944, the Americans on the Allies' right, newly supported by the landing of the U.S. 3rd

IN FOCUS: JULY PLOT

There was something else, besides the progress of the Allies, to demoralize the German commanders—the failure and the aftermath of a conspiracy against Hitler, known as the July Plot, which involved an attempt by German military leaders to assassinate Hitler on July 20, 1944, to seize control of the government, and to seek more favourable peace terms from the Allies.

Alarmed at the calamitous course of events and disgusted by the crimes of the Nazi regime, certain conservative but anti-Nazi civilian dignitaries and military officers had formed themselves into a secret opposition, with Karl Friedrich Goerdeler (a former chief mayor of Leipzig) and Colonel General Ludwig Beck (a former chief of the army general staff) among its leaders. From 1943 this opposition canvassed the indispensable support of the active military authorities with some notable success: General Friedrich Olbricht (chief of the General Army Office) and several of the serving commanders, including Rommel and Kluge, became implicated to various extents. Apart from General Henning von Tresckow, however, the group's most dynamic member was Colonel Graf Claus von Stauffenberg, who as chief of staff to the chief of the army reserve from July 1, 1944, had access to Hitler. Finally, it was decided to kill Hitler and to use the army reserve for a coup d'état in Berlin, where a new regime under Beck and Goerdeler should be set up. On July 20, therefore, Stauffenberg left a bomb concealed in a briefcase in the room where Hitler was conferring at his headquarters in East Prussia. The bomb duly exploded; but Hitler survived, and the coup in Berlin miscarried. The Nazi reaction was savage: besides 200 immediately implicated conspirators, 5,000 people who were more remotely linked with the plot or were altogether unconnected with it were put to death. Kluge committed suicide on August 17, Rommel on October 14. Fear permeated and paralyzed the German high command in the weeks that followed.

Army under Patton, broke through the German defenses at Avranches, the gateway from Normandy into Brittany. On August 7 a desperate counterattack by four panzer divisions from Mortain, east of Avranches, failed to seal the breach, and American tanks poured southward through the gap and flooded the open country beyond. Though some of the U.S. forces were then swung southwestward in the hope of seizing the Breton ports in pursuance of the original prescription of "Overlord" and though some went on in more southerly directions toward the crossings of the Loire, others were wheeled eastward—to trap, in the Falaise "pocket," a large part of the German forces retreating southward from the pressure of the Allies' left at Caen. The Americans' wide eastward flanking maneuver after the breakout speedily produced a general collapse of the German position in northern France.

Meanwhile, more and more Allied troops were being landed in Normandy. On August 1, two army groups were constituted: the 21st (comprising the British and Canadian armies) under Montgomery; and the 12th (for the Americans) under Bradley. By the middle of August an eastward wheel wider than that which had cut off the Falaise pocket had brought the Americans to Argentan, southeast of Falaise and level with the British and Canadian advance on the left (north) of the Allies' front, so that a concerted drive eastward could now be launched. On August 19 a U.S. division successfully crossed the Seine at Mantes-Gassicourt. Already on August 17 the Americans on the Loire had taken Orléans. The clandestine French Resistance in Paris rose against the Germans on August 19. A French division under General Jacques Leclerc, pressing forward from Normandy, received the surrender of the German forces there and liberated the city on August 25.

The German forces would have had ample time to pull back to the Seine River and to form a strong defensive barrier line there had it not been for Hitler's stubbornly stupid orders that there should be no withdrawal. It was his folly that enabled the Allies to liberate France so quickly. The bulk of the German armoured forces and many infantry divisions were thrown into the Normandy battle and kept there by Hitler's "no withdrawal" orders until they collapsed and a large part of them were trapped. The fragments were incapable of further resistance, and their retreat (which was largely on foot) was soon outstripped by the British and American mechanized columns. More than 200,000 German troops were taken prisoner in France, and 1,200 German tanks had been destroyed in the fighting. When the Allies approached the German border at the beginning of September, after a sweeping drive from Normandy, there was no organized resistance to stop them from driving on into the heart of Germany.

Meanwhile, "Operation Dragoon" (formerly "Anvil") was launched on Aug. 15, 1944, when the U.S. 7th Army and the French 1st Army landed on the French Riviera, where there were only four

U.S. paratroopers landing in southern France, 1944. U.S. Air Force photograph

German divisions to oppose them. While the Americans drove first into the Alps to take Grenoble, the French took Marseille on August 23 and then advanced eastward through France up the Rhône Valley, to be rejoined by the Americans north of Lyon early in September. Both armies then moved swiftly northeastward into Alsace.

In the north, however, some discord had arisen among the Allied commanders after the crossing of the Seine. Whereas Montgomery wanted to concentrate on a single thrust northeastward through Belgium into the heavily industrialized Ruhr Valley (an area vital to Germany's war effort), the U.S. generals argued for continuing to advance eastward through France on a broad front, in accordance with the pre-invasion plan. Eisenhower, by way of compromise, decided on August 23 that Montgomery's drive into Belgium should have the prior claim on resources until Antwerp should have been captured but that thereafter the pre-invasion plan should be resumed.

Consequently, Montgomery's 2nd Army began its advance on August 29, entered Brussels on September 3, took Antwerp, with its docks intact, on September 4, and went on, three days later, to force its way across the Albert Canal. The U.S. 1st Army, meanwhile, supporting Montgomery on the right, had taken Namur on the day of the capture of Antwerp and was nearing Aachen. Far to the south, however, Patton's U.S. 3rd Army, having raced forward to take Verdun on August 31, was already beginning to cross the Moselle River near Metz on September 5, with the obvious possibility of achieving a breakthrough into Germany's economically important Saarland. Eisenhower, therefore, could no longer devote a preponderance of supplies to Montgomery at Patton's expense.

Montgomery nevertheless attempted a thrust to cross the Rhine River at Arnhem, the British 1st Airborne Division being dropped ahead there to clear the way for the 2nd Army. The Germans were just able to check the thrust, thus isolating the parachutists, many of whom were taken prisoner. By this time, indeed, the German defense was rapidly stiffening as the Allies approached the German frontiers. The U.S. 1st Army spent a month grinding down the defenses of Aachen, which fell at last on October 20 (the first city of prewar Germany to be captured by the western Allies). And the 1st Canadian Army, on the left of the British 2nd, did not clear the Schelde estuary west of Antwerp, including Walcheren Island, until early November. Likewise, Patton's 3rd Army was held up before Metz.

The Allies' amazing advance of 350 miles (563 km) in a few weeks was thus brought to a halt. In early September the U.S. and British forces had had a combined superiority of 20 to 1 in tanks and 25 to 1 in aircraft over the Germans, but by November 1944 the Germans still held both the Ruhr Valley and the Saarland, after having been so near collapse in the west in early September that one or the other of those prizes could

October 18, 1944: German refugees prepare to leave their homes in the town of Aachen, in an attempt to escape the battle between American and German forces. Fred Ramage/Hulton Archive/Getty Images

have easily been taken by the Allies. The root of the Allied armies' sluggishness in September was that none of their top planners had foreseen such a complete collapse of the Germans as occurred in August 1944. They were therefore not prepared, mentally or materially, to exploit it by a rapid offensive into Germany itself. The Germans thus obtained time to build up their defending forces in the west, with serious consequences both for occupied Europe and the postwar political situation of the Continent.

RUSSIAN ADVANCES ON THE EASTERN FRONT

After a successful offensive against the Finns on the Karelian Isthmus had culminated in the capture of Viipuri (Vyborg) on June 20, 1944, the Red Army on June 23 began a major onslaught on the Germans' front in Belorussia. The attackers' right wing took the bastion town of Vitebsk (Vitebskaya) and then wheeled southward across the highway from Orsha to Minsk. Their left wing, under General Konstantin Konstantinovich Rokossovsky, broke

architect. Safeguarding it was the primary concern of his next three and a half years.

Already in 1944, with victory in prospect, party politics had revived, and by May 1945 all parties in the wartime coalition wanted an early election. But whereas Churchill wanted the coalition to continue at least until Japan was defeated, Labour wished to resume its independence. Churchill as the popular architect of victory seemed unbeatable, but as an election campaigner he proved to be his own worst enemy, indulging in extravagant prophecies of the appalling consequences of a Labour victory and identifying himself wholly with the Conservative cause. His campaign tours were a triumphal progress, but it was the war leader, not the party leader, whom the crowds cheered. Labour's careful but sweeping program of economic and social reform was a better match for the nation's mood than Churchill's flamboyance, and Churchill saw his party reduced to 213 seats in a Parliament of 640. After losing the 1945 election, Churchill became Leader of the Opposition, until 1951, when he was once more elected Prime Minister. He served as Prime Minister until 1955.

CHARLES DE GAULLE

(b. Nov. 22, 1890, Lille, France—d. Nov. 9, 1970, Colombey-les-deux-Églises)

Charles de Gaulle was a soldier, writer, statesman, and architect of France's Fifth Republic.

At the outbreak of World War II, de Gaulle commanded a tank brigade attached to the French Fifth Army. In May 1940, after assuming command as temporary brigadier general in the 4th Armoured Division—the rank that he retained for the rest of his life—he twice had the opportunity to apply his theories on tank warfare. On June 6 he entered the government of Paul Reynaud as undersecretary of state for defense and war, and he undertook several missions to England to explore the possibilities of continuing the war. When the Reynaud government was replaced 10 days later by that of Marshal Pétain, who intended to seek an armistice with the Germans, de Gaulle left for England. On June 18 he broadcast from London his first appeal to his compatriots to continue the war under his leadership. On August 2, 1940, a French military court tried and sentenced him in absentia to death, deprivation of military rank, and confiscation of property.

In his country, to the politicians on the political left, a career officer who was a practicing Roman Catholic was not an immediately acceptable political leader, while to those on the right he was a rebel against Pétain, who was a national hero and France's only field marshal. Broadcasts from London, the action of the Free French Forces, and the contacts of resistance groups in France either with de Gaulle's own organization or with those of the British secret services brought national recognition of his leadership; but full recognition by his allies came only after the liberation of Paris in August 1944.

In London de Gaulle's relations with the British government were never easy, and de Gaulle often added to the strain, at times through his own misjudgment or touchiness. In 1943 he moved his headquarters to Algiers, where he became president of the French Committee of National Liberation, at first jointly with General Henri Giraud. De Gaulle's successful campaign to edge out Giraud gave the world proof of his skill in political maneuvering.

On Sept. 9, 1944, de Gaulle and his shadow government returned from Algiers to Paris. There he headed two successive provisional governments, but on Jan. 20, 1946, he abruptly resigned, apparently because of his irritation with the political parties forming the coalition government. He returned to power in 1958 with the establishment of the Fifth Republic.

HIROHITO
(b. April 29, 1901, Tokyo, Japan—d. Jan. 7, 1989, Tokyo)

Hirohito was emperor of Japan from 1926 until his death in 1989. He was the longest-reigning monarch in Japan's history.

Hirohito became emperor of Japan on Dec. 25, 1926, following the death of his father. His reign was designated Shōwa, or "Enlightened Peace." The Japanese constitution invested him with supreme authority, but in practice he merely ratified the policies that were formulated by his ministers and advisers. Many historians have asserted that Hirohito had grave misgivings about war with the United States and was opposed to Japan's alliance with Germany and Italy but that he was powerless to resist the militarists who dominated the armed forces and the government. Other historians assert that Hirohito might have been involved in the planning of Japan's expansionist policies from 1931 to World War II. Whatever the truth may be, in 1945, when Japan was close to defeat and opinion among the country's leaders was divided between those favouring surrender and those insisting on a desperate defense of the home islands against an anticipated invasion by the Allies, Hirohito settled the dispute in favour of those urging peace. He broke the precedent of imperial silence on Aug. 15, 1945, when he made a national radio broadcast to announce Japan's acceptance of the Allies' terms of surrender. In a second historic broadcast, made on Jan. 1, 1946, Hirohito repudiated the traditional quasi-divine status of Japan's emperors.

Under the nation's new constitution, drafted by U.S. occupation authorities, Japan became a constitutional monarchy. Sovereignty resided in the people, not in the emperor, whose powers were severely curtailed.

ADOLF HITLER
(b. April 20, 1889, Braunau am Inn, Austria—d. April 30, 1945, Berlin, Ger.)

Adolf Hitler was the leader of the National Socialist (Nazi) Party (from 1920/21) and chancellor (Kanzler) and Führer of

Germany (1933–45). He was chancellor from Jan. 30, 1933, and, after President Paul von Hindenburg's death, assumed the twin titles of Führer and chancellor (August 2, 1934).

In 1932 Hitler opposed Hindenburg in the presidential election, capturing 36.8 percent of the votes on the second ballot. On Jan. 30, 1933, Hindenburg offered him the chancellorship of Germany. Once in power, Hitler established an absolute dictatorship. As he had made clear in *Mein Kampf*, the reunion of the German peoples was his overriding ambition. Beyond that, the natural field of expansion lay eastward, in Poland, the Ukraine, and the U.S.S.R. He saw Fascist Italy as his natural ally, Britain as a possible ally, and France as a natural enemy that would have to be cowed or subdued before Germany could expand in the east.

Before such expansion was possible, it was necessary to remove the restrictions placed on Germany at the end of World War I by the Treaty of Versailles. In 1933 Hitler withdrew from the Disarmament Conference and from the League of Nations. His greatest stroke came in March 1936, when he used the excuse of a pact between France and the Soviet Union to march into the demilitarized Rhineland. Meanwhile the alliance with Italy, foreseen in *Mein Kampf*, rapidly became a reality as a result of the sanctions imposed by Britain and France against Italy during the Ethiopian war. In October 1936, a Rome-Berlin axis was proclaimed by Italian dictator Benito Mussolini. Shortly afterward came the Anti-Comintern Pact with Japan, and a year later all three countries joined in a pact.

In November 1937, at a secret meeting of his military leaders, Hitler outlined his plans for future conquest (beginning with Austria and Czechoslovakia). In February 1938 Hitler invited the Austrian chancellor, Kurt von Schuschnigg, to Berchtesgaden and forced him to sign an agreement including Austrian Nazis within the Vienna government. When Schuschnigg attempted to resist, Hitler ordered the invasion of Austria. The enthusiastic reception that Hitler received convinced him to settle the future of Austria by outright annexation (Anschluss).

Hitler proceeded at once with his expansionist plans. Konrad Henlein, leader of the German minority in Czechoslovakia, was instructed to agitate for impossible demands on the part of the Sudetenland Germans. Britain's and France's willingness to accept the cession of the Sudetenland areas to Germany presented Hitler with the choice of substantial gains by peaceful agreement. The intervention by Mussolini and British Prime Minister Neville Chamberlain appear to have been decisive. Hitler accepted the Munich Agreement on Sept. 30, 1938. He also declared that these were his last territorial demands in Europe. Only a few months later, he proceeded to occupy the rest of Czechoslovakia.

Hitler then turned on Poland. First he confirmed his alliance with Italy, and then on Aug. 23, 1939, he signed a nonaggression pact with Joseph Stalin—the greatest diplomatic bombshell in centuries. The German invasion of Poland (September 1) was followed two days later by a British and French declaration of war on Germany.

When the successful campaign against Poland failed to produce the desired peace accord with Britain, Hitler ordered the army to prepare for an immediate offensive in the west. This led to two major changes in planning. The first was Hitler's order to forestall an eventual British presence in Norway by occupying that country and Denmark in April 1940. The second was Hitler's adoption of General Erich von Manstein's plan for an attack through the Ardennes (which began May 10) instead of farther north. This was a brilliant and startling success. The German armies reached the Channel ports (which they had been unable to reach during World War I) in 10 days. Holland surrendered after 4 days and Belgium after 16 days. On June 10 Italy entered the war on the side of Germany. On June 22 Hitler signed a triumphant armistice with the French on the site of the Armistice of 1918.

Hitler then proceeded to plan the invasion of Britain and the Soviet Union. Meanwhile, Mussolini invaded Greece, where the failures of the Italian armies made it necessary for German forces to come to their aid in the Balkans and North Africa. The campaigns in the Mediterranean theatre, although successful, were limited, compared to the invasion of Russia. Hitler would spare few forces from "Operation Barbarossa," the planned invasion of the Soviet Union.

The attack against the U.S.S.R. was launched on June 22, 1941. The German army advanced swiftly into the Soviet Union, corralling almost three million Russian prisoners, but it failed to destroy its Russian opponent. In December 1941, a few miles before Moscow, a Russian counteroffensive dashed Hitler's hopes of a quick victory. On December 7, the Japanese attacked U.S. forces at Pearl Harbor. Hitler's alliance with Japan forced him to declare war on the United States, which finally tipped the balance of the war.

At the end of 1942, defeat at El-Alamein and at Stalingrad and the American landing in French North Africa brought the turning point in the war. After the arrest of Mussolini in July 1943 and the Italian armistice, Hitler not only directed the occupation of all important positions held by the Italian army but also ordered the rescue of Mussolini, with the intention that he should head a new Fascist government. On the Eastern Front, however, there was less and less possibility of holding up the advance.

The Allied invasion of Normandy (June 6, 1944) marked the beginning of the end. In December 1944 Hitler moved his headquarters to the west to direct an offensive in the Ardennes aimed at splitting the American and the British armies. When this failed, his hopes for victory became ever more visionary, based on the use of new weapons (German rockets had been fired on London since June 1944) or on the breakup of the Allied Powers.

After January 1945 Hitler never left the Chancellery in Berlin or its bunker. He at last accepted the inevitability of defeat and thereupon prepared to take his own life. At midnight on April 28–29 he married Eva Braun. Immediately afterward he dictated his political testament, justifying his career and appointing Admiral Karl Dönitz as head of the state and Joseph Goebbels as chancellor. On April 30 he said farewell to Goebbels and the few others remaining, then retired to his suite and shot himself. His wife took poison. In accordance with his instructions, their bodies were burned.

BENITO MUSSOLINI

(b. July 29, 1883, Predappio, Italy—d. April 28, 1945, near Dongo)

Benito Mussolini was Italian prime minister (1922–43) and the first of 20th-century Europe's Fascist dictators.

On Oct. 31, 1922, Mussolini became the youngest prime minister in Italian history. The elections in 1924, though undoubtedly fraudulent, secured his personal power as dictator. Mussolini might have remained a hero until his death had not his callous xenophobia and arrogance, his misapprehension of Italy's fundamental necessities, and his dreams of empire led him to seek foreign conquests. His eye rested first upon Ethiopia, which, after 10 months of preparations, rumours, threats, and hesitations, Italy invaded in October 1935. A brutal campaign of colonial conquest followed. Europe expressed its horror; but, having

done so, did no more. The League of Nations imposed sanctions but ensured that the list of prohibited exports did not include any, such as oil, that might provoke a European war. If the League had imposed oil sanctions, Mussolini said, he would have had to withdraw from Ethiopia within a week. But he faced no such problem, and on the night of May 9, 1936, he announced that Italy had its empire.

Italy had also found a new ally. Intent upon his own imperial ambitions in Austria, Adolf Hitler had actively encouraged Mussolini's African adventure, and under Hitler's guidance Germany had been the one powerful country in western Europe that had not turned against Mussolini. The

Benito Mussolini, Italian prime minister (1922–43) and the first of 20th-century Europe's Fascist dictators, gesticulates during a 1934 speech. Keystone/Hulton Archive/Getty Images

way was now open for the Pact of Steel—a Rome-Berlin Axis and a brutal alliance between Hitler and Mussolini.

Mussolini watched as Germany advanced westward, and when France seemed on the verge of collapse, Mussolini felt he could delay no longer. So, on June 10, 1940, the fateful Italian declaration of war was made.

From the beginning the war went badly for Italy; France surrendered before there was an opportunity for even a token Italian victory. Indeed, from then on Mussolini was obliged to face the fact that he was the junior partner in the Axis alliance. The Germans kept the details of most of their military plans concealed, presenting their allies with a fait accompli for fear that prior discussion would destroy surprise. And thus the Germans made such moves as the occupation of Romania and the later invasion of the Soviet Union without any advance notice to Mussolini.

It was to "pay back Hitler in his own coin," as Mussolini openly admitted, that he decided to attack Greece through Albania in 1940 without informing the Germans. The result was an extensive and ignominious defeat, and the Germans were forced unwillingly to extricate him from its consequences. The 1941 campaign to support the German invasion of the Soviet Union also failed disastrously and condemned thousands of ill-equipped Italian troops to a nightmarish winter retreat. Hitler had to come to his ally's help once again in North Africa. After the Italian surrender in North Africa in 1943, the Germans began to take precautions against a likely Italian collapse. When the Western Allies successfully invaded Sicily in July 1943, it was obvious that collapse was imminent.

On July 25 Mussolini was arrested by royal command on the steps of the Villa Savoia after an audience with the king. Mussolini was imprisoned in a hotel high on the Gran Sasso d'Italia in the mountains of Abruzzi, from which his rescue by the Germans was deemed impossible. Nevertheless, by crash-landing gliders on the slopes behind the hotel, German commandos on Sept. 12, 1943, effected his escape by air to Munich.

Mussolini agreed to Hitler's suggestion that he establish a new Fascist government in the north. But the Repubblica Sociale Italiana thus established at Salò was, as Mussolini himself grimly admitted to visitors, no more than a puppet government at the mercy of the German command. And there, Mussolini awaited the inevitable end.

As German defenses in Italy collapsed and the Allies advanced rapidly northward, Mussolini made for the Valtellina; but only a handful of men could be found to follow him. He tried to cross the frontier disguised as a German soldier in a convoy of trucks retreating toward Innsbruck, in Austria. But he was recognized and killed on April 28, 1945. Huge, jubilant crowds celebrated the fall of the dictator and the end of the war.

HENRI-PHILIPPE PÉTAIN
(b. April 24, 1856, Cauchy-à-la-Tour, France—d. July 23, 1951, Île d'Yeu)

Henri-Philippe Pétain was a national hero for his victory at the Battle of Verdun in

World War I but was discredited as chief of state of the French government at Vichy in World War II. He died under sentence in a prison fortress.

Following the German attack of May 1940 in World War II, Paul Reynaud, who was then head of the government, named Pétain vice premier, and on June 16, at the age of 84, Marshal Pétain was asked to form a new ministry. Seeing the French army defeated, the "hero of Verdun" asked for an armistice. After it was concluded, the Chamber of Deputies and the Senate, meeting in Vichy, conferred upon him almost absolute powers as "chief of state."

With the German army occupying two-thirds of the country, Pétain believed he could repair the ruin caused by the invasion and obtain the release of the numerous prisoners of war only by cooperating with the Germans. In the southern part of France, left free by the armistice agreement, he set up a paternalistic regime the motto of which was "Work, Family, and Fatherland." Reactionary by temperament and education, he allowed his government to promulgate a law dissolving the Masonic lodges and excluding Jews from certain professions.

He was, however, opposed to the policy of close Franco-German collaboration advocated by his vice premier Pierre Laval, whom he dismissed in December 1940, replacing him with Admiral François Darlan. Pétain then attempted to practice a foreign policy of neutrality and delay. He secretly sent an emissary to London, met with the Spanish dictator Francisco Franco, whom he urged to refuse free passage of Adolf Hitler's army to North Africa, and maintained a cordial relationship with Admiral William Leahy, the U.S. ambassador to Vichy until 1942.

When, in April 1942, the Germans forced Pétain to take Laval back as premier, he himself withdrew into a purely nominal role. Yet he balked at resigning, convinced that, if he did, Hitler would place all of France directly under German rule. After Allied landings in November 1942 in North Africa, Pétain secretly ordered Admiral Darlan, then in Algeria, to merge the French forces in Africa with those of the Allies. But, at the same time, he published official messages protesting the landing. His double-dealing was to prove his undoing.

In August 1944, after the liberation of Paris by General Charles de Gaulle, Pétain dispatched an emissary to arrange for a peaceful transfer of power. De Gaulle refused to receive the envoy. At the end of August the Germans transferred Pétain from Vichy to Germany. Brought to trial in France for his behaviour after 1940, he was condemned to death in August 1945. His sentence was immediately commuted to solitary confinement for life. He was imprisoned in a fortress on the Île d'Yeu off the Atlantic coast, where he died at the age of 95.

FRANKLIN D. ROOSEVELT
(b. Jan. 30, 1882, Hyde Park, New York, U.S.—d. April 12, 1945, Warm Springs, Georgia)

Franklin Delano Roosevelt was the 32nd president of the United States (1933–45), and the only president elected to the office four times. Roosevelt led the United States through two of the greatest crises of the 20th century: the Great Depression and World War II. In so doing, he greatly expanded the powers of the federal government through a series of programs and reforms known as the New Deal, and he served as the principal architect of the successful effort to rid the world of German National Socialism and Japanese militarism.

From the beginning of his presidency, Roosevelt had been deeply involved in foreign-policy questions. Roosevelt extended American recognition to the government of the Soviet Union, launched

President Franklin Delano Roosevelt. Library of Congress Prints and Photographs Division

the Good Neighbor Policy to improve U.S. relations with Latin America, and backed reciprocal agreements to lower trade barriers between the U.S. and other countries.

Congress, however, was dominated by isolationists who believed that American entry into World War I had been mistaken and who were determined to prevent the United States from being drawn into another European war. Beginning with the Neutrality Act of 1935, Congress passed a series of laws designed to minimize American involvement with belligerent nations.

When World War II broke out in Europe in September 1939, Roosevelt called Congress into special session to revise the neutrality acts to permit belligerents—i.e., Britain and France—to buy American arms on a "cash-and-carry" basis. Over the objections of isolationists, the cash-and-carry policy was enacted. When France fell to the Germans in the spring and early summer of 1940, and Britain was left alone to face the Nazi war machine, Roosevelt convinced Congress to intensify defense preparations and to support Britain with "all aid short of war." In the fall of that year Roosevelt sent 50 older destroyers to Britain, which feared an imminent German invasion, in exchange for eight naval bases.

In March 1941, after a bitter debate in Congress, Roosevelt obtained passage of the Lend-Lease Act, which enabled the United States to accept noncash payment for military and other aid to Britain and its allies. Later that year he authorized the United States Navy to provide protection for lend-lease shipments, and in the fall he instructed the navy to "shoot on sight" at German submarines. All these actions moved the United States closer to actual belligerency with Germany.

In August 1941, on a battleship off Newfoundland, Canada, Roosevelt and British Prime Minister Winston Churchill issued a joint statement, the Atlantic Charter, in which they pledged their countries to the goal of achieving "the final destruction of the Nazi tyranny." Reminiscent of the Four Freedoms that Roosevelt outlined in his annual message to Congress in January 1941, the statement disclaimed territorial aggrandizement and affirmed a commitment to national self-determination, freedom of the seas, freedom from want and fear, greater economic opportunities, and disarmament of all aggressor nations.

Yet it was in the Pacific sector rather than the Atlantic sector that war came to the United States. When Japan joined the Axis powers of Germany and Italy, Roosevelt began to restrict exports to Japan of supplies essential to making war. Throughout 1941, Japan negotiated with the United States, seeking restoration of trade in those supplies, particularly petroleum products. When the negotiations failed to produce agreement, Japanese military leaders began to plan an attack on the United States.

By the end of November, Roosevelt knew that an attack was imminent (the United States had broken the Japanese code), but he was uncertain where it would

take place. To his great surprise, the Japanese bombed Pearl Harbor, Hawaii, destroying nearly the entire U.S. Pacific fleet and hundreds of airplanes and killing about 2,500 military personnel and civilians. On December 8, at Roosevelt's request, Congress declared war on Japan; on December 11 Germany and Italy declared war on the United States.

From the start of American involvement in World War II, Roosevelt took the lead in establishing a grand alliance among all countries fighting the Axis powers. One early difference centred upon the question of an invasion of France. Churchill wanted to postpone such an invasion until Nazi forces had been weakened, and his view prevailed until the great Normandy Invasion was finally launched on "D-Day," June 6, 1944. Meanwhile, American and British forces invaded North Africa in November 1942, Sicily in July 1943, and Italy in September 1943.

Relations with the Soviet Union posed a difficult problem for Roosevelt. Throughout the war the Soviet Union accepted large quantities of lend-lease supplies but seldom divulged its military plans or acted in coordination with its Western allies. Roosevelt, believing that the maintenance of peace after the war depended on friendly relations with the Soviet Union, hoped to win the confidence of Joseph Stalin. He, Stalin, and Churchill seemed to get along well when they met at Tehrān in November 1943. By the time the "Big Three" met again at the Yalta Conference in the Crimea, U.S.S.R., in February 1945, the war in Europe was almost over. At Yalta, Roosevelt secured Stalin's commitment to enter the war against Japan soon after Germany's surrender and to establish democratic governments in the nations of eastern Europe occupied by Soviet troops. Stalin kept his pledge concerning Japan but proceeded to impose Soviet satellite governments throughout eastern Europe.

By the time of his return from Yalta, Roosevelt was so weak that for the first time in his presidency he spoke to Congress while sitting down. Early in April 1945 he traveled to his cottage in Warm Springs, Georgia—the "Little White House"—to rest. On the afternoon of April 12, while sitting for a portrait, he suffered a massive cerebral hemorrhage, and he died a few hours later.

JOSEPH STALIN

(b. Dec. 21 [Dec. 9, Old Style], 1879, Gori, Georgia, Russian Empire—d. March 5, 1953, Moscow, Russia, U.S.S.R.)

Joseph Stalin was secretary-general of the Communist Party of the Soviet Union (1922–53) and premier of the Soviet state (1941–53). For a quarter of a century, he dictatorially ruled the Soviet Union and transformed it into a major world power.

During World War II Stalin emerged, after an unpromising start, as the most successful of the supreme leaders thrown up by the belligerent nations. In August 1939, after first attempting to form an anti-Hitler alliance with the Western powers, he concluded a pact with Hitler, which encouraged the German dictator to attack Poland and begin World War II. Anxious to strengthen his western frontiers while his new but palpably treacherous German ally was still engaged in the West, Stalin annexed eastern Poland, Estonia, Latvia, Lithuania, and parts of Romania. He also attacked Finland and extorted territorial concessions.

Stalin's prewar defensive measures were exposed as incompetent by the German blitzkrieg that surged deep into Soviet territory after Hitler's unprovoked attack on the Soviet Union of June 22, 1941. When the Germans menaced Moscow in the winter of 1941, Stalin remained in the threatened capital,

Joseph Stalin, 1950. Sovfoto

helping to organize a great counter-offensive. The battle of Stalingrad (in the following winter) and the Battle of Kursk (in the summer of 1943) were also won by the Soviet Army under Stalin's supreme direction, turning the tide of invasion against the retreating Germans, who capitulated in May 1945.

Stalin participated in high-level Allied meetings, including those of the "Big Three" with Churchill and Roosevelt at Tehrān (1943) and Yalta (1945).

TŌJŌ HIDEKI
(b. Dec. 30, 1884, Tokyo, Japan—d. Dec. 23, 1948, Tokyo)

Tōjō Hideki was a soldier, statesman, and prime minister of Japan during most of World War II (1941–44). After Japan's defeat, he was tried and executed for war crimes.

A graduate of the Imperial Military Academy and the Military Staff College, Tōjō served briefly as military attaché in Japan's embassy in Berlin after World War I. In 1937 he was named chief of staff of the Kwantung Army in Manchuria. He returned to Tokyo in 1938 as vice-minister of war and was one of the leading advocates of Japan's Tripartite Pact with Germany and Italy (1940). In July 1940 he was appointed minister of war in the cabinet of Premier Prince Konoe Fumimaro. Tōjō succeeded Konoe as prime minister on Oct. 16, 1941, and pledged his government to a Greater East Asia program, a "New Order in Asia." He retained control of the ministry of war and was also minister of commerce and industry from 1943.

A hardworking and efficient bureaucrat, Tōjō was also one of the most aggressive militarists in the Japanese leadership. He led his country's war efforts after the attack on the U.S. base at Pearl Harbor, and under his direction smashing victories were initially scored throughout Southeast Asia and the Pacific. After prolonged Japanese military reverses in the Pacific, Tōjō assumed virtual dictatorial powers, taking over the post of the chief of the General Staff. But the successful U.S. invasion of the Marianas so weakened his government that he was removed as chief of staff on July 16, 1944, and on July 18 his entire cabinet resigned.

On Sept. 11, 1945, after Japan's formal surrender, Tōjō shot himself in a suicide attempt, but he was nursed back to health and on April 29, 1946, with other Japanese wartime leaders, was indicted and tried for war crimes before the International Military Tribunal for the Far East. He was found guilty and hanged.

HARRY S. TRUMAN
(b. May 8, 1884, Lamar, Mo., U.S.—d. Dec. 26, 1972, Kansas City, Mo.)

Harry S. Truman was the 33rd president of the United States (1945–53). He led his nation through the final stages of World War II and through the early years of the Cold War, vigorously opposing Soviet expansionism in Europe and sending U.S.

forces to turn back a Communist invasion of South Korea.

Roosevelt died suddenly of a cerebral hemorrhage on April 12, 1945. Truman was sworn in as president on the same day as Roosevelt's death. He began his presidency with great energy, making final arrangements for the San Francisco meeting to draft a charter for the United Nations, helping to arrange Germany's unconditional surrender on May 8, and traveling to Potsdam in July for a meeting with Allied leaders to discuss the fate of postwar Germany. While in Potsdam Truman received word of the successful test of an atomic bomb at Los Alamos, New Mexico, and it was from Potsdam that Truman sent an ultimatum to Japan to surrender or face "utter devastation." When Japan did not surrender and his advisers estimated that up to 500,000 Americans might be killed in an invasion of Japan, Truman authorized the dropping of atomic bombs on the cities of Hiroshima (August 6) and Nagasaki (August 9), killing more than 100,000 men, women, and children. This remains perhaps the most controversial decision ever taken by a U.S. president, one which scholars continue to debate today. Japan surrendered August 14, the Pacific war ending officially on September 2, 1945.

Scarcely had the guns of World War II been silenced than Truman faced the threat of Soviet expansionism in eastern Europe. Early in 1946, Truman brought Winston Churchill to Missouri to sound

President Harry S. Truman at work, April 1945. Library of Congress Prints and Photographs Division

the alarm with his "iron curtain" address. The following year, Truman put the world on notice through his Truman Doctrine that the United States would oppose Communist aggression everywhere; specifically, he called for economic aid to Greece and Turkey to help those countries resist Communist takeover. Later in 1947, the president backed Secretary of State George Marshall's strategy for undercutting Communism's appeal in western Europe by sending enormous amounts of financial aid (ultimately about $13 billion) to rebuild devastated European economies. Both the Truman Doctrine and the Marshall Plan (officially the European Recovery Program) achieved their objectives, but they also contributed to the global polarization that characterized five decades of Cold War hostility between East and West.

CHAPTER 9

MILITARY COMMANDERS

W orld War II was astounding in the number of people who were involved in the war effort (about 100 million), as well as the number of people who died (some 70 million) as a direct result. What was also astounding was the ability of the military commanders from every side to incorporate or adapt to the array of new technologies, strategies, and tactics that were developed during this war. Modern warfare was born during World War II. The following brief biographies of Allied and Axis military commanders concentrate on their actions during World War II.

ALLIED COMMANDERS

UNITED STATES

HENRY HARLEY ARNOLD
(b. June 25, 1886, Gladwyne, Pa., U.S.—d. Jan. 15, 1950, Sonoma, Calif.)

Henry (Hap) Arnold was an air strategist and commanding general of the U.S. Army Air Forces in World War II.

Arnold also served as air representative on the U.S. Joint Chiefs of Staff and on the Anglo-American Combined Chiefs of Staff. In these capacities he was an influential architect of the plans and strategy that resulted in Allied victory. In December 1944 he was one of four army leaders promoted to the five-star rank of general of the army. He retired from service in 1946, and in 1949 his title was changed to general of the air force. He was the only air commander ever to attain the rank of five stars.

Omar Nelson Bradley
(b. Feb. 12, 1893, Clark, Mo., U.S.—d. April 8, 1981, New York, N.Y.)

Omar Bradley commanded the U.S. Army's Twelfth Army Group, which helped ensure the Allied victory over Germany during World War II. Later he served as first chairman of the U.S. Joint Chiefs of Staff (1949–53).

At the opening of World War II, Bradley was commandant of the U.S. Army Infantry School, Fort Benning, Georgia, and he later commanded the 82nd and 28th infantry divisions. After being placed at the head of the II Corps for the North African campaign, under General George S. Patton, he captured Bizerte, Tunisia, in May 1943. This victory contributed directly to the fall of Tunisia and the surrender of more than 250,000 Axis troops. Bradley then led his forces in the Sicilian invasion, which was successfully concluded in August.

Later in 1943 Bradley was transferred to Great Britain, where he was given command of the U.S. First Army in 1944. Placed under the command of British Field Marshal Bernard Montgomery, he took part in planning the invasion of France. In June 1944 he joined his troops in the assault on the Normandy beaches and in the initial battles inland. At the beginning of August, he was elevated to command of the U.S. Twelfth Army Group. Under his leadership the First, Third, Ninth, and Fifteenth armies, the largest force ever placed under an American group commander, successfully carried on operations in France, Luxembourg, Belgium, The Netherlands, Germany, and Czechoslovakia until the end of European hostilities.

Dwight D. Eisenhower
(b. Oct. 14, 1890, Denison, Texas, U.S.— d. March 28, 1969, Washington, D.C.)

Dwight D. Eisenhower was the 34th president of the United States (1953–61). He served as supreme commander of the Allied forces in western Europe during World War II.

When the United States entered World War II in December 1941, Army Chief of Staff General George C. Marshall appointed Eisenhower to the army's war plans division in Washington, D.C., where he prepared strategy for an Allied invasion of Europe. Eisenhower had been made a brigadier general in September 1941 and was promoted to major general in March 1942. He was also named head of the operations division of the War Department. In June Marshall selected him over 366 senior officers to be commander of U.S. troops in Europe. Eisenhower's rapid advancement, after a long army career spent in relative obscurity, was due not only to his knowledge of

Brigadier General Dwight D. Eisenhower, c. 1941–42. Encyclopædia Britannica, Inc.

military strategy and talent for organization but also to his ability to persuade, mediate, and get along with others.

Eisenhower was promoted to lieutenant general in July 1942 and named to head Operation Torch, the Allied invasion of French North Africa. This first major Allied offensive of the war was launched on Nov. 8, 1942, and successfully completed in May 1943. A full general since that February, Eisenhower then directed the amphibious assault of Sicily and the Italian mainland, which resulted in the fall of Rome on June 4, 1944.

During the fighting in Italy, Eisenhower participated in plans to cross the

English Channel for an invasion of France. On Dec. 24, 1943, he was appointed supreme commander of the Allied Expeditionary Force, and the next month he was in London making preparations for the massive thrust into Europe. On June 6, 1944, he gambled on a break in bad weather and gave the order to launch the Normandy Invasion, the largest amphibious attack in history. On August 25 Paris was liberated. After winning the Battle of the Bulge—a fierce German counterattack in the Ardennes in December—the Allies crossed the Rhine on March 7, 1945. Germany surrendered on May 7, ending the war in Europe. In the meantime, in December 1944, Eisenhower had been made a five-star general.

WILLIAM F. HALSEY, JR.
(b. Oct. 30, 1882, Elizabeth, N.J., U.S.—
d. Aug. 16, 1959, Fishers Island, N.Y.)

William Halsey led vigorous naval campaigns in the Pacific theatre during World War II. He was a leading exponent of warfare using carrier-based aircraft and became known for his daring tactics.

A graduate of the U.S. Naval Academy at Annapolis, Md., in 1904, Halsey served as a destroyer commander in World War I. He became a naval aviator in 1935 and reached the rank of vice admiral in 1940. After the Japanese attack on Pearl Harbor (December 1941), Halsey's task force was virtually the only operational battle group left in the Pacific. While the United States rebuilt its fleet, he directed surprise forays on Japanese-held islands in the Marshalls and Gilberts as well as on Wake Island. In April 1942 his group maneuvered close enough to Tokyo for Lieutenant Colonel James Doolittle's planes to carry out the first bombing of the Japanese capital. Consistent successes led to his appointment in October 1942 as commander of the South Pacific force and area. During the next two months, he played a vital role in the Battle of Santa Cruz Islands and the naval Battle of Guadalcanal (November 12–15) and was promoted to admiral. From 1942 to mid-1944 Halsey directed the U.S. campaign in the Solomon Islands.

In June 1944 Halsey became commander of the 3rd Fleet and led his carrier task force in brilliant air strikes. He was responsible for covering and supporting U.S. land operations as well as finding and destroying much of the Japanese fleet in the Battle of Leyte Gulf (October). He led U.S. forces in the final naval operations around Okinawa in the Ryukyu Islands from May 28, 1945, to September 2, when the Japanese surrendered. Halsey was promoted to the rank of fleet admiral in December 1945, and he retired in 1947.

ERNEST JOSEPH KING
(b. Nov. 23, 1878, Lorain, Ohio, U.S.—d. June 25, 1956, Portsmouth, N.H.)

Ernest King was commander in chief of U.S. naval forces and chief of naval operations throughout most of World War II. He masterminded the successful U.S.

military campaign against Japan in the Pacific.

King graduated from the United States Naval Academy at Annapolis, Maryland, in 1901 and was commissioned in the navy in 1903. He became a rear admiral in 1933 and a vice admiral in 1938, and he was appointed head of the Atlantic Fleet in January 1941. A few days after the Japanese bombing of Pearl Harbor, King succeeded Admiral Husband J. Kimmel as commander in chief of the U.S. fleet, with the rank of admiral. In March 1942 he also took over the post of chief of naval operations, becoming the most important figure in

Ernest Joseph King, chief of U.S. naval operations, 1942–45. National Archives, Washington, D.C.

the navy (and the only man ever to hold both appointments). He was also a member of the U.S. Joint Chiefs of Staff and of the Anglo-American Combined Chiefs of Staff Committee, and he attended most of the high-level international conferences of the war.

King prosecuted the war against Japan with great energy, and he provided a counterbalance to the defeat-Germany-first strategy of other Allied leaders. King's global strategy was largely responsible for the destruction of the Japanese navy and merchant marine during the war. He picked Admiral Chester W. Nimitz to command the U.S. Pacific Fleet, and his other personnel choices were equally inspired. King also implemented the system whereby the U.S. Navy's far-flung warships were supplied and repaired at sea by relays of special ships so that they could remain at sea for months at a time. By 1945 the U.S. Navy had grown under King's direction to 92,000 ships and other craft and about four million men.

DOUGLAS MACARTHUR
(b. Jan. 26, 1880, Little Rock, Ark., U.S.—d. April 5, 1964, Washington, D.C.)

Douglas MacArthur commanded the Southwest Pacific Theatre in World War II, administered postwar Japan during the Allied occupation that followed, and led United Nations forces during the first nine months of the Korean War.

Recalled to active duty in July 1941, MacArthur conducted a valiant delaying action against the Japanese in the Philippines after war erupted in December. He was ordered to Australia in March 1942 to command Allied forces in the Southwest Pacific Theater. He soon launched an offensive in New Guinea that drove the Japanese out of Papua by January 1943. In a series of operations in 1943–44, MacArthur's troops seized strategic points in New Guinea from Lae to Sansapor, while capturing the Admiralties and western New Britain. The simultaneous northward movement of South Pacific forces in the Solomons, over whom MacArthur maintained strategic control, neutralized Rabaul and bypassed many Japanese units.

After winning a decision to invade the Philippines next rather than Formosa, MacArthur attacked Morotai, Leyte, and Mindoro in autumn 1944. Not until the Leyte operation did he have overwhelming logistical support. His earlier plans had been executed despite inadequacies of personnel and matériel and with little assistance from the Pacific Fleet. MacArthur seriously questioned his superiors' decision to give priority to the European war over the Pacific conflict and to the Central Pacific Theater over his Southwest Pacific area.

His largest, costliest operations occurred during the seven month Luzon campaign in 1945. That spring he also undertook the reconquest of the southern Philippines and Borneo. Meanwhile, he left the difficult mopping-up operations in New Guinea and the Solomons to the

Australian Army. He was promoted to general of the army in December 1944 and was appointed commander of all U.S. army forces in the Pacific four months later. He was in charge of the surrender ceremony in Tokyo Bay on Sept. 2, 1945.

George Catlett Marshall
(b. Dec. 31, 1880, Uniontown, Pa., U.S.— d. Oct. 16, 1959, Washington, D.C.)

George Marshall was the U.S. Army chief of staff during World War II (1939–45) and later U.S. secretary of state (1947–49) and of defense (1950–51). The European Recovery Program he proposed in 1947 became known as the Marshall Plan. He received the Nobel Prize for Peace in 1953.

Marshall was sworn in as chief of staff of the U.S. Army on Sept. 1, 1939, the day World War II began with Germany's invasion of Poland. For the next six years, Marshall directed the raising of new divisions, the training of troops, the development of new weapons and equipment, and the selection of top commanders. When he entered office, the U.S. forces consisted of fewer than 200,000 officers and men. Under his direction it expanded in less than four years to a well-trained and well-equipped force of 8,300,000. Marshall raised and equipped the largest ground and air force in the history of the United States, a feat that earned him the appellation of "the organizer of victory" from the wartime British prime minister, Winston Churchill. As a representative of the U.S. Joint Chiefs of Staff at the international conferences in Casablanca, Morocco, in Washington, D.C., in Quebec, in Cairo, and in Tehrān, Marshall led the fight for an Allied drive on German forces across the English Channel, in opposition to the so-called Mediterranean strategy of the British. So valuable was his service to President Franklin D. Roosevelt that he was kept on at the Joint Chiefs of Staff in Washington while command over the cross-Channel invasion was given to General Dwight D. Eisenhower.

Chester William Nimitz
(b. Feb. 24, 1885, Fredericksburg, Texas, U.S.—d. Feb. 20, 1966, near San Francisco, Calif.)

Chester Nimitz was commander of the U.S. Pacific Fleet during World War II. One of the navy's foremost administrators and strategists, he commanded all land and sea forces in the central Pacific area.

After the Japanese attack on Pearl Harbor (December 1941), Nimitz was elevated to commander in chief of the Pacific Fleet, a command that brought both land and sea forces under his authority. By June 1942 he had proudly announced the decisive victory at the Battle of Midway and the Coral Sea, where enemy losses were 10 times greater than those of the United States at Pearl Harbor. In succeeding years, the historic battles of the Solomon Islands (1942–43), the Gilbert Islands (1943), the Marshalls, Marianas, Palaus, and Philippines (1944), and Iwo

Jima and Okinawa (1945) were fought under his direction.

The Japanese capitulation was signed aboard his flagship, the USS *Missouri*, in Tokyo Bay on Sept. 2, 1945. In December 1944 Nimitz had been promoted to the Navy's newest and highest rank—that of fleet admiral.

GEORGE SMITH PATTON
(b. Nov. 11, 1885, San Gabriel, Calif., U.S.—d. Dec. 21, 1945, Heidelberg, Ger.)

George Patton was an outstanding practitioner of mobile tank warfare in the European and Mediterranean theatres during World War II. His strict discipline, toughness, and self-sacrifice elicited exceptional pride within his ranks, and the general was colourfully referred to as "Old Blood-and-Guts" by his men.

After serving with the U.S. Tank Corps in World War I, Patton became a vigorous proponent of tank warfare. He was made a tank brigade commander in July 1940. On April 4, 1941, he was promoted to major general, and two weeks later he was made commander of the 2nd Armored Division. Soon after the Japanese surprise air attack on Pearl Harbor, he was made corps commander in charge of both the 1st and 2nd armoured divisions and organized the desert training centre at Indio, California. Patton was commanding general of the western task force during the U.S. operations in North Africa in November 1942. He was promoted to the rank of lieutenant general in March

1943 and led the U.S. Seventh Army in Sicily, employing his armour in a rapid drive that captured Palermo in July.

The apogee of his career came with the dramatic sweep of his Third Army across northern France in the summer of 1944 in a campaign marked by great initiative, ruthless drive, and disregard of classic military rules. Prior to the Normandy Invasion, he was publicly placed in command of the First U.S. Army Group, a fictitious army whose supposed marshaling in eastern England helped to deceive German commanders into thinking that the invasion would take

General George Patton stands to the side of an M2 medium tank in Tunisia, 1942. National Archives, Washington, D.C.

(Left to right) *Dwight D. Eisenhower, Omar Bradley, and George Patton at Bastogne, Belgium, February 1945.* Encyclopædia Britannica, Inc.

place in the Pas-de-Calais region of France. Patton's armoured units were not operational until August 1, almost two months after D-Day, but by the end of the month they had captured Mayenne, Laval, Le Mans, Reims, and Châlons. They did not stop until they hurtled against the strong German defenses at Nancy and Metz in November. In December his forces played a strategic role in defending Bastogne in the massive Battle of the Bulge. By the end of January 1945, Patton's forces had reached the German frontier. On March 1 they took Trier, and in the

next 10 days they cleared the entire region north of the Moselle River, trapping thousands of Germans. They then joined the Seventh Army in sweeping the Saar and the Palatinate, where they took 100,000 prisoners.

Patton's military achievements caused authorities to soften strong civilian criticism of some of his actions, including his widely reported striking of a hospitalized shell-shocked soldier in August 1943. (Patton publicly apologized for the incident.) His public criticisms of the Allied postwar denazification policy in

Germany led to his removal from the command of the Third Army in October 1945.

CARL SPAATZ
(b. June 28, 1891, Boyertown, Pa., U.S.— d. July 14, 1974, Washington, D.C.)

Carl Spaatz was the leading U.S. combat air commander in World War II and the first chief of staff of the independent U.S. Air Force.

Spaatz served as a combat pilot during World War I and then acquired extensive staff and command experience between 1919 and 1942. He went to England in 1940 to evaluate German military power, and in July 1942, after the United States had entered the war, he took command of the Eighth Air Force in England. Early in 1943 he was shifted to the Mediterranean theatre, where he commanded the Northwest Africa Air Forces and then directed air assaults against Italy. In January 1944 he became commander of the U.S. Strategic Air Forces in Europe. In this capacity he directed the daylight precision bombing of Germany and occupied lands from both England and Italy until the end of the war in Europe—complementing the nighttime saturation bombings directed by Arthur Harris, his counterpart in the Royal Air Force Bomber Command. In preparation for the Normandy Invasion of June 1944, Spaatz's air forces mounted huge bombing runs against Germany's aircraft industry and then its petroleum and synthetic fuel industries.

Spaatz moved to the Pacific theatre in July 1945, and, though personally opposed to the use of atomic bombs against Japanese cities, he directed the final strategic bombing of Japan that included, under orders of President Harry S. Truman, the dropping of atomic bombs on Hiroshima and Nagasaki. He became chief of staff of the newly independent U.S. Air Force (September 1947), but, not enjoying the administrative work, he retired in 1948.

GREAT BRITAIN

ALAN FRANCIS BROOKE, 1ST VISCOUNT ALANBROOKE, BARON ALANBROOKE OF BROOKEBOROUGH
(b. July 23, 1883, Bagnères-de-Bigorre, France—d. June 17, 1963, Hartley Wintney, Hampshire, Eng.)

Alanbrooke was a British field marshal and chief of the Imperial General Staff during World War II.

Alanbrooke began service in World War II as commander of the II Army Corps in France. After the retreat to Dunkirk, he was responsible for covering the evacuation (May 26–June 4, 1940) of the British Expeditionary Force. In July he took command of the Home Forces, and he served in that capacity until he was promoted to chief of staff by Prime Minister Winston Churchill in December 1941. He held this post until 1946. As chairman of the Chiefs of Staff Committee, Alanbrooke represented the members' views ably and firmly to the prime minister and to the U.S. Joint Chiefs of Staff and thus exercised strong influence on Allied strategy. Alanbrooke was also recognized as a brilliant field commander, though he was never given any of the great overseas commands—including, to his great frustration, command over the Allied invasion of western Europe.

Harold (Rupert Leofric George) Alexander, 1st Earl Alexander (of Tunis)
(b. Dec. 10, 1891, London, Eng.—d. June 16, 1969, Slough, Buckinghamshire)

Harold Alexander, a prominent British field marshal in World War II, was noted for his North African campaigns against Field Marshal Erwin Rommel and for his later commands in Italy and western Europe.

In World War II Alexander commanded the British 1st Corps at Dunkirk, where he helped direct the evacuation of 300,000 troops; he was the last man to leave the beaches. In Burma (February 1942) he successfully extricated British and Indian troops before the advancing Japanese.

In the summer of 1942 Alexander was made British commander in chief in the Mediterranean theatre, where he formed a highly successful duo with his chief field commander, General Bernard Montgomery. Together they reorganized British forces and drove the Germans back from Egypt and across North Africa until the surrender of the Germans in Tunis in May 1943. Alexander continued to drive the Germans from Sicily and southern Italy as commander of the Fifteenth Army Group (with Montgomery and the U.S. general George Patton as his field

commanders), and in November 1944 he became commander in chief of all Allied forces in Italy.

Andrew Browne Cunningham
(b. Jan. 7, 1883, Dublin, Ire.—d. June 12, 1963, London, Eng.)

Andrew Cunningham was an outstanding combat commander early in World War II and served as first sea lord of the British Admiralty from 1943 to 1946.

Cunningham was promoted to vice admiral in 1936, and he was serving as commander in chief of the Mediterranean fleet when World War II began in September 1939. Though his forces were heavily outnumbered by the Italian navy from June 1940 (when Italy entered the war), Cunningham set out to establish British naval supremacy in the Mediterranean. With France knocked out of the war, he was able to secure the disarming of Admiral René Godfroy's French squadron at Alexandria, Egypt. Cunningham then went on the offensive against the Italian navy. His air attacks on the Italian fleet anchored at Taranto (November 1940) put three Italian battleships out of action, and in the Battle of Cape Matapan (March 28, 1941) his forces sank three of Italy's largest cruisers.

With British dominance over the Italian navy firmly established by 1941, Cunningham's principal opponent became the Luftwaffe (German air force), which inflicted heavy losses on his ships in operations around Crete and Malta and on British convoys bound for North

Africa. After spending six months in Washington, D.C., as the Royal Navy's representative to the Anglo-American Combined Chiefs of Staff Committee, Cunningham returned to combat command in November 1942 as naval commander in chief of the Mediterranean and North Africa. Acting as General Dwight D. Eisenhower's naval deputy, Cunningham commanded the large fleet that covered the Anglo-American landings in North Africa (Operation Torch; November 1942) and then commanded the naval forces used in the joint Anglo-American amphibious invasions of Sicily (July 1943) and Italy (September 1943).

Having been promoted (January 1943) to admiral of the fleet, Cunningham returned to London in October 1943 to serve as first sea lord and chief of naval staff, the highest post in the Royal Navy and one in which he reported directly to Prime Minister Winston Churchill through the Chiefs of Staff Committee. He was responsible for overall strategic direction of the navy for the remainder of the war.

HUGH CASWALL TREMENHEERE DOWDING, 1ST BARON DOWDING
(b. April 24, 1882, Moffat, Dumfriesshire, Scot.—d. Feb. 15, 1970, Tunbridge Wells, Kent, Eng.)

Hugh Dowding was a British air chief marshal and head of Fighter Command during the Battle of Britain (1940) in World War II; he was largely responsible for defeating the German Air Force in its attempt to gain control of British skies in preparation for a German invasion of England.

A squadron commander in the Royal Flying Corps in World War I, Dowding remained in the new Royal Air Force. After serving in command, staff, and training positions in Britain and Asia, he became chief of the newly created Fighter Command in 1936. He vigorously promoted the development of radar and the Spitfire and Hurricane fighters that contributed significantly to the defeat of the Luftwaffe during the Battle of Britain. Although the Fighter Command was outnumbered, Dowding's strategic and tactical skill enabled it to retain air superiority and thwart Germany's aims. He retired in November 1942.

SIR ARTHUR TRAVERS HARRIS, 1ST BARONET
(b. April 13, 1892, Cheltenham, Gloucestershire, Eng.—d. April 5, 1984, Goring-on-Thames, Oxfordshire)

Arthur ("Bomber") Harris was the British air officer who initiated and directed the "saturation bombing" that the Royal Air Force inflicted on Germany during World War II.

Harris was made an air commodore in 1937, was named air vice-marshal in 1939, and rose to air marshal in 1941 and to commander in chief of the RAF Bomber Command in February 1942. A firm believer in mass raids, Air Marshal Harris developed the saturation technique of mass bombing—that of concentrating clouds of bombers in a giant raid on a single city, with the object of completely demolishing its civilian quarters. Conducted in tandem with American precision bombing of specific military and industrial sites by day, saturation bombing was intended to break the will and ability of the German people to continue the war. Harris applied this method with great destructive effect in Germany—most notably in the firebombings of Hamburg and Dresden. During the preparations for the Normandy Invasion in early 1944, Harris was subordinate to American commanders such as Dwight D. Eisenhower and Carl Spaatz and directed the destruction of transportation and communication centres in cities all across German-occupied France.

BERNARD LAW MONTGOMERY, 1ST VISCOUNT MONTGOMERY (OF ALAMEIN, OF HINDHEAD)
(b. Nov. 17, 1887, London, Eng.—d. March 24, 1976, near Alton, Hampshire)

Bernard Montgomery was a British field marshal and one of the outstanding Allied commanders in World War II.

Early in World War II, Montgomery led a division in France, and, after the evacuation of Allied troops from Dunkirk, he commanded the southeastern section of England in anticipation of a German invasion.

In August 1942 Prime Minister Winston Churchill appointed him commander of the British Eighth Army in North Africa, which had recently been defeated and pushed back to Egypt by German General Erwin Rommel. There Montgomery restored the troops' shaken confidence and, combining drive with caution, forced Rommel to retreat from Egypt after the Battle of El-Alamein (November 1942). Montgomery then pursued the German armies across North Africa to their final surrender in Tunisia in May 1943. Under the command of U.S. General Dwight D. Eisenhower, he shared major responsibility in the successful Allied invasion of Sicily (July 1943) and led his Eighth Army steadily up the east coast of Italy until called home to lead the Allied armies into France in 1944.

Again under Eisenhower, Montgomery reviewed the plan for Operation Overlord (as the Normandy Invasion was code-named) and recommended expanding the size of the invading force and landing area. Eisenhower approved the expansion plan (code-named Neptune), and Montgomery commanded all ground forces in the initial stages of the invasion, launched on D-Day, June 6, 1944. Beginning August 1, his Twenty-first Army Group consisted of Miles Dempsey's British Second Army and Henry Crerar's First Canadian Army. Promoted to the rank of field marshal, Montgomery led the group to victory across northern France, Belgium, The Netherlands, and northern Germany, finally receiving the surrender of the German northern armies on May 4, 1945, on Lüneburg Heath.

Louis Mountbatten, 1st Earl Mountbatten (of Burma), Viscount Mountbatten of Burma, Baron Romsey of Romsey

(b. June 25, 1900, Frogmore House, Windsor, Eng.—d. Aug. 27, 1979, Donegal Bay, off Mullaghmore, County Sligo, Ire.)

Louis Mountbatten was a British statesman, naval leader, and the last viceroy of India. He had international royal-family background. His career involved extensive naval commands, the diplomatic negotiation of independence for India and Pakistan, and the highest military defense leaderships.

In command of the destroyer *Kelly* and the 5th destroyer flotilla at the outbreak of World War II, Mountbatten was appointed commander of an aircraft carrier in 1941. In April 1942 he was named chief of combined operations and became acting vice admiral and a de facto member of the chiefs of staff. From this position he was appointed supreme allied commander for Southeast Asia (1943–46), prompting complaints of nepotism against his cousin the king. He successfully conducted the campaign against Japan that led to the recapture of Burma (Myanmar).

Soviet Union

Vasily Ivanovich Chuikov

(b. Feb. 12 [Jan. 31, Old Style], 1900, Serebryannye Prudy, near Moscow, Russian Empire—d. March 18, 1982, Moscow, Russia, U.S.S.R.)

Vasily Chuikov was the Soviet general (and later marshal) who in World War II commanded the defense at the Battle of Stalingrad, joined in turning Adolf Hitler's armies back, and led the Soviet drive to Berlin.

Chuikov took part in the Soviet invasion of Poland (1939) and in the Russo-Finnish War (1939–40), and had just finished serving as military attaché in China when he was called to Stalingrad to command that city's defense.

In August 1942 the Germans launched a direct attack against Stalingrad, committing up to 22 divisions with more than 700 planes, 500 tanks, 1,000 mortars, and 1,200 guns. Chuikov, in response, allegedly declared, "We shall hold the city or die here." Much of the fighting in the city and on its perimeters was at close quarters, with bayonets and hand grenades. About 300,000 Germans were killed or captured in the course of the campaign; Soviet casualties totaled more than 400,000. In November the Soviet forces began to counterattack and by the end of the year were on the offensive. General Chuikov subsequently led his forces into the Donets Basin and then into the Crimea and north to Belorussia before spearheading the Soviet drive to Berlin. Chuikov personally accepted the German surrender of Berlin on May 1, 1945.

Georgy Konstantinovich Zhukov

(b. Dec. 1 [Nov. 19, Old Style], 1896, Kaluga province, Russia—d. June 18, 1974, Moscow)

Georgy Zhukov was a marshal of the Soviet Union and the most important Soviet military commander during World War II.

During the Winter War, which the Soviet Union fought against Finland at the outset of World War II, Zhukov served as chief of staff of the Soviet army. He was then transferred to command the Kiev military district and in January 1941 was appointed chief of staff of the Red Army. After the Germans invaded the Soviet Union (June 1941), he organized the defense of Leningrad (St. Petersburg) and was then appointed commander in chief of the Western Front. He directed the defense of Moscow (autumn 1941) as well as the massive counteroffensive (December 1941) that drove the Germans' Army Group Centre back from central Russia.

In August 1942 Zhukov was named deputy commissar of defense and first deputy commander in chief of Soviet armed forces. He became the chief member of Joseph Stalin's personal supreme headquarters and figured prominently in the planning or execution of almost every major engagement in the war. He oversaw the defense of Stalingrad (late 1942) and planned and directed the counteroffensive that encircled the Germans' Sixth Army in that city (January 1943). He was named a marshal of the Soviet Union soon afterward. Zhukov was heavily involved in the Battle of Kursk (July 1943) and directed the Soviet sweep across Ukraine in the winter and spring of 1944. He commanded the Soviet offensive through Belorussia (summer-autumn 1944), which resulted in the collapse of the Germans' Army Group Centre and of German occupation of Poland and Czechoslovakia. In April 1945 he personally commanded the final assault on Berlin and then remained in Germany as commander of the Soviet occupation force. On May 8, 1945, he represented the Soviet Union at Germany's formal surrender. He then served as the Soviet representative on the Allied Control Commission for Germany.

FRANCE

MARIE-PIERRE KOENIG
(b. Oct. 10, 1898, Caen, France—d. Sept. 2, 1970, Neuilly-sur-Seine)

Marie-Pierre Koenig was one of the leading commanders of General Charles de Gaulle's Free French Forces in World War II.

After active duty during World War I and later in North Africa, Koenig campaigned in Norway and France during the early part of World War II. Evacuated to England in June 1940, he joined de Gaulle's movement and rose steadily in the Free French Forces, distinguishing himself in the conquest of Gabon in 1940 and in the defense of Bir Hakeim, Libya, against terrific attacks by German General Erwin Rommel's panzer (armoured) divisions in 1942. He then served as assistant army chief of staff and as Free French delegate to General Dwight D. Eisenhower's supreme Allied headquarters in England. In June 1944 he became head of the French Forces of the Interior, the Resistance army in German-occupied France, and in August he was named military governor of liberated Paris. He had become commander of the French army in Germany by the end of the war.

JACQUES-PHILIPPE LECLERC
(b. Nov. 22, 1902, Belloy-Saint-Léonard, France—d. Nov. 28, 1947, Colomb-Béchar [now Béchar], Alg.)

Jacques-Philippe Leclerc was the French general and war hero who achieved fame as the liberator of Paris.

In 1939, as a captain of infantry, Leclerc was wounded and captured by the Germans, but he managed to escape to England. Upon hearing that General Charles de Gaulle was rallying Free French Forces from London, he took the name Leclerc (so as to spare his family in France any reprisals) and joined de Gaulle. Promoted to colonel by de Gaulle, he achieved a number of military victories in French Equatorial Africa. After being promoted to brigadier general, he staged a spectacular 1,000-mile (1,600-km) march from Chad to Tripoli, Libya, to join the forces of the British Eighth Army, capturing Italian garrisons along the way. He was promoted to major general in 1943.

He took part in the Normandy Invasion of 1944 as commander of the Free French 2nd Armoured Division, which debarked on August 1 and took part in the drive to Alençon and Argentan by U.S. General George S. Patton's Third Army. On August 20 the 2nd Armoured Division was ordered by Supreme Allied Commander Dwight D. Eisenhower to liberate the French capital, and on August 25 the commander of the German garrison in Paris, Dietrich von Choltitz, surrendered to Leclerc. The next day Leclerc and de Gaulle formally entered Paris in triumph.

Leclerc went on to liberate Strasbourg (Nov. 23, 1944) and then led his men on into Germany, capturing Berchtesgaden. In July 1945 Leclerc was named commander of the French expeditionary force to the Far East. That same year he

Jacques-Philippe Leclerc, during the liberation of Paris, August 1944. National Archives, Washington, D.C.

legally changed his name from Philippe-Marie, vicomte de Hauteclocque, to Jacques-Philippe Leclerc de Haute-clocque, using his wartime name.

AXIS COMMANDERS

GERMANY

LUDWIG BECK
(b. June 29, 1880, Biebrich, Ger.—d. July 20, 1944, Berlin)

Ludwig Beck, who was chief of the German army general staff (1935–38), opposed Adolf Hitler's expansionist policies and was a central figure in the unsuccessful July Plot to assassinate Hitler in 1944.

After Hitler came to power, Beck rose rapidly, becoming chief of the elite general staff in 1935, but he resigned in 1938 after protesting the decision to conquer Czechoslovakia and after failing to organize army opposition to Hitler. He became the recognized leader of the conspirators against Hitler and was seen as a possible president of Germany with Hitler out of the way. After the failure of the plot to kill Hitler on July 20, 1944, Beck attempted suicide, receiving the coup de grâce from an attending sergeant.

KARL DÖNITZ
(b. Sept. 16, 1891, Grünau-bei-Berlin, Ger.—d. Dec. 22, 1980, Aumühle, W. Ger.)

Karl Dönitz was the German naval officer who commanded Germany's World War II U-boat fleet and for a few days succeeded Adolf Hitler as German head of state.

In the aftermath of Hitler's accession to power, Dönitz clandestinely supervised—despite the Treaty of Versailles's absolute ban on German submarine construction—the creation of a new U-boat fleet, over which he was subsequently appointed commander (1936). In the early part of the war, Dönitz did as much damage to the Allies as any German commander through his leadership of the U-boats in the Battle of the Atlantic. In the midst of World War II, in January 1943, he was called to replace Admiral Erich Raeder as commander in chief of the German navy. His loyalty and ability soon won him the confidence of Hitler. On April 20, 1945, shortly before the collapse of the Nazi regime, Hitler appointed Dönitz head of the northern military and civil command. Finally—in his last political testament—Hitler named Dönitz his successor as president of the Reich, minister of war, and supreme commander of the armed forces. Assuming the reins of government on May 2, 1945, Dönitz retained office for only a few days. In 1946 he was sentenced to 10 years' imprisonment by the International Military Tribunal at Nürnberg.

HERMANN GÖRING
(b. Jan. 12, 1893, Rosenheim, Ger.—d. Oct. 15, 1946, Nürnberg)

Hermann Göring was a leader of the Nazi Party and one of the primary architects of the Nazi police state in Germany. He was condemned to hang as a war criminal by the International Military Tribunal at Nürnberg in 1946 but took poison instead and died the night his execution was ordered.

Göring was the most popular of the Nazi leaders, not only with the German people but also with the ambassadors and diplomats of foreign powers. He used his impregnable position after the ascension of Adolf Hitler to enrich himself. The more ruthless aspect of his nature was shown in the recorded telephone conversation by means of which Göring blackmailed the surrender of Austria before the *Anschluss* (political union) with Germany in 1938. It was Göring who led the economic despoliation of the Jews in Germany and in the various territories that fell under Hitler's power.

Although Göring's Luftwaffe helped conduct the blitzkrieg that smashed Polish resistance and weakened country after country as Hitler's campaigns progressed, the Luftwaffe's capacity for defense declined as Hitler's battlefronts extended from northern Europe to the Mediterranean and North Africa, and Göring lost face when the Luftwaffe failed to win the Battle of Britain or to prevent the Allied bombing of Germany. On the plea of ill health, Göring retired as much as Hitler would let him into private life among his art collection (further enriched with spoils from the Jewish collections in the occupied countries).

In 1939 Hitler declared Göring his successor and in 1940 gave him the special rank of Reichsmarschall des Grossdeutschen Reiches ("Marshal of the Empire"). Hitler did not displace him until the last days of the war, when, in accordance with the decrees of 1939, Göring attempted to assume the Führer's powers, believing him to be encircled and helpless in Berlin. Nevertheless, Göring expected to be treated as a plenipotentiary when, after Hitler's suicide, he surrendered himself to the Americans.

HEINZ WILHELM GUDERIAN
(b. June 17, 1888, Kulm, Ger.—d. May 14, 1954, Schwangau bei Füssen, W. Ger.)

Heinz Guderian was a German general and tank expert who became one of the principal architects of armoured warfare and the blitzkrieg between World Wars I and II. He contributed decisively to Germany's victories in Poland, France, and the Soviet Union early in World War II.

Attracting Adolf Hitler's attention in 1935, Guderian rose rapidly and was able to put many of his revolutionary ideas into practice. His *Achtung! Panzer!* (1937; *Attention! Tanks!*) incorporated many of the theories of the British general J.F.C. Fuller and General Charles de Gaulle, who advocated the creation of independent armoured formations with strong air and motorized infantry support, intended to increase mobility on the battlefield by quick penetrations of enemy lines and by trapping vast bodies of men and weapons in encircling movements. Unlike most of his reform-minded contemporaries in other armies, Guderian found a sympathetic supporter in his commander in chief, Hitler. Consequently the German army, despite opposition from conservative elements, developed a tactical superiority at the outbreak of World War II that repeatedly ensured victory.

Designated chief of Germany's mobile troops in November 1938, Guderian proved the soundness of his theories in the Polish campaign of September 1939 and spearheaded the drive to the French coast of the English Channel (May 1940) that eliminated France from the war. In the Russian campaign he reached the outskirts of Moscow before being driven back in October 1941. Incurring Hitler's disfavour for withdrawing his troops in the face of a Russian counteroffensive during the winter of 1941–42, he was dismissed, but he returned in March 1943 as inspector general of armoured troops, with authority to establish priorities in the production of armoured vehicles as well as to direct their employment. He simplified and accelerated tank production and, after the July 20, 1944, attempt on Hitler's life, became acting chief of staff. Hitler's interference nullified most of Guderian's actions, however, and he resigned on March 5, 1945.

ALFRED JODL
(b. May 10, 1890, Würzburg, Ger.—d. Oct. 16, 1946, Nürnberg)

Alfred Jodl was head of the German armed forces operations staff and helped plan and conduct most of Germany's military campaigns during World War II.

A competent staff officer and Adolf Hitler's faithful servant to the end, Jodl was named chief of operations of the Oberkommando der Wehrmacht (OKW; Armed Forces High Command) on Aug. 23, 1939, just before the invasion of Poland. With Wilhelm Keitel, OKW chief of staff, he became a key figure in Hitler's central military command and was involved in implementing all of Germany's campaigns except the beginning of the Russia invasion in the second half of 1941. On May 7, 1945, he signed the capitulation of the German armed forces to the western Allies at Reims, France. As chief of operations staff, he had signed many orders for the shooting of hostages and for other acts contrary to international law. He was executed after trial and conviction for war crimes by the International Military Tribunal at Nürnberg.

WILHELM KEITEL
(b. Sept. 22, 1882, Helmscherode [now in Bad Gandersheim], Ger.—d. Oct. 16, 1946, Nürnberg)

Wilhelm Keitel was a field marshal and head of the German Armed Forces High Command during World War II. One of Adolf Hitler's most loyal and trusted lieutenants, he became chief of the Führer's personal military staff and helped direct most of the Third Reich's World War II campaigns.

In 1935 Keitel became chief of staff of the Wehrmachtamt (Armed Forces Office), under the minister of war, and in 1938 he advanced to head of the Oberkommando der Wehrmacht (OKW; Armed Forces High Command), which Hitler had created as a central control agency for Germany's military effort. He held that post until the end of World War II. Keitel participated in all major conferences, dictated the terms of the French surrender in June 1940, and signed operational orders—including directives authorizing the shooting of commandos or political commissars taken prisoner in uniform and other directives making it possible to detain civilians without due process.

Keitel was present, though not injured, at the bombing of Hitler's field headquarters in the July Plot. He directed the efforts to reassert control over the conspirators, and he was a member of the "court of honour" that expelled many of them from the German military—thus securing their conviction and their sentencing to death by a civilian court.

After the war the International Military Tribunal convicted Keitel of planning and waging a war of aggression, of war crimes, and of crimes against humanity. Denied his request for a military execution by firing squad, he was hanged at Nürnberg.

ALBERT KESSELRING
(b. Nov. 20, 1885, Marktstedt, Bavaria, Ger.—d. July 16, 1960, Bad Nauheim, W. Ger.)

Albert Kesselring was a German field marshal who, as German commander in chief, south, became one of Adolf Hitler's top defensive strategists during World War II.

In 1936 Kesselring was promoted to lieutenant general and chief of the General Staff of the Luftwaffe. Early in World War II Kesselring commanded air fleets in Poland (September 1939) and France (May–June 1940) and during the Battle of Britain (1940–41). Having already had experience in the bombing of civilian population centres such as Warsaw and Rotterdam, he apparently concurred in Hermann Göring's decision to redirect Luftwaffe bombing toward London. This proved to be a fateful decision because the resulting discontinuance of attacks on British airfields gave the Royal Air Force Fighter Command time to recover and eventually defeat the German air offensive against England.

After participating in the attack on the Soviet Union (summer 1941), Kesselring became commander in chief, south (late 1941), to bolster Italy's efforts in North Africa and against Malta. Though unable to take Malta, he commanded Erwin Rommel and the Axis campaign in North Africa. After the Allied invasions of Sicily and Italy in the summer of 1943, Kesselring fought a brilliant defensive action that prevented an Allied victory in that theatre for more than a year. Injured in October 1944, he became commander in chief, west, in March 1945, replacing Field Marshal Gerd von Rundstedt, but proved unable to stop the Anglo-American drive into Germany and surrendered the southern half of the German forces on May 7, 1945.

In 1947 a British military court in Venice tried and convicted Kesselring of war crimes—for ordering the shooting of 335 Italian civilian hostages in the so-called Ardeatine cave massacre of March 1944, an atrocity committed in reprisal for an attack by Italian partisans on German soldiers. Sentenced to death on May 6, 1947, Kesselring later won commutation to life imprisonment, and in 1952 he was pardoned and freed.

Erich von Manstein
(b. Nov. 24, 1887, Berlin, Ger.—d. June 11, 1973, Irschenhausen, near Munich, W. Ger.)

Erich von Manstein was a German field marshal who many military historians consider the most talented German field commander in World War II.

At the start of World War II, Manstein served as chief of staff to General Gerd von Rundstedt in the invasion of Poland (1939). Manstein had in the meantime devised a daring plan to invade France by means of a concentrated armoured thrust through the Ardennes Forest. Though this plan was rejected by the German High Command, Manstein managed to bring it to the personal attention of Adolf Hitler, who enthusiastically adopted it.

After leading an infantry corps in the assault on France in June 1940, Manstein was promoted to general that month. He commanded the 56th Panzer Corps in the invasion of the Soviet Union (1941), and nearly captured Leningrad. Promoted to command of the 11th Army on the southern front (September 1941), Manstein managed to take 430,000 Soviet prisoners, after which he withstood the Soviet counteroffensive that winter and went on to capture Sevastopol in July 1942. Soon after, he was promoted to field marshal. He almost succeeded in relieving the beleaguered 6th Army in Stalingrad in December 1942–January 1943, and in February 1943 his forces recaptured Kharkov, in the most successful German counteroffensive of the war. Thereafter he was driven into retreat, and in March 1944 he was dismissed by Hitler. After the war, Manstein was tried for war crimes, and, though acquitted of the most serious charges, was imprisoned until his release in 1953 because of ill health.

Erwin Rommel
(b. Nov. 15, 1891, Heidenheim, Ger.—d. Oct. 14, 1944, Herrlingen, near Ulm)

Erwin Rommel became the most popular German general at home and gained the open respect of his enemies with his spectacular victories as commander of the Afrika Korps in World War II.

In February 1941, Rommel was appointed commander of the German troops dispatched to aid the all-but-defeated Italian army in Libya. The deserts of North Africa became the scene of his greatest successes—and of his defeat at the hands of a vastly superior enemy. In the North African theatre of war, the "Desert Fox," as he came to be called by both friend and foe because of his audacious surprise attacks, acquired a formidable reputation, and soon Hitler, impressed by such successes, promoted him to field marshal.

Rommel had difficulty following up these successes, however. North Africa was, in Hitler's view, only a sideshow. Nonetheless, despite the increasing difficulties of supply and Rommel's request to withdraw his exhausted troops, in the summer of 1942 Hitler ordered an attack on Cairo and the Suez Canal. Rommel and his German-Italian army were stopped by the British at El-Alamein (Al-'Alamayn, Egypt), 60 miles (100 km) from Alexandria. At that time Rommel won astounding popularity in the Arab world, where he was regarded as a "liberator" from British rule. At home the propaganda ministry portrayed him as the invincible "people's marshal" (*Volksmarschall*). But the offensive against Egypt had overtaxed his resources. At the end of October 1942, he was defeated in the Second Battle of El-Alamein and had to withdraw to the German bridgehead in Tunis. In March 1943 Hitler ordered him home.

In 1944 Rommel was entrusted with the defense of France's Channel coast against a possible Allied invasion. The master of the war of movement then developed an unusual inventiveness in the erection of coastal defense works. From his experience in North Africa with Allied air interdiction, Rommel believed the only successful defense of the beaches lay in preventing the enemy a bridgehead by all possible means. To do so, he boldly advocated the placement of reserve forces immediately behind coastal defense works for counterattacks. His superiors, most notably Gerd von Rundstedt,

demurred, however, insisting on a more traditional placement of reserves farther behind the lines to maximize the forces' potential range of movement after the place of invasion became known. This disagreement and the dissonance it fostered within organizations charged with repelling the Allies weakened the effectiveness of the German defense when the invasion finally came along the Normandy coast.

On July 17, 1944, at the height of the invasion battle, Rommel's car was attacked by British fighter-bombers and forced off the road. It somersaulted, and Rommel was hospitalized with serious head injuries. In August he had recovered sufficiently to be able to return to his home to convalesce. In the meantime, after the failure of the attempt on Hitler's life on July 20, 1944, Rommel's contacts with the conspirators had come to light. Hitler did not want the "people's marshal" to appear before the court as his enemy and thence be taken to the gallows. He sent two generals to Rommel to offer him poison with the assurance that his name and that of his family would remain unsullied if he avoided a trial. On October 14 Rommel took poison, thus ending his life. He was later buried with full military honours.

GERD VON RUNDSTEDT
(b. Dec. 12, 1875, Aschersleben, near Magdeburg, Ger.—d. Feb. 24, 1953, Hannover, W. Ger.)

Gerd von Rundstedt was one of Adolf Hitler's ablest field marshals during World War II. He held commands on both the Eastern and Western fronts, played a major role in defeating France in 1940, and led much of the opposition to the Allied offensive in the West in 1944–45.

Rundstedt was active in Germany's secret rearmament both before and after Hitler came to power. He retired in 1938 as senior field commander but returned to active duty to command an army group in the Polish campaign at the outbreak of World War II. Later, on the Western Front, he took part in the implementation of the plan that defeated France in 1940. As head of Army Group B, he led the breakthrough that sealed France's fate. He was, however, partly to blame for the order to halt the German armour, allowing the British to escape from Dunkirk. During the invasion of the Soviet Union, beginning in June 1941, he commanded the German southern wing, which overran almost all of Ukraine before winter. When a Soviet counteroffensive forced a retreat, Hitler dismissed the aged field marshal.

Returning to duty in July 1942, Rundstedt became commander in chief in western Europe and fortified France against an expected Allied invasion. Unable to defeat the Anglo-American invasion forces in 1944, he was replaced in July but returned in September to direct the Ardennes offensive (Battle of the Bulge) that disrupted the military timetable of the western Allies for several months. Relieved for the third time in March 1945, he was captured by U.S. troops in May but was released because of ill health.

JAPAN

YAMAMOTO ISOROKU
(b. April 4, 1884, Nagaoka, Japan—d. April 18, 1943, Solomon Islands)

Yamamoto Isoroku was the Japanese naval officer who conceived of the surprise attack on the U.S. naval base at Pearl Harbor.

Yamamoto commanded the aircraft carrier *Akagi* in 1928. Promoted to rear admiral in 1929, Yamamoto served as chief of the Technological Division of the Naval Air Corps, where he championed the development of fast carrier-borne fighter planes, a program that produced the famous Zero fighters. In 1934 Yamamoto commanded the First Carrier Division, and in 1935 he headed the Japanese delegation to the London Naval Conference, where Japan abandoned 15 years of uneasy naval détente among the world powers. In 1936, as a vice admiral, he became the vice minister of the navy. Yamamoto commanded the First Fleet in 1938, and he became commander in chief of the Combined Fleet in 1939. In these later capacities, Yamamoto used his growing seniority to turn the navy away from battleships, which he viewed as obsolete, in favour of tactics based on aircraft carriers—carrier tactics that he later incorporated into the plan to attack Pearl Harbor.

As the senior seagoing admiral in the Japanese fleet, Yamamoto prepared for war against the United States. Contrary to popular belief, Yamamoto argued for a war with the United States once Japan made the fateful decision to invade the rich lands of Southeast Asia. Others in the naval ministry hoped to avoid war with America even while making war with Dutch and British possessions in Asia. When the Japanese emperor Hirohito adopted Yamamoto's view, the admiral focused his energy on the coming fight with the U.S. Pacific Fleet. Well aware of the immense industrial capacity of the United States, but misunderstanding the potential resolve of the American public, Yamamoto asserted Japan's only

Yamamoto Isoroku, commander in chief of Japan's Combined Fleet during World War II. U.S. Naval Historical Center (Photo number: NH 63430)

chance for victory lay in a surprise attack that would cripple the American naval forces in the Pacific and force the United States into a negotiated peace, thereby allowing Japan a free reign in greater East Asia. Any long war with the United States, Yamamoto believed, would spell disaster for Japan. Although he was not the author of the detailed plan to attack Pearl Harbor, he certainly championed it within government circles. On Dec. 7, 1941, his carriers, under the immediate command of Vice Adm. Nagumo Chūichi, scored a stunning tactical victory over the U.S. Pacific Fleet at anchorage in Pearl Harbor. An unbroken string of naval victories followed this attack for six months, and Yamamoto's prestige reached new heights by the late spring of 1942.

Yet the great tactical success of the Pearl Harbor strike obscured a strategic calamity. Far from encouraging the United States to sue for peace, the attack enflamed the American public. The surprise bombing, designed to avert a long conflict with the United States, instead helped ensure a prolonged and total war. Yamamoto stumbled further at the Battle of Midway (June 4–6, 1942), where he hoped to destroy U.S. ships not caught at Pearl Harbor, notably the U.S. Navy's aircraft carriers. But the strike at Midway failed, partly because the United States had excellent intelligence information regarding Japanese forces but also because Yamamoto's plans were too complex and his objectives confused. The Japanese battle plan included the movement of eight separate task forces, a diversionary attack in the Aleutian Islands, and the occupation of the Midway Islands, all while attempting the destruction of the American carriers. Yamamoto's ensuing campaign for Guadalcanal and the Solomon Islands in the South Pacific was not much better, as he refused to commit his forces in anything other than piecemeal fashion as Allied forces there conducted the kind of attrition war Japan could ill afford.

Still, American assessment of Yamamoto was great enough that, when intelligence information revealed the Japanese admiral's flight plan in April 1943, U.S. commanders in the Pacific undertook to ambush and shoot down his plane. On April 18, 1943, during an inspection tour of Japanese bases in the South Pacific, Yamamoto's plane was shot down near Bougainville Island, and the admiral perished.

Yamashita Tomoyuki
(b. Nov. 8, 1885, Kōchi, Japan—d. Feb. 23, 1946, Manila, Phil.)

Yamashita Tomoyuki led the successful Japanese attacks on Malaya and Singapore during World War II.

An able strategist, Yamashita trained Japanese soldiers in the technique of jungle warfare and helped conceive the military plan for the Japanese invasion of the Thai and Malay peninsulas in 1941–42. In the course of a 10-week campaign, Yamashita's 25th Army overran all of Malaya and obtained the surrender of the huge British naval base at Singapore on Feb. 15, 1942. Soon afterward Yamashita was retired by Prime Minister Tōjō Hideki to an army training command in Manchuria, and he did not see active service again until after Tōjō's fall in 1944, when he was sent to command the defense of the Philippines. His forces were badly defeated in both the Leyte and the Luzon campaigns, but he held out until after the general surrender was announced from Tokyo in August 1945. Yamashita was tried for war crimes, and, though he denied knowing of atrocities committed under his command, he was convicted and eventually hanged.

CHAPTER 10

WASTELAND: THE WORLD AFTER 1945

THE RUIN OF EUROPE AND JAPAN

Harry Truman had been an artilleryman in World War I and remembered well the lunar landscape of the Western Front. Yet, while driving from Potsdam to Berlin in July 1945, he exclaimed, "I never saw such destruction!" Almost all the great cities of central and eastern Europe were jagged with ruined buildings, pitted roads, wrecked bridges, and choked waterways. Amid it all were the gaunt survivors, perhaps 45,000,000 of them homeless, including 25,000,000 in those lands—Poland, the Ukraine, and Russia—that had been overrun and scorched two or three times. European communications and transportation reverted to 19th-century levels: 90 percent of French trucks and 82 percent of French locomotives were out of commission, as were over half the rolling stock in Germany and two-thirds of the Balkan railroads. European coal production was at 40 percent of prewar levels, and more than half the continent's merchant marine no longer existed. Some 23 percent of Europe's farmland was out of production by war's end. Of course, people could be fed with American aid while the rubble was cleared away and utilities restored, but World War II cost Europe more in monetary terms than all its previous wars put together. The war also set in motion the greatest *Völkerwanderung*—movement of peoples—since the barbarian incursions of the late Roman Empire. During the

Nazi onslaught some 27,000,000 people fled or were forced out by war and persecution, and 4,500,000 more were seized for slave labour. When the Red Army advanced westward, millions more fled before it to escape reprisals or Communism. All told, about 60,000,000 people of 55 ethnic groups from 27 countries were uprooted. Finally, 7,000,000 Axis prisoners of war were in Allied hands, along with 8,000,000 Allied prisoners of war liberated from the Axis and 670,000 survivors of Nazi death camps.

The landscape in much of Japan was just as barren, its cities flattened by bombing, its industry and shipping destroyed. Large parts of China had been under foreign occupation for up to 14 years and—like Russia after World War I—still faced several years of destructive civil war. Indeed, World War II had laid waste every major industrial region of the globe except North America. The result was that in 1945–46 the United States accounted for almost half the gross world product of goods and services and enjoyed a technological lead symbolized by, but by no means limited to, its atomic monopoly. On the other hand, Americans as always wanted to demobilize rapidly and return to the private lives and careers interrupted by Pearl Harbor. The Soviet Union, by contrast, was in ruin, but its mighty armies occupied half a dozen states in the heart of Europe, while local Communist parties agitated in Italy and France. The United States and the Soviet Union thus appeared to pose asymmetrical threats to each other.

U.S. VISION OF RECONSTRUCTION

American planners envisioned postwar reconstruction in terms of Wilsonian internationalism but were determined to avoid the mistakes that resulted after 1918 in inflation, tariffs, debts, and reparations. In 1943 the United States sponsored the United Nations Relief and Rehabilitation Administration to distribute food and medicine to the stricken peoples in the war zones. At the Bretton Woods Conference (summer of 1944) the United States presided over the creation of the International Monetary Fund and the World Bank. The dollar was returned to gold convertibility at $35 per ounce and would serve as the world's reserve currency, while the pound, the franc, and other currencies were pegged to the dollar. Such stability would permit the recovery of world trade, while a General Agreement on Tariffs and Trade (ratified in 1948) would ensure low tariffs and prevent a return to policies of economic nationalism. Treasury Secretary Henry Morgenthau tried to entice the Soviets to join the Bretton Woods system, but the U.S.S.R. opted out of the new economic order.

The American universalist program seemingly had more luck in the political realm. Roosevelt was convinced that the League of Nations had been doomed by the absence of the United States and the Soviet Union and thus was anxious to win Soviet participation in the compromises at Yalta. The Big Four powers accordingly drafted the Charter of the United Nations at the San Francisco Conference in April 1945. Roosevelt wisely appointed several leading Republicans to the U.S. delegation, avoiding Wilson's fatal error and securing the Senate ratification of the UN Charter on July 28, 1945, by a vote of 89–2. Like Wilson, Roosevelt and Truman hoped that future quarrels could be settled peacefully in the international body.

THE END OF EAST–WEST COOPERATION

By the time of the Potsdam Conference, Truman was already aware of Soviet unwillingness to permit representative governments and free elections in the countries under its control. The U.S.S.R. compelled the King of Romania to appoint a Communist-dominated government, Tito's Communists assumed control of a coalition with royalists in Yugoslavia, Communists dominated in Hungary and Bulgaria (where a reported 20,000 people were liquidated), and the Red Army extended an invitation to "consult" with 16 underground Polish leaders only to arrest them when they surfaced. As Stalin said to the Yugoslav Communist Milovan Djilas: "In this war each side imposes its system as far as its armies can reach. It cannot be otherwise." On April 23, 1945, Truman scolded Molotov for these violations of the Yalta Accords and, when Molotov protested such undiplomatic conduct, replied, "Carry out your agreements and you won't get talked to like

that." On May 11, three days after the German surrender, Truman abruptly ordered the termination of Lend-Lease aid to the U.S.S.R. Two weeks later Stalin replied in like terms to the envoy Harry Hopkins by way of protesting the suspension of Lend-Lease, Churchill's alleged plan to revive a *cordon sanitaire* on Russia's borders, and other matters. Hopkins, however, assured him of American goodwill and acquiesced in the imprisonment of the Polish leaders and the inclusion of only a few London Poles in the new government. The United States and Britain then recognized the Warsaw regime, assuring Soviet domination of Poland.

The short-lived détente was to be consummated at Potsdam, the last meeting among the Big Three. In the midst of the conference, however, the British electorate rejected Churchill at the polls, and the Labour Party leader Clement Attlee replaced him in the councils of the great. Aside from the Soviet promise to enter the war against Japan and Truman's hint that the United States had developed the atomic bomb, the Potsdam Conference dealt with postwar Europe. The U.S.S.R. was authorized to seize one-third of the German fleet, extract reparations-in-kind from its eastern German occupation zone, and benefit from a complicated formula for delivery of industrial goods from the western zones, 15 percent to be counted as payment for foodstuffs and other products sent from the Soviet zone. The conference provided for peace treaties with the defeated countries once they had "recognized democratic governments" and left their drafting to the Council of Foreign Ministers. Finally, the Potsdam nations agreed to prosecute Germans for war crimes in trials that were conducted at Nürnberg for a year after November 1945. Potsdam, however, left the most divisive issues—the administration of Germany and the configuration of eastern European governments—to future discussion. At the first such meeting, in September, the new U.S. secretary of state, James F. Byrnes, asked why Western newsmen were not allowed into eastern Europe and why governments could not be formed there that were democratic yet still friendly to Russia. Molotov asked on his own account why the U.S.S.R. was excluded from the administration of Japan.

Truman enumerated the principles of American foreign policy in his Navy Day speech of October 27. Its 12 points echoed the Fourteen Points of Woodrow Wilson, including national self-determination; nonrecognition of governments imposed by foreign powers; freedom of the seas, commerce, expression, and religion; and support for the United Nations. Confusion reigned in Washington, however, as to how to implement these principles in league with Moscow. As the political commentator James Reston observed, two schools of thought seemed to compete for the ear of the president. According to the first, Stalin was committed to limitless expansion and would only be encouraged by concessions. According to the second, Stalin was amenable to a

structure of peace but could not be expected to loosen his hold on eastern Europe so long as the United States excluded him from, for instance, Japan. Truman and the State Department drifted between these two poles, searching for a key to unlock the secrets of the Kremlin and hence the appropriate U.S. policy.

Truman's last attempt to win the Soviets to his universalist vision was the Byrnes mission to Moscow in December 1945. There the Soviets promptly accepted an Anglo-American plan for a UN Atomic Energy Agency meant to control the development and use of nuclear power. Stalin also conceded that it might prove possible to make some changes in the Romanian and Bulgarian parliaments, though conceding nothing that might weaken his hold on the satellites. George F. Kennan of the U.S. embassy in Moscow called the concessions "fig leaves of democratic procedure to hide the nakedness of Stalinist dictatorship," while Truman's own dissatisfaction with the results at Moscow and growing domestic criticism of his "coddling" of the Russians were pushing him toward a drastic reformulation of policy.

Why, in fact, did Stalin engage in such a hurried takeover of eastern Europe when it was bound to provoke the United States (magnifying Soviet insecurity) and waste the opportunity for access to U.S. loans and perhaps even atomic secrets? Was not Stalin's policy, in retrospect, simply unwise? Such questions cannot be answered with assurance, since less is known about the postwar Stalinist era

PRIMARY SOURCE: WINSTON CHURCHILL'S SPEECH ON THE IRON CURTAIN

British Prime Minister Winston Churchill came to the United States in 1946 and on March 5 at Westminster College in Fulton, Missouri, delivered an address on East-West relations and the prospects for maintaining peace. A portion of the address is reprinted below. Vital Speeches of the Day, New York, March 15, 1946: "Alliance of English-Speaking People."

A shadow has fallen upon the scenes so lately lighted by the Allied victory. Nobody knows what Soviet Russia and its Communist international organization intends to do in the immediate future, or what are the limits, if any, to their expansive and proselytizing tendencies . . .

We understand the Russians need to be secure on her western frontiers from all renewal of German aggression. We welcome her to her rightful place among the leading nations of the world. Above all we welcome constant, frequent, and growing contacts between the Russian people and our own people on both sides of the Atlantic. It is my duty, however, to place before you certain facts about the present position in Europe—I am sure I do not wish to, but it is my duty, I feel, to present them to you.

From Stettin in the Baltic to Trieste in the Adriatic, an iron curtain has descended across the Continent. Behind that line lie all the capitals of the ancient states of central and eastern Europe. Warsaw, Berlin, Prague, Vienna, Budapest, Belgrade, Bucharest, and Sofia, all these famous cities and the populations around them lie in the Soviet sphere and all are subject in one form or another, not only to Soviet influence but to a very high and increasing measure of control from Moscow. Athens alone, with its immortal glories, is free to decide its future at an election under British, American, and French observation. The Russian-dominated Polish government has been encouraged to make enormous and wrongful inroads upon Germany, and mass expulsions of millions of Germans on a scale grievous and undreamed of are now taking place.

The Communist parties, which were very small in all these Eastern states of Europe, have been raised to preeminence and power far beyond their numbers and are seeking everywhere to obtain totalitarian control. Police governments are prevailing in nearly every case, and so far, except in Czechoslovakia, there is no true democracy. Turkey and Persia are both profoundly alarmed and disturbed at the claims which are made upon them and at the pressure being exerted by the Moscow government . . .

Whatever conclusions may be drawn from these facts—and facts they are—this is certainly not the liberated Europe we fought to build up. Nor is it one which contains the essentials of permanent peace . . . .

On the other hand I repulse the idea that a new war is inevitable; still more that it is imminent. It is because I am so sure that our fortunes are in our own hands and that we hold the power to save the future that I feel the duty to speak out now that I have an occasion to do so. I do not believe that Soviet Russia desires war. What they desire is the fruits of war and the indefinite expansion of their power and doctrines. But what we have to consider here today, while time remains, is the permanent prevention of war and the establishment of conditions of freedom and democracy as rapidly as possible in all countries . . .

(1945–53) than any other in Soviet history, but the most tempting clue is again to be found in Stalin's domestic calculations. If the Soviet Union were to recover from the war, not to mention compete with the mighty United States, the population would have to be spurred to even greater efforts, which meant intensifying the campaign against alleged foreign threats. What was more, the Soviets had only recently regained control of populations that had had contact with foreigners and, in some cases, collaborated with the invaders. Ukrainians in particular had tried to establish an autonomous status under the Nazis, and they persisted in guerrilla activity against the Soviets until 1947. If Soviet citizens were allowed widespread contact with foreigners through economic cooperation, international institutions, and cultural exchanges, loyalty to the Communist regime might be weakened. Firm control of his eastern European neighbours helped assure Stalin of firm control at home. Indeed, he now ordered the utter isolation of Soviet life to the point that returning prisoners of war were interned lest they "infect" their neighbours with notions of the outside world. Perhaps Stalin did not really fear an attack from the "imperialists" or consider a Soviet invasion of western Europe, but neither could he welcome the Americans and British as genuine comrades in peace without undermining the ideology and the emergency that justified his own iron rule.

A swift return to Communist orthodoxy accompanied the clampdown on foreign contacts. During the war the U.S.S.R.'s leading economist, Evgeny Varga of the Institute of World Economy and World Politics, argued that government controls in the United States had moderated the influence of monopolies, permitting both dynamic growth and a mellower foreign policy. The U.S.S.R. might therefore benefit from East–West cooperation and prevent the division of the world into economic blocs. Stalin appeared to tolerate this nontraditionalist view as long as large loans from the United States and the World Bank were a possibility. But the suspension of Lend-Lease, opposition to a Soviet loan in the State Department, and Stalin's renewed rejection of consumerism doomed these moderate views on the world economy.

The new Five-Year Plan, announced at the start of 1946, called for continued concentration on heavy industry and military technology. The war and victory, said Stalin, had justified his harsh policies of the 1930s, and he called on Soviet scientists to overtake and surpass Western science. Soviet economists perforce embraced the traditional view that Western economies were about to enter a new period of inflation and unemployment that would increase the imperialist pressure for war. Andrey Zhdanov, the Communist leader of Leningrad, was a bellwether. In 1945 he wanted to reward the Soviet people with consumer goods for their wartime sacrifices; in early 1947 he espoused the theory of the "two camps," the peace-loving, progressive camp led by the Soviet Union and the militaristic, reactionary camp led by the United States.

American confusion came to an end after Feb. 9, 1946, when Stalin's great speech inaugurating the Five-Year Plan reiterated clearly his implacable hostility to the West. Kennan responded with his famous "Long Telegram" from Moscow (February 22), which for years to come served as a primer on Soviet behaviour for many in Washington. The Kremlin's "neurotic view of world affairs," he wrote, was the product of centuries of Russian isolation and insecurity vis-à-vis the more advanced West. The Soviets, like the tsars, viewed the influx of Western ideas as the greatest threat to their continued power, and they clung to Marxist ideology as a cover for their disregard for "every single ethical value in their methods and tactics." The U.S.S.R. was not Nazi Germany—it would not seek war and was averse to risk taking—but it would employ every means of subverting, dividing, and undermining the West through the actions of Communists and fellow travelers. Kennan's advice was to expect nothing from negotiations but to remain confident and healthy, lest the United States become like those with whom it was contending.

Kennan's analysis implied several important conclusions: that the Wilsonian vision inherited from Roosevelt was fruitless; that the United States must take the lead in organizing the Western world; and that the Truman administration must prevent a renewal of isolationism and persuade the American people to shoulder their new responsibilities. Churchill, though out of office, aided this agenda when he warned the American people (with Truman's confidential endorsement) from Fulton, Mo., on March 5, 1946, that an "iron curtain" had descended across the European continent.

CHAPTER 11

THE FINAL SOLUTION

WANNSEE CONFERENCE

At a meeting of Nazi officials on Jan. 20, 1942, in the Berlin suburb of Wannsee, plans for the "final solution" (*Endlösung*) to the so-called "Jewish question" (*Judenfrage*) were adopted. On July 31, 1941, Nazi leader Reichsmarschall Hermann Göring had issued orders to Reinhard Heydrich, SS (Nazi paramilitary corps) leader and Gestapo (Secret Police) chief, to prepare a comprehensive plan for this "final solution." The Wannsee Conference, held six months later, was attended by 15 Nazi senior bureaucrats led by Heydrich and including Adolf Eichmann, chief of Jewish affairs for the Reich Central Security Office.

The conference marked a turning point in Nazi policy toward the Jews. An earlier idea, to deport all of Europe's Jews to the island of Madagascar, off of Africa, was abandoned as impractical in wartime. Instead, the newly planned final solution would entail rounding up all Jews throughout Europe, transporting them eastward, and organizing them into labour gangs. The work and living conditions would be sufficiently hard as to fell large numbers by "natural diminution." Those that survived would be "treated accordingly."

The men seated at the table were among the elite of the Reich. More than half of them held doctorates from German universities. They were well informed about the policy toward

Jews. Each understood that the cooperation of his agency was vital if such an ambitious, unprecedented policy was to succeed.

Among the agencies represented were the Department of Justice, the Foreign Ministry, the Gestapo, the SS, the Race and Resettlement Office, and the office in charge of distributing Jewish property. (Although Judaism is a religion, the Nazis viewed it as a racial identification.) Also at the meeting was a representative of the General Government, the Polish occupation administration, whose territory included more than 2 million Jews. The head of Heydrich's office for Jewish affairs, Adolf Eichmann, prepared the conference notes.

Heydrich himself introduced the agenda:

> *Another possible solution of the [Jewish] problem has now taken the place of emigration—i.e., evacuation of the Jews to the east . . . Such activities are, however, to be considered as provisional actions, but practical experience is already being collected which is of greatest importance in relation to the future final solution of the Jewish problem.*

The men needed little explanation. They understood that "evacuation to the east" was a euphemism for concentration camps and that the "final solution" was to be the systematic murder of Europe's Jews, which is now known as the Holocaust. The final protocol of the Wannsee Conference never explicitly mentioned extermination, but, within a few months after the meeting, the Nazis installed the first poison-gas chambers in Poland in what came to be called extermination camps. Responsibility for the entire project was put in the hands of Heinrich Himmler and his SS and Gestapo.

THE EXTERMINATION CAMPS

In early 1942 the Nazis built extermination camps at Treblinka, Sobibor, and Belzec in Poland. The death camps were to be the essential instrument of the "final solution." The *Einsatzgruppen* had traveled to kill their victims. With the extermination camps, the process was reversed. The victims traveled by train, often in cattle cars, to their killers. The extermination camps became factories producing corpses, effectively and efficiently, at minimal physical and psychological cost to German personnel. Assisted by Ukrainian and Latvian collaborators and prisoners of war, a few Germans could kill tens of thousands of prisoners each month. At Chelmno, the first of the extermination camps, the Nazis used mobile gas vans. Elsewhere, they built permanent gas chambers linked to the crematoria where bodies were burned. Carbon monoxide was the gas of choice at most camps. Zyklon-B, an especially lethal killing agent, was employed primarily at Auschwitz and later at other camps.

Crushed by German force, Warsaw ghetto Jews of all ages surrender following their uprising of April–May 1943. Keystone/Hulton Archive/Getty Images

Auschwitz, perhaps the most notorious and lethal of the concentration camps, was actually three camps in one: a prison camp (Auschwitz I), an extermination camp (Auschwitz II–Birkenau), and a slave-labour camp (Auschwitz III–Buna-Monowitz). Upon arrival, Jewish prisoners faced what was called a *Selektion*. A German doctor presided over the selection of pregnant women, young children, the elderly, handicapped, sick, and infirm for immediate death in the gas chambers. As necessary, the Germans selected able-bodied prisoners for forced labour in the factories adjacent to Auschwitz where one German company, IG Farben, invested 700,000 million Reichsmarks in 1942 alone to take advantage of forced labour. Deprived of adequate food, shelter, clothing, and medical care, these prisoners were literally worked to death. Periodically, they would face another *Selektion*. The Nazis would transfer those unable to work to the gas chambers of Birkenau.

While the death camps at Auschwitz and Majdanek used inmates for slave labour to support the German war effort, the extermination camps at Belzec, Treblinka, and Sobibor had one task alone: killing. At Treblinka, a staff of 120, of whom only 30 were SS (the Nazi paramilitary corps), killed some 750,000 to 900,000 Jews during the camp's 17 months of operation. At Belzec, German records detail a staff of 104, including about 20 SS, who killed some 600,000 Jews in less than 10 months. At Sobibor, they murdered about 250,000. These camps began operation during the spring and summer of 1942, when the ghettos of German-occupied Poland were filled with Jews. Once they had completed their missions—murder by gassing, or "resettlement in the east," to use the language of the Wannsee protocols— the Nazis closed the camps. There were six extermination camps, all in German-occupied Poland, among the thousands of concentration and slave-labour camps throughout German-occupied Europe.

The impact of the Holocaust varied from region to region, and from year to year in the 21 countries that were directly affected. Nowhere was the Holocaust more intense and sudden than in Hungary. What took place over several years in Germany occurred over 16 weeks in Hungary. Entering the war as a German ally, Hungary had persecuted its Jews but not permitted their deportation. After Germany invaded Hungary on March 19, 1944, this situation changed dramatically. By mid-April the Nazis had confined Jews to ghettos. On May 15, deportations began, and over the next 55 days, the Nazis deported some 438,000 Jews from Hungary to Auschwitz on 147 trains.

Policies differed widely among Germany's Balkan allies. In Romania it was primarily the Romanians themselves who slaughtered the country's Jews. Toward the end of the war, however, when the defeat of Germany was all but certain, the Romanian government found more value in living Jews who could be held for ransom or used as leverage with the West. Bulgaria permitted the deportation of Jews from neighbouring Thrace and Macedonia, but government leaders faced stiff opposition to the deportation of native Bulgarian Jews.

German-occupied Denmark rescued most of its own Jews by spiriting them to Sweden by sea in October 1943. This was possible partly because the German presence in Denmark was relatively small. Moreover, while anti-Semitism in the general population of many other countries led to collaboration with the Germans, Jews were an integrated part of Danish culture. Under these unique circumstances, Danish humanitarianism flourished.

In France, Jews under Fascist Italian occupation in the southeast fared better than the Jews of Vichy France, where collaborationist French authorities and police provided essential support to the understaffed German forces. The Jews in those parts of France under direct German occupation fared the worst. Although allied with Germany, the Italians did not participate in the Holocaust until Germany occupied northern Italy after the overthrow of the Fascist leader, Benito Mussolini.

Throughout German-occupied territory the situation of Jews was desperate. They had meagre resources and few allies and faced impossible choices. A few people came to their rescue, often at the risk of their own lives. Swedish diplomat Raoul Wallenberg arrived in Budapest on July 9, 1944, in an effort to save Hungary's sole remaining Jewish community. Over the next six months, he worked with other neutral diplomats, the Vatican, and Jews themselves to prevent the deportation of these last Jews. Elsewhere, Le Chambon-sur-Lignon, a French Huguenot village, became a haven for 5,000 Jews. In Poland, where it was illegal to aid Jews and where such action was punishable by death, the Zegota (Council for Aid to Jews) rescued a similar number of Jewish men, women, and children. Financed by the Polish government in exile and involving a wide range of clandestine political organizations, the Zegota provided hiding places, financial support, and forged identity documents.

Some Germans, even some Nazis, dissented from the murder of the Jews and came to their aid. The most famous was Oskar Schindler, a Nazi businessman, who had set up operations using involuntary labour in German-occupied Poland in order to profit from the war. Eventually, he moved to protect his Jewish workers from deportation to extermination camps. In all occupied countries, there were individuals who came to the rescue of Jews, offering a place to hide, some food,

or shelter for days, weeks, or even for the duration of the war. Most of the rescuers did not see their actions as heroic but felt bound to the Jews by a common sense of humanity. Israel later recognized rescuers with honorary citizenship and commemoration at Yad Vashem, Israel's memorial to the Holocaust.

JEWISH RESISTANCE

It is often asked why Jews did not make greater attempts at resistance. Principally they had no access to arms and were surrounded by native anti-Semitic populations who collaborated with the Nazis or condoned the elimination of the Jews. In essence the Jews stood alone against a German war machine zealously determined to carry out the "final solution." Moreover, the Nazis went to great lengths to disguise their ultimate plans. Because of the German policy of collective reprisal, Jews in the ghettos often hesitated to resist. This changed when the Germans ordered the final liquidation of the ghettos, and residents recognized the imminence of their death.

Jews resisted in the forests, in the ghettos, and even in the death camps. They fought alone and alongside resistance groups in France, Yugoslavia, and Russia. As a rule, full-scale uprisings occurred only at the end, when Jews realized the inevitability of impending death. On April 19, 1943, nine months after the massive deportations of Warsaw's Jews to Treblinka had begun, the Jewish resistance, led by 24-year-old

IN FOCUS: WHY WASN'T AUSCHWITZ BOMBED?

The question "Why wasn't Auschwitz bombed?" is not only historical. It is also a moral question emblematic of the Allied response to the plight of the Jews during the Holocaust.

Yet bombing a concentration camp filled with innocent, unjustly imprisoned civilians also posed a moral dilemma for the Allies. To be willing to sacrifice innocent civilians, one would have had to perceive accurately conditions in the camp and to presume that interrupting the killing process would be worth the loss of life in Allied bombings. In short, one would have had to know that those in the camps were about to die. Such information was not available until the spring of 1944.

On April 10, 1944, two men escaped from Auschwitz: Rudolph Vrba and Alfred Wetzler. They made contact with Slovak resistance forces and produced a substantive report on the extermination camp at Auschwitz-Birkenau. In great detail, they documented the killing process. Their report, replete with maps and other specific details, was forwarded to Western intelligence officials along with an urgent request to bomb the camps. Part of the report, forwarded to the U.S. government's War Refugee Board

During German occupation, Jewish men and women—like those seen here at the extermination camp in Auschwitz, Poland—were forced to wear yellow stars to identify themselves as being Jewish.
Imagno/Hulton Archive/Getty Images

by Roswell McClelland, the board's representative in Switzerland, arrived in Washington on July 8 and July 16, 1944. While the complete report, together with maps, did not arrive in the United States until October, U.S. officials could have received the complete report earlier if they had taken a more urgent interest in it.

In August, U.S. Assistant Secretary of War John J. McCloy wrote to Leon Kubowitzki of the World Jewish Congress, noting that the War Refugee Board had asked if it was possible to bomb Auschwitz. McCloy responded:

"After a study it became apparent that such an operation could be executed only by the diversion of considerable air support essential to the success of our forces now engaged in decisive operations elsewhere and would in any case be of such doubtful efficacy that it would not warrant the use of our resources. There has been considerable opinion to the effect that such an effort, even if practicable, might provoke even more vindictive action by the Germans."

We know that, in the end, the pessimists won. They argued that nothing could be done, and nothing was done. The proposals of the optimists, those who argued that something could be done, were not even considered. Given what happened at Auschwitz-Birkenau during the summer of 1944, many have seen the failure to bomb as a symbol of indifference. Inaction helped the Germans achieve their goals and left the victims with little power to defend themselves. The Allies did not even offer bombing as a gesture of protest.

Mordecai Anielewicz, mounted the Warsaw Ghetto Uprising. In Vilna partisan leader Abba Kovner, recognizing the full intent of Nazi policy toward the Jews, called for resistance in December 1941 and organized an armed force that fought the Germans in September 1943. In March of that year, a resistance group led by Willem Arondeus, a homosexual artist and author, bombed a population registry in Amsterdam to destroy the records of Jews and others sought by the Nazis. At Treblinka and Sobibor uprisings occurred just as the extermination camps were being dismantled and their remaining prisoners were soon to be killed. This was also true at Auschwitz, where the *Sonderkommando* ("Special Commando"), the prisoner unit that worked in the vicinity of the gas chambers, destroyed a crematorium just as the killing was coming to an end in 1944.

By the winter of 1944–45, with Allied armies closing in, desperate SS officials tried frantically to evacuate the camps and conceal what had taken place. They wanted no eyewitnesses remaining. Prisoners were moved westward, forced to march toward the heartland of Germany. There were over 50 different marches from Nazi concentration and extermination camps during this final winter of Nazi domination, some covering hundreds of miles. The prisoners were given little or no food and water, and almost no time to rest or take care of bodily needs. Those who paused or fell behind were shot. In January 1945, just hours before the Red Army arrived at Auschwitz, the Nazis marched

some 60,000 prisoners to Wodzisław and put them on freight trains to the camps at Bergen-Belsen, Gross-Rosen, Buchenwald, Dachau, and Mauthausen. Nearly one in four died en route.

In April and May of 1945, American and British forces en route to military targets entered the concentration camps in the west and caught a glimpse of what had occurred. Even though tens of thousands of prisoners had perished, these camps were far from the most deadly. Still, even for the battle-weary soldiers who thought they had already seen the worst, the sights and smells and the emaciated survivors they encountered left an indelible impression. At Dachau they came upon 28 railway cars stuffed with dead bodies. Conditions were so horrendous at Bergen-Belsen that some 28,000 inmates died after they were freed, and the entire camp had to be burned to prevent the spread of typhus. Allied soldiers had to perform tasks for which they were ill-trained: to heal the sick, comfort the bereaved, and bury the dead. As for the victims, liberation was not a moment of exultation. Viktor Frankl, a survivor of Auschwitz, recalled, "Everything was unreal. Unlikely as in a dream. Only later—and for some it was very much later or never—was liberation actually liberating."

The Allies, who had early and accurate information on the murder of the Jews, made no special military efforts to rescue them or to bomb the camps or the railroad tracks leading to them. They felt that only after victory could something be done about the Jewish situation. Warnings were issued, condemnations

IN FOCUS: WARSAW GHETTO UPRISING

On April 19, 1943, Polish Jews under Nazi occupation in Warsaw began an armed resistance to being deported to the Treblinka extermination camp. The revolt was crushed four weeks later, on May 16.

As part of Adolf Hitler's "final solution" for ridding Europe of Jews, the Nazis had established ghettos in areas under German control to confine Jews until they could be executed. The Warsaw ghetto, enclosed at first with barbed wire but later with a brick wall 10 feet (3 m) high and 11 miles (18 km) long, comprised the old Jewish quarter of Warsaw. The Nazis herded Jews from surrounding areas into this district until by the summer of 1942 nearly 500,000 of them lived within its 840 acres (340 hectares). Many had no housing at all, and those who did were crowded in at about nine people per room. Starvation and disease (especially typhus) killed thousands each month.

Beginning July 22, 1942, transfers to the death camp at Treblinka began at a rate of more than 5,000 Jews per day. Between July and September 1942, the Nazis shipped about 265,000 Jews from Warsaw to Treblinka. Only some 55,000 remained in the ghetto. As the deportations continued, despair gave way to a determination to resist. A newly formed group, the Jewish Fighting Organization (Żydowska Organizacja Bojowa; ŻOB), slowly took effective control of the ghetto.

On Jan. 9, 1943, Heinrich Himmler, the chief of the SS, visited the Warsaw ghetto. He ordered the deportation of another 8,000 Jews. The January deportations caught the Jews by surprise, and ghetto residents thought that the end had come. Making use of the many hiding places that they had created since April, Jews did not report as ordered. The resistance sprang into action. Jewish fighters could strike quickly, then escape across the rooftops. German troops, on the other hand, moved cautiously and would not go down to cellars. When the German deportation effort ended within a few days, Jews interpreted this as a victory. From then on, the resistance dominated the ghetto. The resistance fortified hideouts and strengthened fighting units in preparation for the next battle.

Having withdrawn, the Germans suspended deportations until April 19, when Himmler launched a special operation to clear the ghetto in honour of Adolf Hitler's birthday, April 20. April 19 was also the first day of Passover, the Jewish holy days celebrating freedom from slavery in Egypt. Before dawn, 2,000 SS men and German army troops moved into the area with tanks, rapid-fire artillery, and ammunition trailers. While most remaining Jews hid in bunkers, by pre-arrangement, the ŻOB and a few independent bands of Jewish guerrillas, in all some 1,500 strong, opened fire with their motley weaponry—pistols, a few rifles, one machine gun, and homemade bombs destroying a number of tanks, killing German troops, and holding off reinforcements trying to enter the ghetto. The Germans withdrew in the evening. The next day the fighting resumed and casualties mounted. The Germans used gas, police dogs, and flamethrowers in an effort to rout the Jews from their bunkers, leaving the city under a pall of smoke for days. On the third day the Germans' tactics shifted. They no longer entered the ghetto in large groups but roamed it in small bands. Then they made a decision to burn the entire ghetto.

The Germans had planned to liquidate the ghetto in three days. The Jews held out for nearly a month. Resistance fighters succeeded in hiding in the sewers, even though the Germans tried first to flood them and then force them out with smoke bombs. Not until May 8 did the Nazis manage to take *the ŻOB headquarters bunker. Civilians hiding there surrendered, but many of the surviving ŻOB fighters took their own lives to avoid being captured alive; so died Mordecai Anielewicz, the charismatic young commander of the underground army. The one-sided battle continued until May 16, becoming sporadic as Jewish ammunition was exhausted. Total casualty figures for the uprising are uncertain, but the Germans likely lost several hundred soldiers during the 28 days that it took them to kill or deport over 40,000 Jews. SS Major General Jürgen Stroop supervised the coup de grace: the dynamiting of the Great Synagogue of Warsaw. Thereupon he wrote his report: "The Warsaw Ghetto Is No More."*

were made, plans proceeded to try the guilty after the war, but no concrete action was undertaken specifically to halt the genocide. An internal memo to U.S. Secretary of the Treasury Henry Morgenthau, Jr., from his general counsel in January 1944 characterized U.S. State Department policy as "acquiescence to the murder of the European Jews." In response Morgenthau helped spur the creation of the War Refugee Board, which made a late and limited effort to rescue endangered Jews, mainly through diplomacy and subterfuge.

WORLD WAR II
IN RETROSPECT

World War II and Hitler's attempts to dominate all of Europe are inextricably linked with the evils visited upon the Jews during the Holocaust. Today the Holocaust is viewed as the emblematic manifestation of absolute evil. Its revelation of the depths of human nature and the power of malevolent social and governmental structures has made it an essential topic of ethical discourse in fields

as diverse as law, medicine, religion, government, and the military.

Many survivors report they heard a final plea from those who were killed: "Remember! Do not let the world forget."

Aside from the terrible human costs World War II exacted, from the extermination of the Jews and the interment of the Japanese in America to the dropping of the atomic bomb, it has had a lasting geopolitical impact as well, resulting in the extension of the Soviet Union's power to nations of eastern Europe, enabling a communist movement eventually to achieve power in China, and marking the decisive shift of power in the world away from the states of western Europe and toward the United States and the Soviet Union.

As Americans looked forward at the end of the war, the notes sounded were those of rebuilding and moving ahead. Reflected in everything from the GI Bill to the Marshall Plan to the uptempo music of Big Band Swing, the Allied victory created a palpable optimism, a sense that by winning the war, we had made the world a better place.

Appendix: Tables

GERMAN AIRCRAFT PRODUCTION BY YEAR		
YEAR	COMBAT TYPES	OTHER TYPES
1933	0	368
1934	840	1,128
1935	1,823	1,360
1936	2,530	2,582
1937	2,651	2,955
1938	3,350	1,885
1939	4,733	3,562

ALLIED AIR STRENGTH, SEPTEMBER 1939			
AIRCRAFT	BRITISH	FRENCH	POLISH
BOMBERS	536	463	200
FIGHTERS	608	634	300
RECONNAISSANCE	96	444	—
COASTAL COMMAND	216	—	—
FLEET AIR ARM	204	194	—

WORLD WAR II CASUALTIES					
COUNTRY	MILITARY KILLED, DIED OF WOUNDS, OR IN PRISON[1]	MILITARY WOUNDED	MILITARY PRISONERS OR MISSING[2]	CIVILIAN DEATHS DUE TO WAR	ESTIMATED TOTAL DEATHS
ALLIED POWERS					
BELGIUM	12,000	—	—	76,000	88,000
BRAZIL	943	4,222	—	—	1,000
BRITISH COMMON-WEALTH	373,372	475,047	251,724[3]	92,673	466,000
AUSTRALIA	23,365	39,803	32,393	—	24,000
CANADA	37,476	53,174	10,888	—	38,000
INDIA	24,338	64,354	91,243	—	—
NEW ZEALAND	10,033	19,314	10,582	—	10,000
SOUTH AFRICA	6,840	14,363	16,430	—	7,000
UNITED KINGDOM	264,443	277,077	213,919	92,673[4]	357,000
COLONIES	6,877	6,972	22,323	—	7,000
CHINA[5]	1,310,224	1,752,951	115,248	—	—
CZECH-OSLOVAKIA[6]	10,000	—	—	215,000	225,000
DENMARK	1,800	—	—	2,000[7]	4,000
FRANCE[8]	213,324	400,000	—	350,000	563,000
GREECE[9]	88,300	—	—	325,000	413,000
NETHERLANDS	7,900	2,860	—	200,000	208,000
NORWAY	3,000	—	—	7,000	10,000
POLAND[10]	123,178	236,606	420,760	5,675,000	5,800,000
PHILIPPINES	27,000	—	—	91,000	118,000
UNITED STATES[11]	292,131	671,801	139,709	6,000	298,000

Country	Military killed, died of wounds, or in prison[1]	Military wounded	Military prisoners or missing[2]	Civilian deaths due to war	Estimated total deaths
U.S.S.R.[12]	11,000,000	—	—	7,000,000	18,000,000
Yugoslavia	305,000	425,000	—	1,200,000	1,505,000
Axis Powers					
Bulgaria[13]	10,000	—	—	10,000	20,000
Finland	82,000	50,000	—	2,000	84,000
Germany[14]	3,500,000	5,000,000	3,400,000	780,000	4,200,000
Hungary[13]	200,000	—	170,000	290,000	490,000
Italy[15]	242,232	66,000	350,000	152,941	395,000
Japan	1,300,000[16]	4,000,000	810,000	672,000	1,972,000
Romania[13]	300,000	—	100,000	200,000	500,000

1 Figures for deaths, insofar as possible, exclude those who died of natural causes or were suicides. **2** As far as possible the figures in this column exclude those who died in captivity. **3** Figures for all Commonwealth nations include those still missing in 1946, some of whom may be presumed dead. **4** This figure comprises 60,595 killed in aerial bombardment, 30,248 in the merchant marine service, 624 in women's auxiliary services, and 1,206 in the Home Guard. **5** The figures for China comprise casualties of the Chinese Nationalist forces during 1937–45, as reported in 1946, and do not include figures for local armies and Communists. Estimates of 2,200,000 military dead and 22,000,000 civilian deaths appear in some compilations but are of doubtful accuracy. **6** Czech military figures include only those who fought on the Allied side, not Sudeten Germans and others who served in the German Army. **7** Includes merchant marine personnel who served with Allies. **8** French military casualties include those dead from all causes in the campaign of 1939–40, those of Free French, of rearmed French units that fought with Allies during 1942–45, and of French units that fought with Axis forces in Syria and North Africa during 1941–42 (1,200 dead). **9** These figures released in 1946 are possibly too high. Merchant seamen are included with military dead. **10** Military figures drawn from statement released by Polish government in 1946 and include casualties in the campaign of 1939, those of the underground, of Polish forces serving with British and Soviet armies, and those incurred in the Warsaw uprising. Civilian casualty figures, which include 3,200,000 Jews, are based on this statement as modified by the calculations of population experts. **11** Military figures include those of Army Ground and Air Forces, and those of the Navy, Marines, and Coast Guard. There were an additional 115,187 deaths of U.S. servicemen from non-battle causes. Civilians listed in 1946 as dead or missing include 5,638 of the merchant marine service. **12** Available estimates of

Soviet casualties vary widely. A Soviet officer who served with the high command in Berlin and left the Soviet service in 1949 placed total military losses at 13,600,000–8,500,000 dead or missing in battle; 2,600,000 dead in prison camps; 2,500,000 died of wounds—and estimated civilian casualties at 7,000,000. These figures have been widely accepted in Germany, but most U.S. compilations, based on Soviet announcements, list 6,000,000 to 7,500,000 battle deaths. Calculations made on the basis of population distribution by age and sex in the 1959 U.S.S.R. census give some credence to the higher figures, for they seem to indicate losses of from 15,000,000 to 20,000,000 males of military age in World War II. The figures used here are a compromise estimate, not intended to obscure the fact that Soviet casualties are, in reality, unknown in the West. **13** Estimates based on fragmentary data. **14** Military estimates include men from outside Germany who served with the German armed forces and are based on the assumption that about 1,000,000 of the 1,250,000 men still listed as missing in Soviet territory in 1955 were dead. In addition, perhaps 250,000 military personnel died of natural causes, committed suicide, or were executed. Civilian figures are for Germany and Austria only, and they do not include an estimated 2,384,000 German deaths during 1944-46 resulting from Soviet invasion and forced transfers of population in the eastern provinces given to Poland after the war. **15** Figures for dead include those listed as still missing in compilation made by the Italian government in 1952 (131,419 military personnel and 3,651 civilians), but not 49,144 military deaths from natural causes or suicide. Known dead from enemy action amounted to 110,823, making a total of 159,957 military deaths from all causes if the missing are not included. Of this number, 92,767 occurred before the 1943 Armistice, 67,190 afterward. **16** Based on an estimate of 1,600,000 total military deaths on the assumption that about half of those listed as missing in Soviet territory in 1949 were dead. About 300,000 of these probably resulted from causes not related to battle.

abdication A formal resignation of powers.

amalgam A mixture.

amphibious Occurring on both land and water.

anodyne Something that relieves stress or pain.

appellation A name or title.

archipelago A group of many islands.

armistice A cease-fire so opponents can discuss peace terms.

atoll An island formed from a coral reef with a lagoon in the center.

attrition The weakening of resistance.

audacious Extremely daring.

authoritarian Term for a form of government in which the ruler is an absolute dictator.

autonomous Having political independence.

battalion A large body of troops.

beleaguered Beset by difficulty.

blackshirt A member of the Italian Fascist Party before and during World War II, known for wearing black shirts as part of their uniform.

Bolshevik A radical political group with extreme socialist views; a Communist.

bridgehead A defensive post at the end of a bridge closest to the enemy.

calamitous Disastrous.

capitalist One who supports an economic system with private ownership of capital.

capitulate Surrender under certain terms.

cessation A bringing to a stop.

clandestine Done in secret to conceal an illicit purpose.

collectivization The creating of large, state-run farms rather than individual holdings.

compatriot A person from one's own country.

convoy A group of land vehicles traveling together.

corporatism Control of the state by large interest groups.

culminate To reach a final, climactic conclusion.

despoliation Stripping and taking by force.

détente An easing of tension between rivals by negotiations.

directorate A group of people chosen to govern the affairs of a department.

driblet A small quantity.

embargo A government order that prevents certain or all trade with a foreign nation.

emissary Someone sent to represent someone else.

enervate To lessen the strength of.

enigmatic Mysterious, inexplicable.

eradicate To remove entirely.

euphemism An inoffensive expression that is substituted for one that is distasteful or offensive.

exacerbate To increase the severity of something.

fait accompli An established fact.

Fascism A governmental system led by a dictator having complete power.

Fifth Republic The fifth and current republican constitution of France, which was introduced in 1958.

fissionable Capable of undergoing nuclear fission.

flotilla A group of small naval vessels.

formidable Impressive in strength.

garrison Troops stationed to a fortified military post.

gird To prepare for action.

guerrilla A method of armed force that fights with sabotage and harassment.

ignominious Disgraceful.

imbroglio An intricate or complicated situation.

imperialism A policy of exerting rule over foreign countries for territorial gain.

impregnable Strong enough to withstand attack.

impunity Exemption from punishment.

infantry An army unit of soldiers fighting on foot.

inimical Unfriendly.

interdiction The bombardment of enemy communication lines to delay their advance.

isolationism A national policy of nonparticipation with other nations.

isthmus A narrow strip of land surrounded by water that connects to larger pieces of land.

littoral Pertaining to a coastal region.

napalm A highly flammable explosive in the form of gelled gasoline.

nationalist Advocate of a country's national independence or strong national government.

nepotism Favoritism based on family relationships.

nonbelligerent Not participating in a conflict.

nullify To declare invalid.

orthodoxy A belief that agrees with traditional or conventional standards.

ostensible Seeming a certain way outwardly.

pacifism The belief that violence is not justifiable.

parity Equality.

piecemeal Bit by bit.

plebiscite A vote by the electorate to determine public opinion.

plenipotentiary A diplomat authorized to represent his government.

polarization A sharp division of people into opposing groups.

precipitate To bring about abruptly.

proselytize To convert or try to convert someone to join another faith or doctrine.

protectorate A less powerful state that is partially controlled by a stronger state but is still autonomous in internal affairs.

protocol Code of correct conduct.

proviso A clause in a contract (a condition).

putsch A plotted revolt or attempt to overthrow the government.

reactor pile Nuclear reactor.

reconnaissance Exploration with the purpose of gaining new information.

reprisal An act of retaliation against an enemy.

revisionism The advocacy of the revision of an accepted and long-standing doctrine.

rudimentary Minimal.

salient An outwardly projecting part of a fortification, trench system, or line of defense.

salvo Simultaneous discharge of artillery or firearms.

scapegoat One who bears the blame for others.

scuttled Sunk by means of cutting holes in the bottom of a ship.

sedition The inciting of resistance to the government.

socialism A political theory that supports state ownership of capital.

sortie A sudden attack by an army surrounded by its enemy.

squadron A small unit or formation of troops.

subjugate Bring under complete control by a conquering power.

tandem One following behind the other, as in a line.

tonnage A tax imposed on ships that enter the U.S.

totalitarian A term for a form of government that exercises control over freedom, will, or thought.

tribunal A judicial assembly.

unmitigated Not diminished in intensity.

untenable Unable to defend.

xenophobia A fear or dislike of strangers or foreigners.

BIBLIOGRAPHY

The literature on World War II is vast and ever-growing. Nonfiction books range from popular overviews to multivolume official histories to scholarly analyses of single campaigns or social issues. In addition, numerous motion-picture and television documentaries are available as video recordings.

Surveys

Good histories of the war include Williamson Murray and Allan R. Millett, *A War to Be Won: Fighting the Second World War* (2000); Gerhard L. Weinberg, *A World At Arms: A Global History of World War II* (1994); John Keegan, *The Second World War* (1990, reissued 1997); Mark Calvocoressi, Guy Wint, and John Pritchard, *Total War*, rev. 2nd ed., 2 vol. (1995); and B.H. Liddell Hart, *History of the Second World War* (1970, reissued 1999).

Documentaries

The classic documentary, organized around original film footage and interviews with key individuals still living at the time, is the massive 32-hour series *The World at War* (1974), produced by Jeremy Isaacs and narrated by Sir Laurence Olivier for Thames Television, in cooperation with the Imperial War Museum. American perspectives are given in *World War II with Walter Cronkite*, a multipart series first broadcast by CBS-TV in 1982; and *America Goes to War* (1998), a series on the "home front" produced by Questar Inc. and narrated by another CBS journalist, Eric Sevareid. In addition, the Arts and Entertainment Television Network has produced outstanding biographical documentaries of World War II personalities, including every major political figure and numerous military leaders such as Douglas MacArthur, Bernard Montgomery, Chester Nimitz, George Patton, and Georgy Zhukov.

Scholarly Views

For the origins of the war, see Joachim Remak, *The Origins of the Second World War* (1976); Donald Cameron Watt, *How War Came: The Immediate Origins of the Second World War, 1938–1939* (1989); and Akira Iriye, *The Origins of the Second World War in Asia and the Pacific* (1987).

For specific campaigns of the European theatre, see Richard Hough and Denis Richards, *The Battle of Britain: The Greatest Air Battle of World War II* (1989); Richard Overy, *Russia's War* (1997, reissued 1999); Carlo D'Este, *Bitter Victory: The Battle for Sicily, July–August 1943* (1988, reprinted 1991); John Keegan, *Six Armies in Normandy*, new ed. (1994); Trevor N. Dupuy, David L. Bongard, and Richard C. Anderson, *Hitler's Last Gamble: The Battle of the Bulge, December 1944–January 1945* (1994); and John Toland, *The Last 100*

Days: The Tumultuous and Controversial Story of the Final Days of WW II in Europe (1965, reissued 2003).

Outstanding treatments of the war in the Pacific from the Japanese point of view include Saburo Ienaga, *The Pacific War, 1931–1945* (1978); and Akira Iriye, *Power and Culture: The Japanese-American War, 1941–1945* (1981). The American perspective is found in John Costello, *The Pacific War*, rev. ed. (1985); and Ronald H. Spector, *Eagle Against the Sun: The American War with Japan*, new ed. (2000).

Naval history is treated in Paul S. Dull, *A Battle History of the Imperial Japanese Navy, 1941–1945* (1978); and John Prados, *Combined Fleet Decoded: The Secret History of American Intelligence and the Japanese Navy in World War II* (1995, reissued 2001). The war under the waves is detailed in the following books on submarines by Clay Blair: *Silent Victory: The U.S. Submarine War Against Japan* (1975, reissued 2001); *Hitler's U-Boat War: The Hunters, 1939–1942* (1996, reissued 2000); and *Hitler's U-Boat War: The Hunted, 1942–1944* (1998, reissued 2000). The air war has likewise received special attention, including Richard J. Overy, *The Air War, 1939–1945* (1980, reissued 1991); Michael S. Sherry, *The Rise of American Air Power: The Creation of Armageddon* (1987); and Geoffrey Perret, *Winged Victory: The Army Air Forces in World War II* (1993, reissued 1997).

There is a vast literature on the war's cultural and social aspects. For the war's racial dimensions, see John Dower, *War Without Mercy* (1986, reprinted with corrections, 1993). Stories of the home front are well told in Angus Calder, *The People's War: Britain, 1939–1945* (1969, reissued 1992); Susan M. Hartmann, *The Home Front and Beyond: American Women in the 1940s* (1982, reissued 1995); John Barber and Mark Harrison, *The Soviet Home Front, 1941–1945* (1991); and Ben-Ami Shillony, *Politics and Culture in Wartime Japan* (1981, reissued 2001).

Decisions concerning the atomic bomb and the end of war in the Pacific are outlined in scores of books, many published in 1994 and 1995 as the world marked the 50th anniversary of the atomic bombings of Hiroshima and Nagasaki. In some ways Herbert Feis, *The Atomic Bomb and the End of World War II*, rev. ed. (1966, reissued 1970), remains the standard. For competing views of this important aspect of the war, see also Gar Alperovitz, *The Decision to Use the Atomic Bomb and the Architecture of an American Myth* (1995); and Richard Frank, *Downfall: The End of the Imperial Japanese Empire* (1999, reissued 2001).

Official Histories

In the half-century following the war, Her Majesty's Stationery Office (now known as The Stationery Office) published scores of books under the general title "History of the Second World War." These include F.H. Hinsley et al., *British Intelligence in the Second World War*, 5 vol. (1981–90); S.W. Roskill, *War at Sea*

1939–1945, 3 vol. in 4 (1954–61); and L.F. Ellis et al., *Victory in the West*, 2 vol. (1960–68). The standard for U.S. official histories, published by the Office of the Chief of Military History, is *The United States Army in World War II*, 75 vol. (1944–86), also known as the "Green Books." Other U.S. histories include Samuel Eliot Morison, *History of United States Naval Operations in World War II*, 15 vol. (1947–62, reissued 2001); and Wesley Craven and James Cate (eds.), *The Army Air Forces in World War II*, 7 vol. (1948–58, reissued 1983). *Militärgeschictliches Forschungsamt* (Armed Forces Historical Research Office), *Das Deutsche Reich und der Zweite Weltkrieg*, 10 vol. (1979–), is the official German history; the volumes are being published in English under the title *Germany and the Second World War* (1990–).

INDEX